The Jossey-Bass Series
in Higher Education

Preface

New Perspectives on Teacher Education is addressed to those who, like myself, wish to become informed about the future of teacher education, an audience which should include not only those who profess to be teacher trainers but the whole range of persons with a stake in education. I have in mind students, parents, school board members, teachers, administrators, liberal arts professors, taxpayers, and the citizenry at large.

Why should teacher education warrant the full attention of these diverse groups at this time? Isn't it evident that the teacher shortage is over, thereby removing one divisive issue from society's overworked agenda? But precisely because we no longer need to mass produce teachers we must thoughtfully examine what the future portends. The issue now is one of direct consequences and overall goals. It is an issue which may well be disregarded because, as we all know, our society disengages itself quickly from matters which no longer seem to be pressure packed.

Education has never had an easy time of it. It is constantly the subject of a contest because it does not have well defined boundaries. The classicist argues persuasively that real education is cultivation of the mind. But the vocational voice, highly regarded in our culture, stresses the importance of job-oriented instruction. And the pragmatist seeks to reconcile these divergent views, often with little success. Small wonder that educational critics, a group to which all citizens belong by the very nature of their concern, disagree about educational goals. And because our society has not yet made up its mind about what schools should be about, it is not surprising that teachers sometimes question what it is they are trying to do.

This setting prompted me to invite a number of distinguished individuals to set forth their ideas about new directions in teacher education. The authors I cajoled into accepting my challenge write well and pointedly. All share one essential quality, proven intellectual competence. They are able to capture the pulse of the times and record the essence of the issues before us in teacher education. Thus readers of *New Perspectives on Teacher Education* will find the discussions exciting and useful.

I deliberately sought outstanding writers with differing opinions. We have long recognized in education the limitations of the single author approach, where one viewpoint prevails, and too many of us have been disappointed by committee monographs purporting to report the consensus. Both of these approaches fall short of the healthy dialogue needed to illuminate rather than obfuscate. Many of the observations made in this book clash with conventional wisdom, but they are not irresponsible carpings. When even the idea of going to school is being challenged, an attempt must be made to find a satisfactory rationale for formal schools or for abandoning them. Despite their different persuasions the contributors believe that the public schools will survive.

New Perspectives on Teacher Education is being published at a most opportune time. The current crisis about certification and credentials is a threat to the continuation of schools of education, at least in regard to performance of their past functions. Many scenarios are possible. Once the teacher is prepared in the field under the direct supervision of public school systems, for example, the old pattern of specific college credit requirements will vanish. The monopoly formally exercised by colleges and universities may be broken. Teacher unions could become the certifying agencies of the future. This example is only one possibility. Teacher proof curriculums, performance-based teacher education, total community involvement in the educational process all have their proponents. Whatever the reader's bias, he will certainly be rewarded by a careful study of the arguments presented in *New Perspectives on Teacher Education*. These authors do not content themselves with simple repetition of the time-worn critiques of teacher education; their opinions are stimulating, new, and imaginative.

I am indebted to my collaborators for the quality of their work. An editor can design a book that appears to have internal logic, but it takes talented people to make the best plan a reality. None of my fears that the chapters might contain some of the tired cliches so prevalent in educational literature were realized. Instead, my best hopes were fulfilled. I firmly believe the serious student of education will agree with me once he has finished these pages.

Madison   DONALD J. McCARTY
March 1973

Contents

Contributors

J. Myron Atkin, *dean, School of Education,*
    University of Illinois

Jack A. Bils, *resident in research, Northwestern University*

Robert W. Blanchard, *superintendent of schools,*
    Portland, Oregon

Luvern L. Cunningham, *dean, college of education,*
    The Ohio State University

William H. Drummond, *professor of education,*
    University of Florida

Leon D. Epstein, *professor of political science,*
    University of Wisconsin–Madison

Edgar Z. Friedenberg, *professor of sociology,*
    Dalhousie University

HAROLD HOWE II, *vice-president, Division of Education and Research, The Ford Foundation*

HERBERT M. KLIEBARD, *professor of curriculum and instruction and educational policy studies, University of Wisconsin–Madison*

JAMES D. KOERNER, *program officer, Alfred P. Sloan Foundation*

MARGARET LINDSEY, *professor of education, Teachers College, Columbia University*

DONALD J. McCARTY, *dean, school of education, University of Wisconsin–Madison*

THEODORE R. SIZER, *headmaster, Phillips Academy*

LINDLEY J. STILES, *professor of education for interdisciplinary studies, sociology, and political science, Northwestern University*

WILLIAM TAYLOR, *professor of education, University of Bristol*

HERBERT A. THELEN, *professor of curriculum and instruction, University of Chicago*

New Perspectives on Teacher Education

An Overview

Donald J. McCarty

Teacher education is characterized at the levels of theory and action alike by confusion, by effervescent hopes and mordant fears, by wishful thinking and destructive pessimism. That teacher education finds itself in ferment is not surprising; there has hardly been a time when it has not, often fruitlessly, to be sure.

As for the immediate future, societal influences (tax resistance, loss of confidence in formal schools, wavering federal initiative) will almost certainly reduce spending for basic research in teacher education; the emphasis will be on defusing political pressures by well-publicized action programs. Basic research, the indispensable foundation for solid growth and progress, will be singularly ignored except in outstanding schools of education and private research and testing agencies. It is disquieting to anticipate the rhetoric, fanfare, and political pressure for spectacular achievements, when history reveals that strident calls for revolutionary change result only in high expectations that remain unfulfilled.

The purpose of *New Perspectives in Teacher Education* is to critique the present conditions and to illuminate what the future

might bring. All the chapters are original ones prepared especially
for this volume by distinguished specialists. The authors represent
a wide variety of publics; unfortunately, their appraisals of the
current scene in teacher education are not completely reassuring.

The persistent message flowing from the pens of these
thoughtful authors is that schools are not going to change. There is
almost a desperate defeatism in these pages. Liberal arts professors
are detached from the concerns of teacher education, tight budgets
inhibit significant educational reform, the public likes the schools
the way they are, leadership from state departments and the federal
government is often confusing and disruptive rather than constructive, and teaching is a pseudoprofession, resting on experience and
apprenticeship rather than ideas.

Harsh indictments these when voiced by scholars not inhospitable to exemplary teacher education programs. Glimmers of hope
are raised but only tentatively. If I read these chapters correctly,
the authors think that somehow the answer lies in a spontaneously
developed shared commitment among teacher educators and their
many and diverse publics; a new cooperative spirit might be able to
overcome the lethargy, the bureaucratic tangles, the political power
structures, and the other all too familiar impediments. But are
these utopian dreams or will teacher education revitalize itself?
Whatever one's persuasion, the serious and penetrating dialogue
offered in *New Perspectives in Teacher Education* should be rewarding and challenging to all individuals interested in understanding and coping with the complexities.

This book is built around the theme of improvements in
teacher education and is divided into three parts. The chapters
may be read in sequence if desired; for the person interested in
browsing here and there, I have written brief résumés of each
author's main arguments. These short summations do not do justice
to the elegance of the chapters, but I hope they will direct the
reader's attention to those matters that interest him most.

Herbert Kliebard's opening chapter in Part One points out
that American scholars in education are increasingly asking themselves the question that international scholars have been asking for
years: Is teaching a technical process? Kliebard brings a historical

perspective to his discussion of this essential curricular issue. He argues that instead of unlocking the secrets of successful teaching, technological efforts in the past, in large measure, have hampered other forms of inquiry. Kliebard proposes that we reformulate the question and explore critically the directions uncharted paths may take.

Edgar Friedenberg believes that teacher education programs are quite literally the creatures of the public school system and that the central function of the public school system is to preserve itself and jobs for its members rather than to meet the needs of students, the weakest and most vulnerable of the constitutencies of the schools. Some may consider this a harsh charge, but few would argue against Friedenberg's thesis that schools of education have a single-client relationship with the schools, in contrast to a department of political science, for instance, which makes no attempt to cater to the expectations of politicians exclusively.

Theodore Sizer argues that the public is not interested in radical changes in education; instead, financial stringencies are likely to stabilize the status quo. Moreover, he sees teaching as a pseudoprofession, resting on experience and apprenticeship rather than on ideas. In his view, increased emphasis on systematic inquiry into teaching and learning is needed. Sizer concludes that no academic institution save the school of education now champions such work and that the responsibility for husbanding this essential resource lies with that institution.

Harold Howe makes it patently clear that he considers teaching to be a skill. His definition implies, however, that these skills are complex and not easily mastered: "These skills are based on the ability to size up individuals, to judge their responses, and to make your responses reflect theirs, to diagnose each one's special needs and problems, to present ideas and activities in ways that will motivate interest in learning, to coordinate varied materials into their most effective impact, to sense the nuances of individual and group attitudes and feelings, and to balance all these variables in a kaleidoscopic drama featuring players with different rates of learning, different backgrounds, and totally different feelings." In order to prepare people to meet these giant demands, Howe recom-

mends that schools of education make effective use of the schools
themselves, enlist community resources in training, and involve the
full resources of the university in the educational process.

Robert Blanchard believes that the quality of preparation
given to new entrants into the teaching profession has never been
better. At the same time he pleads for a specialized curriculum to
fit the requirements of our diverse school systems. Through outlining
the agenda of a typical board meeting, Blanchard illustrates the inherent value differences that plague our social system. He suggests
that schools of education develop specific courses in role definition
and decision-making; to date, education has been especially tardy
as a profession in realizing the need to systematically analyze its
decision-making process.

Part Two principally concerns influences on teacher education. Myron Atkin in his analysis of the federal influence on teacher
education states that the federal emphasis, resembling that of the
major foundations, has stressed exemplary efforts, demonstrations,
and some limited research. He intimates that the U.S. Office of
Education does not know what it takes to modify education in any
substantial way; rather it has sacrificed program quality for managerial control in the McNamara tradition. Atkin speculates that the
future of teacher education will more than likely be determined by
negotiation of competing interests among university groups, the
organized profession, and the public, with government less intrusive
than it became in the late 1960s.

State departments of education have only recently become
powerful and dynamic agents for change. William Drummond, a
former member of the state of Washington Department of Public
Instruction, acknowledges that state departments exist in a political
environment. As a result, they characteristically do what they are
required to do by law, often do what they are authorized to do by
law, and may, in rare instances, do what they are not prohibited
from doing by law. Drummond predicts that these departments will
play different and vigorous roles in the future, particularly in attempting to spearhead new initiatives in curriculum and personnel
development.

Is it practical to think that there will be genuinely new
directions in teacher education? According to James Koerner, the

idea is nonsense. Change at glacial speed is the norm. Koerner thinks that improvement is essentially a political problem and that the monolithic and monopolistic education establishment has the tools to dilute and delay reforms proposed by outsiders. Mild meliorism is the best we can hope for. He graphically defends his position by detailing efforts to change teacher-licensing requirements in Massachusetts and California.

According to Lindley Stiles and Jack Bils nothing is more controversial in teacher education, at the moment, than its system of national accrediting. They say that national accrediting may be failing simply because it is an impossible task (too many institutions prepare teachers). They review how the National Council for Accreditation of Teacher Education (NCATE) evolved into its present state and present formidable critiques of its performance. After examining alternatives to national accrediting, they conclude that NCATE will survive, partly because its stamp of approval symbolizes professionalism in teaching, but more because it is the arm of the teacher education establishment.

Part Three treats organizational issues from a number of perspectives. Colleges of education have been caricatured as bastions of conservatism sadly lacking in intellectual vitality. Fortunately, a few enterprising places still do not fit this oversimplified stereotype. Luvern Cunningham sketches how the huge College of Education at Ohio State University attempted to remake its programs in teacher education. His account is poignant testimony to the difficulty of the task as he records the frustrations, agonies, disappointments, and successes of his courageous venture in planned change. Cunningham admits that his self-report is impressionistic and no doubt biased, but his critique is too revealing to be put aside as hortatory. It is an honest case study from which many lessons can be learned about how to effect reform in complex colleges of education.

Teacher education in England and Wales has been struggling with much the same problems as the United States. Although the answers may be slightly different, as William Taylor indicates in his critique of the controversial report of the powerful James Committee, the imponderables are still imponderable. Attention has been drawn to new forms of governance; now opportunities are needed to attend to the structure and content of courses and to the pedagogic practices and procedures of teacher training. Such a statement could well be made about teacher education in this country.

Mindless adoption and installation of ready-made curricular models have consistently plagued teacher educators. Currently, performance-based teacher education qualifies as the most likely candidate. Margaret Lindsey warns that if these adoptions are accompanied by single-handed political power plays, by lack of involvement and preparation of those who must make the model operative in a given setting, the chances of realizing whatever promise the model was thought to possess are greatly reduced. She argues forcibly that future gains lie more in the actions sparked by confrontation and dialogue among concerned agencies and professionals than they do in the production of materials, whether they be instructional modules, taxonomies, or comprehensive conceptual models.

Many scholars have debated whether teaching is a profession. Herbert Thelen offers new insights well worth attending to. He states that the quality of education depends to a high degree on the voluntary exercise of courage, insight, and commitment by thousands of teachers. Their efforts cannot be coordinated by force (supervision)', nor can their behavior be programed by administration (procedures). The basis of quality has to be shared commitment to an educational vision: the concept of a profession. The profession will develop through dialogue that involves all parts and levels of the educational enterprise. The desired outcomes of such dialogue will be public policy for action and private reconstruction of meanings.

The institutional arrangements that liberal arts colleges and departments of education have acquiesced in for many years create a sharp division between content and method. Leon Epstein states that most liberal arts professors have never been interested in systematic methods of teaching. They doubt whether methods are reducible to a science. Neither are liberal arts professors threatened or seriously troubled by whatever it is that schools of education are trying to do. Absence of interest seems more typical than overt hostility. It is no wonder that conscious efforts to develop coopera-

tive working relationships between the two units have not been successful. Overt conflict has been avoided, but both sides keep their
distance from each other.

In the final chapter I point out that the leadership options
of deans of schools of education are limited both by the internal
structure of the university and by its social milieu. In the necessary
interaction between leadership style and social environment, the
boundaries for deans of schools of education are relatively short
and the constraints are strong; these factors hamper the influence
that any single leader may have upon program development. I
emphasize that leadership is part of a total set of forces; however,
if a dean is to have a positive impact, he must initiate proposals
rather than serve primarily as a reactor to the ideas of others.

These delightful chapters are not likely to please reaction-
aries who want to dissolve teacher education to save money or
radicals who consider the education of teachers to be beyond repair.
Teacher education has suffered greatly from what the philosophers
describe as inflated ideals; the antidote is not to declare the process
useless but to make the necessary improvements. The recommendations offered in *New Perspectives in Teacher Education* may help
suggest the new directions so urgently required.

Chapter 1

The Question
in Teacher Education

Herbert M. Kliebard

As she lay dying, Gertrude Stein is reputed to have uttered one last memorable line: "What *is* the answer? . . . In that case, what is the question?" (Sutherland, 1951, p. 203). The question of the question is not only one of the most elusive in a broad philosophical sense, but also probably the most critical in the development and definition of a field of study. "A question," writes Langer, "is really an ambiguous proposition; the answer is its determination. There can be only a certain number of alternatives that will complete its sense. In this way the intellectual treatment of any datum, any experience, any subject, is determined by the nature of our questions and only carried out in the answers" (1948, pp. 15–16). The question sets limits on and creates the framework for the kinds of answers that are sought.

Unfortunately, the fundamental questions that characterize

a field of study are frequently so submerged that they are rarely raised to the level of self-conscious examination and are sometimes only vaguely known at all. This is probably because the members of any scholarly community undergo professional socialization into their fields, which makes the fundamental questions seem entirely normal and natural. Possible alternative questions simply do not arise very readily. In one sense, the function of the question in guiding research is similar to what Kuhn associates with the paradigm: "One of the things a scientific community acquires with a paradigm is a criterion for choosing problems that, while the paradigm is taken for granted, can be assumed to have solutions" (1964, p. 37).

Where can the question (paradigm) in teacher education be found? We must review the questions posed by research on teaching as well as consider the historical evolution of the field of teacher education.

Early Formulations

Teaching is such a natural and spontaneous form of human activity that its origins are lost in prehistory. A "science" of teaching, however, begins in the late nineteenth century. Probably the first scientific studies of teaching to have a major impact on public consciousness were those conducted by Joseph Mayer Rice, whose exposés of American educational practice created a national furor. His early articles in *The Forum* reflected a growing concern about waste, not only in education but also in other aspects of American life. Rice felt that two fundamental questions in education had been subjected to a "mass of philosophical opinion" and had become "waterlogged in a sea of opinions" (1969, p. 5). "How much time shall be devoted to a subject?" and "What results shall be accomplished?" were questions that should be subjected to scientific inquiry. His "plan of application" lay "in subjecting children taught under different systems to one and the same test . . . and comparing the results" (1969, p. 7). Science would provide not only the appropriate standard of achievement to be reached but also the best way to achieve it. Rice estimated, for example, that some schools devoted approximately 70 percent of their instructional time to the three R's. Would a reduction to, say, 50 percent result in a comparable reduction in achievement? Or, does the additional 20 percent represent a waste of instructional time and effort? In the outline of this research procedure lie the roots of the development of the scientific study of teaching and of the attempt to build a program of teacher education on that foundation.

Beginning early in 1895, Rice arranged for the testing of approximately 33,000 children using a standard spelling test that he had devised. Since the early results indicated a range of accuracy of from 33 to 95.3 percent, he at first believed "that the spelling problem had already been solved and that nothing was needed to put all our teachers on the right path beyond a careful study of the methods employed where the highest standards had been secured, and carrying the message to those whose results had been less favorable" (1969, p. 68). Rice discovered, however, upon visiting the classes involved that the favorable results were achieved not by any particular methodology or special technique for teaching spelling, but by the teachers' careful enunciation during testing, which provided obvious clues to the correct spelling of the words.

Undaunted, Rice undertook a second round of testing, this time under his personal supervision. The new results, however, were puzzling. The ranges in achievement were extremely narrow, which made it difficult to attribute success or failure to "mechanical schools" as opposed to "progressive schools" or even "to distinguish the schools attended by the children of cultured parents from those representing the foreign laboring element" (1969, p. 77). Rice finally concluded that there was no relation between the then identifiable methods of teaching spelling and that the results were attributable to "the ability of those who use them" (1969, p. 90). Neither could any relationship be found between the amount of time spent in spelling instruction and achievement in spelling. "Our efforts," he recommended, "should be primarily directed toward supplying our schools with competent teachers" (1969, p. 99). Since not enough teachers are "born to the profession," however, the "only course lies in developing the requisite powers, as well as we can, where they are naturally weak" (1969, p. 99). This could be accomplished by first establishing with precision the job to be done and the time needed to do it and then making the teacher's job dependent on his success in doing it.

Apart from the overtones in Rice's conclusions of what is now called accountability are the seeds of what has become the major effort insofar as teacher education was concerned. Since the number of "born" teachers was obviously too small to staff our burgeoning school systems, research in teaching would have to be directed toward identifying those qualities, characteristics, and behaviors that constituted good teaching; and teacher education, in turn, would be directed toward using that research in order to provide a competent corps of teachers for the schools.

What constitutes good teaching? On the basis of this deceptively complex question, a massive research effort was undertaken, with the ultimate practical aim of developing teacher education programs that would instill the techniques of good teaching into tomorrow's teachers. In general, bad teaching came to be associated with *waste,* a term Rice anticipated, and for a time *economy* enjoyed a vogue as the great enemy of waste; but ultimately, *efficiency* became the term most educators accepted as synonymous with good. A good teacher achieved a prespecified task with maximum efficiency. Given this conception, only two problems remained to be resolved: first, stipulating the specifications or standards of success that define good teaching; and second, discovering the means by which such success could be most efficiently achieved.

Educational leaders and teacher educators were in virtual agreement as to the task before them. Franklin Bobbitt, an extraordinarily prolific writer and influential reformer who was particularly active during the first quarter of this century, set the tone. The new era in education would be governed by SCIENCE—scientific management in the administration of schools, scientific curriculum-making, and the scientific discovery of the qualities of a good teacher. "Efficient *methods,*" Bobbitt declared, "are dependent on definite standards" (1913, p. 45). Notable success had already been achieved in the area of standards by such researchers as S. A. Courtis, L. P. Ayers, and Edward Thorndike. The number of correct arithmetic combinations per minute for each grade level, for example, could already be accurately determined, and teachers' success could be gauged in terms of rate of efficiency in raising achievement to prescribed levels of speed and accuracy. Ultimately, differentiated criteria of success for different categories of students

—future accountants, musicians, bricklayers—could be set, thus accomplishing even greater efficiency and scientific accuracy.

Here also would lie the key to teacher education. The personal qualities that were closely linked with success in achieving the predetermined achievement rates could then be isolated. If it could be known that a stoker or a ditch digger "would better be of sluggish mentality" and that a lawyer or a banker should be possessed of a "keen and ever-alert intelligence" (Bobbitt, 1913, p. 63), then the particular qualities that make for success in teaching could be identified. Citing Frederick Winslow Taylor, the efficiency engineer, and his study of women working in a bicycle factory, Bobbitt, like Rice, felt that the technique for the identification and training of good teachers was already within our grasp. It consisted essentially of two tasks: The first was "to locate a fairly large sample of the best 5 percent of teachers in the profession, those who in their original nature probably possess the native elements, rightly proportioned, of the so-called 'born teacher' "; and the second, "to analyze out and to define in reasonably definite terms the characteristics of personality which this group of teachers exhibits" (Bobbitt, 1913, p. 64).

By the 1920s, little doubt existed as to the appropriate course of action for developing a scientifically based teacher education. Essentially, it was to follow the lines that Taylor had developed in industry and took the form of job analysis. Comparisons were constantly being made with technological and industrial jobs, and concern was frequently expressed that precise lists of abilities in teaching had not yet been formulated. "The teacher-training institution is a vocational school," declared Bobbitt (1924, p. 187). If we can discover the 165 jobs that a plumber has to perform, why are we unable to accomplish the same with the admittedly more complex job of teaching? "To discover the objectives of teacher training, therefore, the investigator will go where teachers are performing all their tasks as they ought to be performed. He will then list the 200 or 500 or 5000 tasks which the competent teacher accomplishes in his work. The *abilities* to perform these tasks, then, are the fundamental teacher-training objectives—the abilities to do the jobs are the objectives. There are no others" (Bobbitt, 1924, p. 188).

W. W. Charters, another exceptionally influential reformer of the 1920s endorsed the same general framework. If, for example, a teacher performs three activities between 8:40 A.M. and 9:00 A.M. —correcting papers, planning a lesson, and greeting students—these activities should be duly noted, and the abilities involved in performing these activities successfully would become the objectives of teacher education programs (1920, pp. 305–306).

Charters, along with Douglas Waples, conducted one of the most massive inquiries into the activities of teachers ever undertaken. The Commonwealth Teacher Training Study, as it was called, was initiated in 1925 as the latest in a series of scientific inquiries into teaching sponsored by the Commonwealth Fund. Apart from Charters and Waples, an impressive staff of scientifically minded investigators was assembled (including Ralph Tyler of the University of North Carolina as supervisor of statistical operations) to discover scientifically the traits and activities that define good teaching. Once discovered, these would become the elements of a new teacher education curriculum.

Instead of assuming that certain activities and traits of teachers were desirable, the study was designed to extract from teachers and supervisors the positive components of the activity of teaching. By polling "competent critics" of teachers, for example, the twenty-five most important traits of teachers were isolated and then broken down into behavioral components. Thus, adaptability could be seen in a teacher who "does not dance nor play cards if the community objects," animation in a teacher who "expresses enthusiasm in eyes," attractive personal appearance in one who "does not wear shoes that are run over at the heels," and cleanliness in one who "washes faces when they need washing" (Charters and Waples, 1929, pp. 223–244).

To secure a comprehensive list of the activities of teachers, 22,000 questionnaires were sent to experienced teachers in forty-two states. Over 6000 usable replies were obtained indicating some 211,890 activities. In addition, various studies of the activities of teachers were analyzed, each yielding roughly three hundred more. Finally, after elimination of duplication and some telescoping, a master check list of the 1010 activities of teaching was developed. The teacher-training institutions had only to use the lists of traits and activities thus formulated to develop a teacher education program that reflected the world of the classroom.

Yet, teacher education institutions remained curiously intractable. Although sporadic efforts were made to inject the products of this research into programs of teacher education, and thousands of check lists were reproduced for use by supervisors, the Commonwealth Teacher Training Study is largely forgotten today.

The major intent of the study, however, is still recognized, and the search for the correct set of teacher behaviors and personality traits (or competencies) continues undiminished. Perhaps the most influential person identified with the movement to isolate the characteristics of good teachers is A. S. Barr. Although his best-known study was published in 1929, his search continued for many years afterward and probably involved hundreds of studies. In his 1929 book, Barr compared forty-seven good social studies teachers with forty-seven poor ones as identified by city and county superintendents in the state of Wisconsin, carrying the scientific study of teaching one step further than the Commonwealth study by deriving his data from observation of classroom performance rather than through questionnaires or opinions of supervisors.

The range of behaviors Barr observed was enormous. They included verbal behavior, such as characteristic expressions, posture, assignments made, and even the physical conditions in the classrooms. Barr reported, for example, a virtual tie (42 to 44) in the most frequently used expression, "all right." For "yes," the expression next in frequency, there was a flat tie (34 to 34) (1929, p. 39). The data on posture were not much more illuminating. Although the category of "folds hands" was won by the good teachers by a score of 7 to 4, most other scores were close, such as the 3 to 3 tie in the category "puts hands to chin or cheek" (1929, p. 64). Although Barr's behavior categories may seem naïve by modern standards, he was carrying forward, in broad outline at least, the central line of inquiry in research on teaching.

Limitations of Teaching Technology

In at least some important respects, the scientific study of teaching currently being supported by the U.S. Office of Education

(USOE), and other prestigious agencies under the banner of teacher competencies follows the same path that Rice trod some eighty years ago, one that is by now well worn. Attired in new rhetorical finery, performance-based or competency-based teacher education not only has captured the imagination of many leading teacher educators but also has become the essential condition for the granting of many federal and even some state funds. State departments of education from Florida to Oregon either have announced their intention to or have begun to implement teacher certification and teacher rating plans involving the specific performance or competence of teachers.

Identifying any precise meaning for the terms and catch-words that are used is difficult however. Even the statement issued by the Committee on Performance-Based Teacher Education of the American Association of Colleges for Teacher Education admits that "no entirely satisfactory description of performance-based teacher education has been framed to date" (Elam, 1972, p. 1). The statement refers to one observer's description of performance-based teacher education as "a multifaceted concept in search of practitioners" (Elam, 1972, p. 1). A more accurate description at this stage would probably be that it is a slogan system in search of followers. Much has gone on under the rubric of competency-based teacher education, but the key notion seems to be that identifiable behaviors, competencies, and characteristics of teaching, once isolated, can form the basis of teacher education and teacher certi-fication. Those who believe in competency-based teacher education, like Rice before them, are directing a major portion of their efforts and expenditures (which are considerable in many cases) toward cutting through the logjam in the "sea of opinions" that surrounds the performance of teachers and toward identifying scientifically demonstrated behaviors that define good or at least competent teaching. As Charters and Barr discovered, the process of isolating those specific behaviors is more complex than appears at first. In fact, it would be difficult to name even a single specific behavior that has been shown to be consistently correlated with a reasonable definition of competent teaching. Why is this?

J. M. Stephens, one of the few professional students of edu-cation to strike out in an alternate direction in trying to explain the persistent failures to isolate critical teacher behaviors, raises the possibility that although teaching is usually considered to be a highly deliberate process, there may be blind, spontaneous (that is, nondeliberative) factors at work that have much to do with the effects and effectiveness of schooling (1955, 1956a, 1956b, 1967). In fact, these nondeliberative, sometimes even unconscious, tendencies may have more to do with what the schools accomplish than do the deliberate particular behaviors that teachers exhibit in the classroom. Fishing or bird-watching, talking to others about what we find interesting and exciting, and expressing approval or disapproval of the performance of others, particularly children: these widely distributed, perhaps even universal, human characteristics are all examples of spontaneous, natural behaviors that may account for what schools do. Wallen and Travers (1963, pp. 448–505) express a similar position.

If this position has merit, it may, Stephens points out (1967, pp. 71–90), explain the persistent phenomenon in educational research of *no significant differences,* a problem that in a wide range of studies comparing one educational technique with another (that is, lecture versus discussion, homogeneous versus heterogeneous grouping) is rarely given serious consideration. One answer to this problem, according to Stephens, is that the spontaneous tendencies of human beings, along with what might be called the culture of the school, account in such large measure for the impact of schooling that the particular modifications we introduce are not sufficient to show up in statistical measures of school achievement.

At the heart of the difference between Stephens' position and the dominant tradition from Rice to USOE's performance-based teacher education programs is the most fundamental question that faces us as teacher educators: Is teaching a *technical* process? When one learns to be a teacher, is one learning a technique? (The term, *technique* is being used here in Ellul's (1964) sense as a standardized way to achieve a predetermined end.) When one teaches teachers or future teachers, does one teach the single right way to accomplish some particular thing? Certainly, this assumption is basic to the concept of what we thought was a science of teaching. It is also the impetus for the expenditure of millions of dollars by the USOE. The sheer intensity of the effort to convince or, in some instances, to compel teachers to express in minute terms the exact behavioral outcomes of their instruction is one crucial manifestation of this assumption. Without this manifestation, a *technique* of teaching can not exist.

Research reported by one of the leading proponents of specific performance objectives and performance-based teacher education is an interesting case in point. Teaching Performance Tests were developed at UCLA to assess the proficiency with which prespecified achievement objectives are achieved. "By holding the instructional goals constant," "it was asserted, it becomes possible to contrast teachers with respect to their skill in accomplishing identical goals" (Popham, 1971, p. 600). This is, of course, the same fundamental assumption that prompted Rice to construct and administer his tests of spelling achievement. The results were the same. Experienced teachers performed no better than college students in teaching social science, and tradesmen did about as well as experienced teachers in teaching auto mechanics and electronics. Again, there were *no significant differences*. Popham, in explaining his conclusion that "experienced teachers are not particularly skilled at bringing about specified behavior changes in learners" (1971, p. 601), lays the blame squarely on teacher training institutions. The reason experienced teachers fail to win the race against their untutored and presumably flabby opponents is that the right techniques for achieving prespecified objectives have not been correctly instilled in them during their preservice or inservice training. Although the investigator declares this to be "a *totally unacceptable* state of affairs," he does not reveal the particular techniques that would have enabled the experienced teachers to win the race.

It is easy to understand the reason for the omission: No one knows what these techniques are—if indeed there are any. Our basic presuppositions make this difficult to admit. Many professors of education prefer to pretend, either to themselves or to others, that they do know what these techniques are. Certainly, a great many students come to their classes expecting professors of education to release the secrets of efficient instruction that in the past have been so closely guarded. No wonder they often leave these courses disappointed. Even the relative effectiveness of the so-called lecture and discussion techniques, one of the most intensely investigated problems in all of research on teaching, is completely unknown. In a remarkable study undertaken at the Center for the Advanced Study of Educational Administration, for example, ninety-one comparative studies in college instruction conducted between 1924 and 1965 were reviewed and reanalyzed. The stark conclusion was: "These data demonstrate clearly and unequivocally that there is no measurable difference among truly distinctive methods of college instruction when evaluated by student performance on final examinations" (Dubin and Taveggia, 1968, p. 35). Even that old chestnut has not been pulled from the fire.

The issue is not the reluctance of teacher education institutions to emphasize a technology of teaching or even the strength of their commitment to the notion that finding and disseminating a technology of teaching is their central task. It goes far beyond the question of whether Stephens' theory of spontaneous schooling has any explanatory power. In view of an unbroken record of failure to answer the question of how to achieve educational aims most effectively, the decision before us is whether we should pursue that question now with increased vigor and determination or whether we should reformulate the question itself.

Certainly, the USOE has committed itself largely to the first alternative, and it seems fair to say that most professional students of teaching prefer to rededicate themselves periodically to the pursuit of their traditional question. N. L. Gage, for example, a leading exponent and practitioner of a science of teaching, sees some reason for optimism. He notes four process variables that promise a significant correlation with desirable outcome variables such as student achievement and positive reactions on the part of students. The four are warmth, indirectness, cognitive organization, and enthusiasm. An examination of the last one may illustrate some problems associated with these tentative signs of optimism. Gage describes two studies in which a positive outcome (student achievement) seems to be related to the teacher's enthusiasm. In the first, two investigators asked teachers to present lessons "in a static, or unenthusiastic fashion (read from a manuscript, with no gestures, eye contact, or inflections), and also in a dynamic, or enthusiastic, fashion (delivered from memory, with much inflection, eye contact, gesturing, and animation" (Gage, 1972, p. 38). After the ten-minute lessons, tests indicated more learning on the part of the latter class. In a second study, twenty teachers were asked to lecture in an "indifferent" manner one week and "enthusiastically" the next. In all but one of the classes, mean achievement scores were higher for the enthusiastic lessons. It appears, that students are able to remember more of their dynamic lessons than they are of their boring lessons.

Whatever the strength of the statistical relationships may be, it is difficult to derive great optimism about a science of teaching from findings such as these. For example, if teachers are asked to teach in a static or indifferent way, they will with reason probably interpret the instructions as an injunction to teach poorly. They are, in effect, being asked to make their lessons as dull as they can. When they are told to teach enthusiastically, the effect is to ask them to give their teaching ability full rein. As reported, then, the experiments could be said to indicate that the teachers involved were reasonably successful in following the instructions of the investigators. In most instances, compared with their efforts to teach well/enthusiastically, their efforts to teach poorly/unenthusiastically were rewarded by poor results on achievement tests. Another important question to consider in examining the findings is whether the relationship between the independent and the dependent variables is linear. Would success, however defined, continue to rise with the level of enthusiasm? Does the research indicate that the best teacher is one who conducts his classes in an absolute frenzy of enthusiasm? Or is anything above the level of zombie sufficient to achieve success?

These objections aside, what if a truly independent variable were found to be consistently related by reliable statistical measures to a desirable outcome variable, say, client satisfaction? Suppose that there is strong relationship between the teacher's use of a high percentage of vertical hand gestures, Harry Truman style, and positive student attitudes as opposed to the use of horizontal hand gestures or to no gestures at all. Would it be reasonable to assume in view of indisputable statistical evidence that vertical hand gestures are a sure road to popularity as a teacher? The task of teacher education institutions would then be to ensure that up and down movements of the arm became an integral part of the repertoire of every certified teacher. The question is not a facetious one. It is related to the well-meaning efforts of some teacher training institutions to teach indirectness, for example, in the Flanders interaction sense, as one of the ingredients in good teaching. Would prospective teachers who master the technique of "accepts or uses ideas of student: clarifying, building, or developing ideas suggested by a student" then be on the high road to success as teachers? The key problem would be whether vertical hand gestures (or indirectness) themselves cause client satisfaction or whether a previously undiscovered cause somehow manifests itself both in the tendency toward the vertical hand gestures and the client satisfaction. In that case, teacher education institutions that were successful in inculcating the appropriate hand movements would be no better insofar as developing popular teachers than would be institutions that systematically ignored this important statistical relationship.

Guidelines to Restating the Question

What has gone on in the name of the scientific study of teaching has been, in large measure, raw empiricism, a blind and almost necessarily futile groping for statistically significant relationships. Even if a persistent statistical relationship were somehow found, the absence of analytical clarification of the concepts involved and the lack of a theoretical framework for the research would preclude the development of any scientific understanding of the relationship and, for that matter, would probably rule out any useful purpose to which the research could be put. Cronbach's description of the typical research in this area is as accurate as any:

> *John Doe contends that programed presentation of college geology is better than conventional lectures. He assembles a writing team and spends two years drafting material, editing every sentence, trying it on pilot classes, and revising. Then Doe runs a grand experiment in which ten classes are taught with his material, while ten classes take the regular lecture course. Unless his writers were painfully inept, the test scores favor the new method, and unless Doe is a very saint of an experimenter, he concludes that programed instruction is more effective than the lecture method. Doe has shown that his pro-*

grams give better results than the lectures in their casual, un-edited, tired old form, but the outcome would very likely to have been reversed if he had put the same two-year effort into tuning up the lectures. Nothing of explanatory value has been learned from his study [1966, p. 80].

One other feature of typical research on teaching is worth noting. One of the reasons there can be nothing of explanatory value in Doe's results is that he has not conceptualized the problem. There is no theoretical framework in which the research is set. The typical research on teaching is essentially a horse race. Sometimes one horse wins, sometimes the other; often, it is a tie. In any case, the outcome of the race adds nothing to our understanding of the complex processes that are involved in teaching. As Hawkins puts it, "To call something an independent variable is not to use a name but to claim an achievement" (1966, p. 6). Certainly, the case for warmth or indirectness or enthusiasm as truly important variables related to success in teaching can never rest on statistical correlations alone.

A second guideline for reformulating the question in teacher education involves the naïveté or, perhaps, the pretentiousness of the research we have been doing. The main research effort of the past eighty years has been built on the assumption that one can skip over all the little intermediate questions that may lie in the path of any given line of inquiry and answer the ultimate question at once. It is as if biologists set as their single-minded purpose the discovery of the secret of life. We might as well admit that the secrets of success in teaching, if they are knowable at all, are a long way from being revealed and are particularly impregnable to a direct assault. The big question is too formidable, too imposing, too cosmic to ask directly. We have to sneak up on it.

The way to do this is to be more modest in the research task we set for ourselves. We have to engage in the slow and sometimes unrewarding process of trying to understand the phenomena with which we are dealing. As Smith expresses it, "The first task of research is to build a body of pedagogical knowledge" (1967, p. 71). Although, on the face of it, this is not a startling pronouncement, at least some research on teaching is designed to improve the process of teaching in the absence of any understanding of what it is.

An important step toward pedagogical knowledge may involve nothing more spectacular than natural history research. Essentially, this involves making observations "in the wild" and seeing what goes on (Hawkins, 1966, p. 6). This has been, generally a neglected phase of the inquiry process in research on teaching, and only in recent years have there been any concerted efforts to study classroom processes as they go forward, independent of any judgments about good and poor teaching. The natural history stage in the inquiry process should not be lightly disregarded. Northrup makes this point clearly: "Nothing is more important . . . for a clarification of scientific method, empirical logic, and philosophy than a clear recognition of the different stages of inquiry. Once this is appreciated the natural history type of scientific knowledge gains the importance which is its due. In no empirical inquiry will anything ever take the place of looking and seeing" (1959, p. 39).

Natural history research is not simply an alternative to the familiar research effort directed toward isolating the components of good teaching. It is a necessary stage in the development of a field of inquiry. "The great point," observes Homans, "is to climb down from the big words of social science, at least as far as common-sense observation. Then, if we wish, we can start climbing up again, but this time with a ladder we can depend on" (1950, p. 13). Curbing our overwhelming sense of urgency and scaling down our grandiose ambition by taking on modest tasks may in the long run bring us rewarding returns on our research efforts in teaching.

The third guideline for the development of a new question in teacher education has already been alluded to. It calls into question one of the basic assumptions that has guided research in teacher education from the time of Rice's refreshingly naïve crusade for educational reform to at least some of the current frenetic efforts of the USOE to discover the behavior and skills—the much-heralded competencies—that resumably hold the key to good teaching. The assumption is that teaching, like typing or bricklaying, consists of a set of standard ways to do a particular thing. The notion appeals to a common human impulse. In approaching any complex activity, we like to think that there must be a trick to it which, once discovered, makes one a skilled practitioner. But we might as well face the likelihood that teaching may not consist of standard best ways to do particular things. Being a good teacher, like being a good statesman or a good mother, may involve infinite possible human excellences and appropriate behaviors, no one much more a guarantor of success than the other. As we attempt to observe and understand teaching, we may discover that teaching, after all, does not involve the exercise of a technical skill.

The technological framework as applied to teaching involves both precise prespecification of outcomes and progressively efficient means toward their achievement. For years, teachers have been invited to accept this framework and cajoled and threatened; yet they seem to be perversely resistant to it. Teachers want their students to learn, but getting them to state learning outcomes or "terminal behaviors" in a particularized form has turned out to be a more formidable task than first imagined (although, under pressure, teachers may go through the motions). Perhaps their resistance is not due to any natural recalcitrance; perhaps their instincts and their experience tell them that the process of teaching can not be made to fit the technological mold. This may have something to do with the interactive setting in which the activity of teaching goes on. "In the interactive setting," Jackson observes, "the teacher commonly encourages his students to do what he thinks will be good for them without giving too much thought to the precise outcome of his instructional efforts" (1968, p. 162). Teachers, in other words, like to engage in worthwhile activities, activities that they think are good for their students. When Jackson interviewed a specially selected group of outstanding teachers, he found that they derived their greatest professional satisfaction not from high scores on achievement tests in their classes, but from the interest and involvement of their students. The technological framework places its highest value on the educational *product,* on predictability and precision; the teachers in Jackson's study valued *process,* an educationally worthwhile activity from which will flow something desirable (Jackson, 1968, pp. 115–155). Studies such as his are illuminating because if one wishes to understand the process of teaching or even to improve it, one cannot afford to ignore teaching as it goes forward in its most familiar setting, the classroom.

Efforts to impose an artificial technological framework on the activities of teaching and learning provide the backdrop for the search for the secrets of good teaching because if teaching means a particular way to accomplish a particular thing, the secret may ultimately be revealed. But once the technological framework is discarded, the search for the best way becomes meaningless, and new, perhaps more fruitful, questions in teacher education may emerge.

The dream of educational reformers like Rice, Charters, Barr, and even the current performance-oriented teacher educators is not an ignoble one. Omar Khayyam, too, was intrigued by "the sovereign Alchemist that in a trice, Life's leaden metal into Gold transmute"; but like the alchemist's ambition, the teacher educator's dream of unlocking the secrets of success in teaching has been, in large measure, misconstrued and misdirected. The long and widely recognized record of failure does not suggest an extensive and frenzied search for the magic formula. Instead, it points toward a radical reformulation of the question in teacher education in modest terms and a critical exploration of the directions of *new* paths.

Chapter 2

Critique of
Current Practice

Edgar Z. Friedenberg

A major difficulty in formulating a useful critique of current practice in teacher education is that what the critic would criticize depends almost wholly on the relationship of teacher education to schooling that he accepts. Persons who believe that the schools are doing a useful job fairly well (if there be such persons) might still wish to suggest ways in which changes in teacher education would result in the schools' doing an even better job. Persons who believe that the schools, or some major proportion of them such as the large urban systems, are doing a poor job would almost certainly have proposals about how better teacher education could improve them. Critics writing from either point of view share a set of conventional assumptions: that schooling is a major source of education; that such education is useful to students; and that schools which do not benefit their students or which harm them are performing their function badly and require, although they may not welcome them, better-prepared teachers.

This critique, however, is written from a different set of assumptions, assumptions that reflect conclusions reached by major critics of the school system (Wasserman, 1970; Herndon, 1968, 1971; Friedenberg, 1965). In my view, the schools, like other social institutions, are primarily self-serving. They exist primarily to meet the economic needs and, to a lesser degree, the psychological needs of those involved in running them; and they obtain the support and resources that permit them to go on existing by serving the more powerful elements of society. The services they provide are many and diverse. They divide the population into winners and losers, in ways that correspond adequately though imperfectly to the class and ethnic distinctions existing in the society; and they instill in each child throughout childhood and adolescence the expectation as to which of these he or she is to become. By the time most pupils drop out or graduate they have internalized the evaluation that the schools make of their worth and prospects, although they may not consciously accept it; and even if they fight against it, they often do so in self-defeating ways which reveal that they have nevertheless been strongly affected by it.

Schools socialize. They impart values, patterns of anxiety, and habitual modes of response to authority and to peers, which are usually defended as necessary preparation for success in later life as well as in school. This defense, however, is largely a self-fulfilling prophecy, because the school also teaches its pupils how success is defined, characteristically in crass, petit bourgeois terms, and provides the credentials necessary to further progress along most conventional career lines. The only benefit it can confer on a pupil whose goals are different from or in conflict with the value system it imposes comes from the experience of struggling with and defending himself against it, although these are learning experiences that are not to be despised.

Of all the social groups whose interests are involved with that of the school system, the pupils who compose its largely compulsory clientele have the least power. They can not lawfully even be absent; they are not paid; they can not strike; their power to disrupt is limited by their special vulnerability to legal sanctions (compared to adults). Their sole power derives from the fact that only their presence and the benefits they are supposed to receive from their education legitimates the school system, which does depend ultimately on some degree of public consensus that the schools are useful in educating children. Since, however, there is very little consensus and much polarization along social class lines about what kind of education is beneficial and what kind oppressive and stultifying, or permissive and overindulgent, there is little danger of the schools' losing their legitimacy, so long as they manage to remain physically safe and orderly enough not to create a public scandal. Urban schools in North America can no longer even accomplish this.

There seems no convincing reason to believe that young people by being legally designated as pupils and compelled to attend schools learn more that is of value to them than they would if the school system had not been developed. This is not an empirically testable question since the schools do exist and by their existence have usurped the resources—forty billion dollars a year or more in the United States, roughly equal to the cost of the probably even more devastating Indochina war—that might have been devoted to alternative means of helping the young to learn. The schools have also rendered illegal during school hours those alternatives that might still be devised and funded. If choice were permitted, there are certainly more pleasant, and probably more instructive, things that persons between the ages of six and eighteen might be than either pupil or truant. That no choice is permitted is itself the best possible proof of the relative powerlessness of youth among the constituencies affected by the school system.

Starting from these premises, constructing a critique of current practice in teacher education is a complicated job. One must avoid putting the teacher-educators in a double bind in which they are sure to be damned either for doing a useful job badly or for doing a harmful job well. The nature of the difficulties encountered becomes clearer if the task is compared to that of evaluating the effectiveness of and offering suggestions to improve military training. Do you give credit or count off for depersonalization? For the weakening of the conscript's instinct of self-preservation? For reducing his tendency to question the moral basis of the adventure for which he is being trained? Is an officer candidate program better for enrolling only those conscripts with the characteristics traditionally attributed to "good officer material," making the deployment of its resources most efficient or is it obligated to identify and advance candidates whose promise may be obscured by ethnic or personality characteristics not usually esteemed in the corps?

Military training programs do not, however, justify their establishment as in the best interests of their conscripts. Schools do. Like the military, they claim to serve the interests of society as a whole, but this claim is based wholly on the skills and attitudes they presumably develop in their pupils to those pupils' putative advantage. The contribution of the schools to the gross national product could almost be calculated on the basis of "value added" to the student as he is processed: The propaganda directed against dropping out of school often takes the form of data purporting to show the cash value, presumed to reflect the social value, of a high school education in terms of total accrued life income. However crude and misleading this measure may be, it is nevertheless always treated as evidence of an advantage pupils may expect to derive from their schooling, not merely as an index of the effectiveness of the schools in supplying industry and the nation with a trained labor force.

Any critique of current teacher education programs is justified in addressing itself primarily to the effect such training may be expected to have on what students will learn. No school system or educational authority ever questions the premise, however absurd the fact that they do not may seem in the light of what happens in any particular school, that schools exist in order to educate pupils for the pupils' own, although not their sole, advantage. It does not follow from this that the best program of teacher education is one that enables teachers to function with the least friction in the schools that exist, or to earn the most favorable ratings from the administrators who employ them, or to materially increase their chances of steady and continuous employment, with increasing status, in the school system of their choice. A really challenging program of teacher education might, indeed, tend to unsuit those who complete it for service in any school, since it is likely that even the best schools act in fundamental ways as impediments to learning. True, they help learning, too, by bringing together persons

defined as learners, persons defined as teachers, and resource materials deemed instructive. But they do so under conditions of great
constraint and artifice, usually within an inflexible time schedule,
for the purpose of studying a curriculum that has largely become
a cliché, in an atmosphere dominated by lower–middle-class shabby
gentility and cheery cuteness. In the charnel-house schools of the
inner city, the atmosphere is far grimmer. These conditions are not
conducive to learning, unless one takes the school itself as a highly
expressive example of culture in action and treats it as a self-vali-
dating case study for use by its own pupils. And this is never done;
in fact, it would be regarded as unprofessional, since to do it would
require that teachers expose the hidden agenda in their own and
their colleagues' games.

Teacher education, to be most useful to the students whom
teachers will ultimately serve, must prepare teachers to facilitate
learning in contexts very different from those typically provided in
a public school. It must also prepare them to function in existing
schools in ways very different from those that schools now expect.
The most basic criticism of current practice in teacher education is
that it does not usually consider teaching to be at all different from
schooling. Certainly, some progress has been made in including in
the curriculum newer approaches to instruction. There is and there
should be, increasing attention paid to the open classroom and its
uses, to the use of the community as a laboratory in which students
may learn from experiences that involve them more completely than
a field trip could, and to the use of cameras, videotape machines,
and living theatre, not just as devices for presenting material to
students, but for students themselves to use as they are already
taught to use writing to record and express the meaning of their
experience and their own views of reality. Teacher education programs, in fact, have moved far ahead of practice in such innovative
instruction. Not many teachers who take jobs in the schools will
find much opportunity to make frequent use of such innovations,
and the courses that would prepare them to do so still remain elec-
tives in an otherwise largely prescribed program in many institutions. But teacher education has not remained static so far as its
influence on public school practice is concerned. Improved procedures are taught that may form an opening wedge as newer teachers

enter the system. Some results are to be expected, although the process, like administering a suppository to a fretful and elderly crocodile, is not likely to be rewarding either to the impatient or the excessively cautious young teacher.

At a more basic level, there has been no fundamental change. Students in teacher education programs are still thought of, and still think of themselves, as candidates for employment, and probably for careers, in a school system. They may have fantasies of changing it or they may anticipate fitting into it docilely, but they do not consider the possibility of building a life as an educator independent of it, even psychologically independent of it, as a prisoner of war is taught to remain independent of his prison camp. This, I believe, is a major reason that departments or schools of education have such low status in universities. No other discipline commonly accorded departmental or college status in the university has but a single client or accepts so servile a relationship to its client. Departments of economics do not train their students to be just what banks require; medical schools do not teach physicians to concede professional autonomy to the hospitals in which they practice, even though they must use these hospitals on their own terms.

Increasing awareness, within and outside the university, of the growing dependence of research on military contracts, especially in the natural sciences (and the concomitant effects on related departmental policy about the conduct of research and about hiring and retention of personnel) has led to what is probably the most serious crisis of confidence the university has ever faced; and the revelation that certain universities have allowed themselves to be used as a cover for counter-insurgency programs of the United States government created a public scandal. Meanwhile, oblivious of these reverberations, departments and schools of education have gone on defining their role totally as that of serving one of the most consistently authoritarian and coercive of public agencies as if no alternative definition were even possible. Teacher education programs do not teach their students to even consider that they might, much less how they might, plan a career as a teacher eschewing the public school system, although discontent with the public schools keeps mounting and myriad free schools, small, ill-funded, and often unsatisfactory, are created with the hope that they might be livelier and more open situations in which to learn, only to batter themselves to pieces in a few months against the legal barriers that function to protect the near monopoly that the public schools have on education or to fail from attrition because no provision for their support can be drawn from public funds.

Besides the fact that departments and schools of education are totally dependent for survival on the patronage of the public schools, there is another important reason why "educationists" are generally looked down on by their colleagues on university faculties. They are thought to have no subject matter uniquely their own, except for the tricks of the public-school trade. The charge is substantially true. No unique sociological insights or concepts are required in order to analyze and understand the functioning of the school as a social institution. No psychological principles apply just in the schoolroom and nowhere else; the psychology taught in psychology departments is quite adequate to explain why people learn, or do not learn, in school. Some of the philosophical problems raised by education are highly specialized, in as much as they are concentrated in the area of philosophy that deals with the relationship of symbols to phenomena, but this is a classic specialty within academic philosophy itself. Courses in these areas are taught in special pedagogical variants in schools of education, not because they have a specialized content that the departments of sociology or psychology or philosophy can not provide, but because they might prove ideologically unacceptable to such departments.

The one social science discipline that might have a unique and valuable contribution to make to teacher education is omitted from it: political science. School politics, internal and external, are different from other political phenomena studied in political science courses and can not really be approached in the same way. The basic principles are the same, no doubt, but what else is there that costs so much money, employs so many people (most of whom at any one time have tenure), serves a totally subject clientele, continues from year to year without having to demonstrate clearly just what it is producing (not to mention making a profit), and is supported largely by funds garnered from local taxation? Until the last qualification is added the military is a close parallel, but local support and local influence make the schools unique. Systematic study of politics related to the school would be a fascinating addition to teacher education; but it is unlikely to be found there. Something of the sort, although heavily biased toward the perpetuation of the schools, is taught in programs leading to degrees in school administration, but not, routinely, to prospective classroom teachers.

Psychology, on the other hand, which is included in teacher education programs as educational psychology is, I fear, a source of special difficulties because of the assumptions that underlie it. Educators treat psychology as an engineering discipline that teaches them how to perform operations on pupils: how to motivate them, how to measure their capacity and achievement, what kind and size of group to put them into and designate as a class, how to monitor their growth and give them guidance or remedial work to normalize them. This may or may not work; it probably does not most of the time, since the students get wise to what is being done to them and the school is usually subject to too many conflicting demands and regulations to permit the consistent application of any body of psychological theory, however enthusiastically undertaken. Sometimes, it may even work out for the best by boomeranging. There are at least grounds for hope that sex education, if widely adopted in the schools, may somewhat reduce the severity of the current population crisis by making sexuality as distasteful as most other attitudes the school intentionally seeks to instill. If the schools can only do for sex what they have already done for patriotism, lust may have to be removed from the list of cardinal sins, at least in highly schooled societies.

Whether or not educational psychology courses provide prospective teachers with applications that work, they do reinforce the teacher's conviction that teaching is a process by which you do something to a pupil and observe, if possible measure, his response. Educational psychology is activist, manipulative, and intrusive. This is not a defect inherent in the parent discipline itself; psychology need not be used in this way, although it often is by business, government, and industry at least as uncritically as by the schools. There is also a psychology of contemplative states; there is existential psychology, which is precisely not manipulative but seeks rather to be revelatory. Psychology, as a discipline, now embraces mysticism and altered states of consciousness as appropriate subjects for serious study. Educational psychology, however, goes on providing the teacher with the empirical whips she is supposed to crack in the air behind her students as she cries "Mush!"

This is less true, I think, of sociology of education, although there is no reason in principle why it should be. Educational sociology courses, that is, could draw from sociology primarily materials dealing with group dynamics, the Hawthorne effect, and such, and teach prospective teachers to use these as the basis for classroom engineering. The basic content of sociology of education courses, however, seems still to be drawn more frequently from concepts such as status and role as these affect the experiences of students in school, relations of the school to other social institutions, and power and forms of social control. This is useful and relevant material for prospective teachers, although in no way distinctively educational, except insofar as this, too, leads to reinforcement of the assumption that the word *educational* means "of, or referring to, the processes that take place in the schools that exist."

"Field experience," or practice-teaching, is the aspect of teacher education programs most directly and specifically linked to existing school practice as a model. Practice-teaching is probably the most strongly established part of the teacher education program. It has survived decades of curricular innovation substantially unchanged. Practical students, who are a large proportion of those who plan to become teachers, tend to regard it as the most valuable part of their professional program, often as the only valuable part, dismissing the background courses as "theoretical bullshit." Its inclusion in teacher education programs is required by state and provincial licensing requirements, although there may be a degree of flexibility in how these define the nature and length of the practice-teaching requirement.

In the usual program, the student teacher is sent into a school for a period of from a month or two to a semester and assigned, in effect, as an apprentice to a master teacher who is on the regular staff of the school. During this time he is observed at intervals by a supervising teacher from the faculty of the teacher education program in which he is enrolled. He starts out by simply observing or acting as an aide to the master teacher and is expected later on, after assimilating some of this mastery, to take over the class and teach it, if not independently, at least in the master teacher's absence. During this time he is still subject to observation and evaluation by both the master teacher and the supervising teacher. Both submit evaluations that become a part of his record and are intended as a guide to his prospective employers.

This seems a very sensible approach to teacher education, especially supplemented as it is with course work intended to broaden the context of the field experience. Apprenticeships, or, as those whose work is classified as professional prefer to call them, internships, are usually the part of any program of professional education that has the highest face validity. The student begins to get the feel of his future profession, and success and failure take on an objective rather than an arbitrary meaning. They are also the realistic part of the program, where the student can correct any excessively romantic notions he may have of what the profession is really like. But there are serious questions to be raised about the effects of such programs on the rating and subsequent performance of candidates for entry into the profession, and these are especially acute when the profession itself has developed dysfunctional aspects and must change radically in order to retain its social usefulness.

From the barrage of informed criticism directed against the schools and from the mere record of events that occur within them from day to day, it is clear that schooling has developed seriously dysfunctional aspects. It is also clear that it is perilous to think of education—if the word is to retain its positive connotation—as synonymous with schooling. But internships and practice-teaching as a required part of teacher education proceed on the assumption that the institutions in which the internship is served are models. The intern is being trained to practice his profession in a somewhat similar situation, governed by similar customs, styles, and codes of ethics. For the practice teacher, the school is not only a model institution, the master teacher is supposed to be a role model. He is expected to internalize the informal behavioral codes, styles, and ethics he learns as he participates as a teacher in the life of the school. This does not imply that he is expected to regard either the school or the master teacher as excellent, but they are supposed to indicate to him, in the words of the title of one of the most perceptive books about schools ever published, "The Way It Spozed to Be."

An internship is not defined as an opportunity for anthropological study. If it were, nothing could exceed the value of practice-teaching both as a part of the teacher education program and for its contribution to social insight in general. A school is a marvelously revealing microsection of the society it serves. There is simply no better place to study the operations of social class, the dynamics of small groups, the influence of status on channels of communication, alienation and ritualized behavior, systems of social sanctions and other mechanisms for social control, the influence of ideology on perception, juvenile delinquency, drug abuse. The whole assortment of social problems and social dynamics is there in small compass, laid out for participant observation. If practice teachers, in addition to their practice-teaching, were directed to observe and discuss such phenomena as these in the context of the school and were evaluated on their astuteness in perceiving and analyzing them, there could be no question whatever of the value of field experience in their programs. But in practice-teaching, the schools serve as the source of norms, not as a social laboratory with themselves as objects of scrutiny.

The function of practice teaching is to socialize the student into the teaching role in the institutions that exist, not to provide an opportunity to examine and come to understand the way they operate and their role in the larger scheme of things. That socialization is the intent seems obvious in view of the short time that elapses between graduation from high school and return to the schools for field experience: less than four years, and that time spent in college, which is not all that different. Indeed, if the people who enter teacher education programs had not been students so recently and for so long in schools like those in which they are destined to teach, practice-teaching would probably not be so much emphasized. It would not then be charged with one of its major functions, resocialization. One of the greater difficulties in equipping people to reenter the schools as teachers is their earlier socialization as students, which leaves them with a complex of conflicting attitudes toward the school and their roles in it. Practice-teaching does not eradicate this conflict: the conflict is not really rooted out, worked through, and removed. Practice-teaching merely buries it by anticipatory socialization into the new, higher-status role of teacher, much as upwardly mobile lower–middle-class members of ethnic enclaves assume the life style and sexual attitudes of middle-class suburbia while the attitudes and values characteristic of their former life style remain latent in them. This makes practice teachers more rigid as they embrace their new status; the newly converted often try to be more Catholic than the Pope.

Internships, in fact, act fully as much as rites of passage as they do opportunities to learn professional techniques. They are initiations and, as such, close off as much as possible the initiate's earlier, lay experience with the organization to which he has now been admitted. This greatly reduces the innovative effects of the admission of new recruits and helps to explain the glacial immutability of school systems (and the medical profession) to modernization at the hands of their newer members. Other factors, of course, are equally and perhaps more important: The fact that the neophyte has low status, no tenure, and is subject to the judgment of his elders for preferment in the profession also prevents the young teacher from acting very effectively as an agent of change, even though he may personally be very critical of established practice. But practice-teaching serves also to establish the identity of the student teacher as a teacher, thus preventing him from acting on or even recalling with any vividness the resentments, sense of impotence, and humiliation that, along with more positive feelings, are a large part of adults' memories of what it was like to be a pupil. In this way, the profession stabilizes itself.

The functions of socialization and social analysis are, however, incompatible. A program of practice-teaching that encouraged its practice teachers to view the school as an anthropologist might, becoming consciously aware of its folkways, sanctions, and rituals, would impede their identification as teachers. They would be encouraged to remain marginal men, detached intellectuals, which would pose a severe threat to the existing power structure of the profession. Since teacher education programs are so largely the agency of existing school systems, no such program is likely to be encouraged.

There is, in fact, considerable empirical evidence from studies like those of Iannacone and Button (1964, p. 3), Haslam (1971), and Conner and Smith (1967) that student teachers become measurably more rigid and authoritarian in their approach to pupils and to classroom routines during the course of their field experience. I would like to see the practice eliminated from teacher education programs as counter-productive to the stated aims of such programs, but this is unlikely since it contributes greatly to their actual aims. Another way in which its constrictive effects might be minimized at the same time that what value it has in familiarizing prospective teachers with the feel of actual school routines could be retained would be to use a technique that has already begun to be introduced in teacher education programs and in inservice training of teachers. This is the encounter group in which the members of the social group express the feelings that affect social interaction so that they can be consciously dealt with and taken into account in the formulation of policy. The popularity of encounter groups as a form of industrial psychology has its threatening and manipulative aspect, as well as an underlying falseness, particularly when the group is made up of members of an organization who will later be able to impose sanctions on one another for having been excessively frank in this situation. Nevertheless, they do work better than anything else in breaking down established patterns of response derived from status and role rather than from the actual feelings and demands of the protagonists.

Teacher education programs might be much enhanced by bringing together teachers, both master and student, and their pupils for a day of open encounter, presumably after the practice-teaching period, when all the reports are in. Pupils could ask why the student teacher had accepted the routines of the school instead of following his own values, if these appeared to be in conflict, the student teacher could question the sources of the pupils' apathy or superficial compliance, if these became an obstacle to learning, and so forth. All this can of course be done during class if the student teacher is "together" enough to encourage it, but most student teachers are not. The function of the teacher education program is, presumably, to assist them in developing just those competences useful in their profession, which they have so far not developed whether through inexperience, immaturity, or timidity. An encounter group might help with these.

Other specific revisions of the teacher education program, intended to increase its liberalizing effect on teachers and make them more resourceful in facilitating learning in a wide variety of pupils can certainly be suggested. Yet, there is a certain unreality in suggesting improvements directed toward such ends as these. Schools, as Herndon so eloquently asserts, are not going to change (1971, pp. 111–112). Institutions hardly ever do; instead, as they become dysfunctional, others, with different hangups, supersede them. It is far more likely that persons below the age of eighteen will cease to be defined by law as pupils and confined in schools than it is that schools will greatly alter.

Teacher education programs are literally the creatures of the public school system, regardless of their college or university affiliations; and the central function of the public school system in a time of crisis is to preserve itself and the jobs and perquisites of its staff. The growth of unionism in the schools—the New York City system provides some especially striking examples—demonstrates fairly clearly that the fundamental concern of those who operate the schools is to keep their jobs and keep those jobs from demanding more than they can contribute to them, emotionally or intellectually. The pupils must be kept coming so that the teachers will have posts and the money provided by the state, which is based on average daily attendance, can be collected. If teachers strike, as they did unlawfully in New York City, holidays can be abolished and the school year extended to make up the lost time. If students strike, they are truants. They must be there and are enjoined to ask not what the schools can do for them but, rather, what they can do for the schools.

There is nothing unusually iniquitous about this; it is largely true of every institution that serves a captive clientele. But that it is true should set limits to the enthusiasm for liberal reforms that do not alter the distribution of power within the institutions. Programs of foreign aid do not help the poor and enslaved in the countries that receive it; they help keep in power the governments that impoverish and enslave them. Poverty programs do not alleviate the sufferings of the poor; they establish a huge and lucrative poverty industry that benefits social workers and accountants, making use of the poor as essential raw material. And improvements in teacher education programs usually can not benefit students because the difficulties the pupil experiences are inherent in his status as a pupil. It is not possible to do much to help people who have low status from within the system in which that status is defined because having low status means, among other things, that your superiors in status are free to rip off the benefits that were intended for you. And teacher education programs are within that system.

Improvements in education there will certainly be and probably fairly rapidly. But they must be brought about by changes in the status of pupils themselves: changes in compulsory attendance laws and changes easing the establishment of alternative schools and widening their basis for support. Unionization of pupils to countervail against teachers' unions and, especially, the use of such organizations to provide an independent base for activities usually centered in and controlled by individual schools would improve student status immeasurably. High school students in Vancouver, British Columbia, have, for example, been publishing *Interschool,* a newspaper devoted to the concerns of high school students but not associated with any particular high school and hence no more subject to prior restraint on publishing or the demands of an advisor than is any other paper in Canada.

There is a genuine conflict of interest among the cadres that constitute the schools' constituencies: pupils, faculty, administrative staff—local, "downtown," and in the state or provincial capitol—and parents. Assistance directed to the benefit of one can not usually be channelled through the agency of another. This is especially true of assistance intended to improve the lot of pupils, the weakest and most vulnerable of the schools' constituencies, yet the one on which the legitimacy of the entire enterprise rests, and whose continued acquiescence must be insured at all costs. Ultimately it is this fact, and this fact alone, that is likely to make improvement in the teacher education program very limited in its effect on school practice.

Chapter 3

Teacher Education
for the 1980s

Theodore R. Sizer

The needs and character of children and the cultures surrounding them govern the shape of schools and the roles of teachers within them. Teacher education, in turn, must help prepare those teachers for the jobs available to them. Teacher education is thus fourth in line: One cannot plan for the training of educators in the 1980s without prior consideration of children, the culture, and the schools.

Schools, and the expectations of society for them, are unlikely to be very different in 1980 from what they are today. That there will be minimal change should be no surprise: Schools have altered remarkably little, relative to the changes in society and scholarship, since 1900. The factors that have reinforced the status quo in recent decades will be even more pronounced in the next ten years. Formal education will be increasing in rigidity rather than decreasing, and before considering appropriate forms of teacher education for the future, it would be well to review the reasons for this rigidity. They are at the center of an explanation of what most Americans feel schools provide and what they are for.

It is important that educators understand the extent of public satisfaction with existing schools. Professionals often overlook the fact that those flaws in the system that they identify either are not recognized at all by the public or are considered popularly to be virtues rather than vices. For much of the public, schools provide elementary skill and job training, and they serve as a rite of social passage, a place for the collecting of social symbols considered to have great value. Over the years, of course, these rites have meaning only if they remain relatively fixed, a series of hurdles over which grandparents, parents, and children have jumped or should jump. At the end are diplomas and degrees, the outward manifestation of social "success," and one tampers with these at one's peril. Even in those schools that have been hit in recent years by racial or social-class-related turbulence, fundamental reconstruction of the educational program has rarely been seen. In fact, the public response to disorder in schools has most often been to blame the children rather than the system, and remedies have usually been ones of repression rather than of reform. The public likes the schools; when it is dissatisfied, it is because the schools are not meeting their agreed-upon objectives, and not because these objectives themselves are dubious or misdirected (Gallup, 1972).

It is easy to mock public support of often empty social symbols, but in a nation that thinks it has rejected a hereditary delineation of classes, a sorting system that appears meritocratic has considerable and understandable appeal. Schools, as much recent research has amply demonstrated, actually reward the wealthier sectors of the population, providing apparently class-free legitimization to the dominant interests of middle- and upper-income groups. The school system meets an important social need, popularly desired even if, in some abstract order of justice, it is patently unfair. If one eliminated our school system, one would have to invent another.

Given the importance of this symbolic function, it is no surprise to find the curricula of schools and, for that matter, of universities so unchanging. The central core of liberal studies—language, social science, natural science, and mathematics—has remained remarkably fixed since the turn of the century and is likely to continue so well beyond the 1980s. Not only is the public satisfied with these studies, but the scholarly world, immune as it is from serious external challenge, accepts them as gospel as well. Even the most radical universities preserve the traditional curriculum and the departments representing its several components. The profession depends on them: The core subjects representing liberal studies are unassailably entrenched for the next decade or two. Again, it is easy to curse this apparently unthinking acceptance. In the abstract it makes poor sense. In sociopolitical terms, of course, it is wholly plausible.

After the Second World War American education expanded at a rate of revolutionary proportions, a rate that could have caused significant alteration and reform of the schools. Numbers of youngsters in classrooms grew almost geometrically as the baby boom that followed the cessation of hostilities washed in upon the schools. Not surprisingly, there was a teacher shortage, and the number of new teachers in the schools increased significantly. If these young men and women had been trained in dramatically different ways from their predecessors, the schools might have taken a significantly different direction than they did. But they were not, of course, and the opportunity was missed. In the next decade, we do not have a similar opportunity. The number of youngsters in American elementary and secondary schools will increase very slowly, at a markedly lower rate than that the United States experienced from 1950 to 1965. Without rapidly increasing enrollments, there will be no need for large numbers of new, young teachers to enter teaching. New blood, however trained, will enter slowly indeed.

In addition, teacher turnover, traditionally high relative to other professions, may decline. Salaries and perquisites accorded school teachers have, on the whole, run ahead of those in comparable lines of work, and increasingly effective unionization is likely to accelerate this trend. As a group, teachers are reasonably well paid; it is now possible for a person with three or four dependents, employed in a city or a moderately affluent suburb, to support them tolerably well by teaching. The need to leave the classroom when family responsibilities become heavy will, as a result, decrease. Furthermore, the growing social acceptance both of working mothers' and of women's carrying significant outside employment will decrease the number of departures of many young female teachers (save for short periods while their children are infants). The pregnant teacher, the teacher with young children, the part-time teacher are all increasingly accepted by school systems, which have been cajoled by the national discussion of women's rights and the public ridicule of practices that previously had discriminated against females. This will result in a far more stable female teaching force than we have seen before, lessening even further the need for new teachers in the schools. If change is to come about in the 1980s, it will be led by a staff now entering or already in service.

In addition, formal education is moving into a period notable for its psychology of limited resources, a political climate which no longer assumes that growth is inevitable and infinite reform possible. The overblown rhetoric and overcommitted public responsibilities of the middle and late 1960s are now home to roost. There are many complex causes for this, far beyond the scope of this chapter, but it is enough to say that the cheap ride that the American middle class was provided in the 1950s and 1960s by noncompetitive foreign markets and an underpaid industrial sector is no longer possible. Local tax burdens have reached the point of no return, and the politics of the 1970s and 1980s are likely to be ones of making do with a minimum. This will inevitably hit the public sector first—state hospitals, prisons, schools, and transit authorities. Indeed, it already has. Schools, often absorbing the largest percentage of the public costs in many communities, will feel it acutely. However, as during the Depression of the 1930s, there is no reason to believe that tightened belts will lead to significant educational changes. There is a floor of school services below which very few communities will drop. This floor is a traditional one almost precisely like the one that existed in the 1890s: one teacher and thirty-five to forty pupils. An additional effect of the financial crisis has been and will continue to be to force teachers into militant unionization. An accommodation between city authority and union will follow, which will provide for maximum protection of teachers at minimum cost to the community. A precondition for tough bargaining between teachers and community will be acceptance of a relatively static relationship between numbers of teachers to number of pupils. It is highly unlikely that a significant change in the form of instruction or the content of instruction will emerge. Certainly, it has not in negotiations in public trades and professions other than teaching. The public—the kids—is damned. Such a state of affairs is poor soil in which to plant change.

There are other political causes for the likely lack of change in schools. Public education is increasingly losing the support of the liberal intellectuals who for generations served as its spokesmen and articulators of need. The "new realism" that has followed the rhetorical excesses of the Johnson administration has extended to the scholarly world as much as to any other, and the journals today are increasingly filled with articles by debunking social scientists who challenge the success of the enterprises so eagerly forwarded by the optimists of the 1960s. This realism is, of course, in great measure healthy; it would be even more so if it were seized upon by the teaching profession as the basis for reform. But, alas, our profession is notable for its failure to act on evidence relating to its performance from any form of theory: It is a pseudoprofession, resting on experience and apprenticeship rather than on ideas. As a result, the profession erects poor defenses against the charges of social science. The response has often been Luddite: One hears an attack from senior school administrators and from teacher union leaders alike on "useless" research such as that carried out by James Coleman. This kind of criticism of the "new realism" merely reinforces the suspicions of what one might call today the *Public Interest* crowd of American intellectuals. The yowl of rage from educators merely increases the suspicions of the critics (and the arrogance, too), and one finds an unexpected coalition of so-called radical reformers of the Kozol-Holt-Illich stripe and the social-science debunkers such as Moynihan and Jencks arrayed against the educationists. Strange bedfellows!

If change in the schools is unlikely, then the planning task of teacher educators is remarkably easy. What is needed for tomorrow is what was needed yesterday: a sound understanding of the officially prescribed subjects of the curriculum—physics, reading, mathematics, American history, and the rest—and some experience in purveying these to children. Given the low likelihood of public interest in significantly changing the curriculum, extensive theoretical training can be dispensed with. One simply needs to combine sound traditional collegiate training in the subjects that are in the course of study in the schools with well-supervised and sensitive practical instruction in the craft of teaching, this, most likely, provided in the schools.

B. O. Smith gives perhaps the most helpful prescription for teacher education that assumes the status quo (1969). Professional training is to be concentrated in so-called teacher complexes, American variations of British teacher centers; prospective teachers arrive for training in these complexes after mastering, to some degree, one of the subjects of the curriculum (or its equivalent for elementary school teachers). Experienced teachers would also be served by the complexes. The complexes and centers do imply, of course, that, although reform is needed, it is reform within the parameters of the existing school, by existing teachers, and under existing governmental structures. One cannot seriously quarrel with this implication, for it is realistic. Teacher complexes are constructive, if incremental.

The point of view that Smith expresses is basically quite consistent with the recommendations both of Conant (1959, 1963) for American schools in the early 1960s and with Lord James's commission for teacher education in the United Kingdom (1972). Both, even though in somewhat different ways, imply that school organization, school practice, and school aims are givens, relatively unchallengeable, and that the problem of teacher education is the accommodation of new professionals to this relatively fixed system. An intelligent blend of scholarly study and induction as apprentices is sensible within this framework; indeed, it is almost beyond criticism. British and American educators will consume hours of time wrangling over the details of such training, as they have in the past, but the broad outlines of teacher education for the schools are unlikely to be contested. Indeed, the details will probably make very little difference at all, being but variations on a strong, sensible, obvious, but conservative theme.

However, we can escape neither from the findings of the "new realists" nor from the common sense of experienced school teachers. Although we may not wish to use the hyperbole of many of the radical critics, who assert that our children are dying and that teachers are guilty of genocide, it is simple honesty to suggest that the current school system is in many respects outmoded. Teacher educators, even as they realistically allow that little fresh thinking on a wide scale and few brave new educational forms will emerge for children over the next ten years, cannot escape the obligation to promote reform in a least a few teacher training institutions and schools, places where an effort to be honest with the issues of education can begin. In this, one need not be conspiratorial, secretive, hyperbolic, or contemptuous of the motives of the rest of the profession: Humility is the soul of truth. Nor does one need to be insensitive to public pressures, both symbolic and financial, on the schools. Nor does one need to be excessively theoretical. One merely needs to be self-critical.

For example, consider the implications of the following summary of a major study of teachers:

> [Our study] does not lend much support to those who claim that better teacher recruitment and training will appreciably boost student achievement. Effective teachers are about equally likely to be born rich or poor, black or white, male or female. They appear no more likely to graduate from liberal arts colleges than from teachers' colleges, to major in academic subjects rather than education, to attend what they view as "good" rather than "bad" colleges, or to hold higher degrees. Verbally fluent teachers may be slightly more effective than verbally inept teachers, but it is not clear whether they are better at teaching their pupils or only at negotiating their way into schools where pupils overachieve for other reasons [Jencks, 1972, p. 101].

Findings such as this, and this study is modestly reported, strike at the heart of the assumptions upon which we have rested teacher education for generations. We have depended unquestioningly on universities for academic standards. The challenge of the "realists" to the universities is hard to handle, but careful consideration of their evidence must serve as a precondition for any kind of fresh look in the education of children.

Fortunately, much of the "realist" social science squares

with the hunches of wise school teachers. Most teachers will agree with scholars in the behavioral sciences that an interested pupil learns more than a bored one and that the world outside the classroom is often more interesting to him than that inside. It follows that if those academic ends desired by the school (let us accept those for a minute unchallenged) could be related to interests exhibited outside of school, then learning would be more powerful. Obviously, learning and teaching should proceed both in and out of school, in some mix appropriate for the child rather than be dictated by some rigid compulsory school-attendance law.

It is no special surprise to find that youngsters learn more from their peers and their unstructured youthful "surround" than they do from their teachers, more in a cognitive sense as well as in the sense of values and attitudes. Ours is a society awash in information, a congested society where youngsters are constantly thrust among large numbers of people. A classroom as youngsters' principal source of vicarious knowledge, the principal place where they meet individuals their own age, has far less importance today than it did in a thinly populated, isolated age; as a social experience it is redundant for children. School is no longer special. There is stimulation for learning all around, in the street, on television, in the cheap press, and elsewhere. The number of hours a year during which a child is bombarded with images and information far exceeds that afforded him in school, and the battle is no contest. The world out of school now informally teaches many things for which the common schools were in fact created. Educators need to accept this reality and to seize for public uses all agencies that provide powerful learning experience for youngsters—schools, the media, and more. The concept of school needs to be sharply extended.

Teachers and social scientists agree that youngsters learn at different rates and that these rates do not necessarily follow the chronology of age. A mass of literature on grouping and tracking supports this view, but the fact remains that our schools operate primarily by age groups. Youngsters enter school at five or six, and they go through eight or nine grades before entering something called high school. They graduate with their age group, even though everybody all along the way knows that some youngsters are ahead of others by any relevant standard of intellectual competence, physical competence, or social maturity. Furthermore, common sense shows that as the power to learn relates to the power of interest, many older people who previously eschewed learning desire it in their twenties or thirties or later. They are readier for learning after their teens than during them. For them, there was compulsory attendance when they did not want it but few formal opportunities later when they want them, few opportunities to rejoin the educating stream. Existing high school equivalency exams are, by and large, an insult to the intelligence and maturity of older people. Community colleges and adult education programs are hardly widespread or demanding enough to meet a need that common sense suggests should exist in large numbers. Why can not educators act on their common sense and on the evidence of social scientists both by breaking the grip of chronological promotion and by providing formal education for youngsters and adults on some basis other than full-time incarceration in schools until the age of sixteen (or later)?

Many teachers and social scientists agree that there are differing modes of learning, each appropriate to achieving a particular pedagogical objective. Some are highly sequential, some are analytic, some intuitive, some a mix of these. The initial learning of a language is a different kind of mental exercise from the development of prose style in one's mother tongue. The mode of thought required by a chemistry laboratory experiment is different from that provoked with the wrestling over conflicting claims arising from some incident in history. Nonetheless, virtually all instruction in our schools today is carried on in a roughly common mode, with classes conducted for similar lengths of time for a similar number of hours per week in similar groups, irrespective of the objectives of the course, the mode of thinking and acting required for it, or the particular disposition of a particular set of pupils and teacher. Such arrangements make sense for scheduling officers, but for few others.

Few teachers need a social scientist or a theologian to persuade them that there can be no such thing as a moral-free or moral-neutral school or a school from which all sectarian religious views are excluded. Furthermore, our commonsensical teacher would agree that there is no such thing as a school free from political ideology, from a faculty and a student body that exhibit in one way or another a set of political and social values. Few schools exist that contain within themselves widely diverse ideologies: Indeed, such may be impossible. Given the educational objective (perhaps) to provide youngsters with a range of political and moral points of view as well as the intellectual equipment to sort them out, one might come to the conclusion that there is a need for youngsters to attend several different schools at a time, ones providing different value frames and political positions. At the least, the unitary schools found in socially segregated American communities might be recognized as political and moral agencies, hardly institutions that are value-free. If we can not provide youngsters with formal education that offers a variety of values (a shocking admission), we can at least expose the current delusion that we in education are neutral. We must, as teachers, be respectfully self-conscious about our values and biases.

It is obvious that a self-confident, self-aware student is more able to capitalize on abstract learning than is a youngster personally at sea. A youngster who believes in himself believes in his future and is likely to devote energy and effort to improve that future. The child's future is, of course, what education is all about: Schooling for him is an investment. However, some classroom teachers act as if self-confidence is but a secondary responsibility, being the primary responsibility of someone called counselor. The notion that a teacher of mathematics or of British history has a responsibility to build the confidence of a youngster often does not cross that teacher's mind. Somehow he believes that it is quite acceptable to terrorize, harass, and insult youngsters (however unwittingly) in the interests of inculcating a subject; children's sensitivity and self-regard is of secondary concern in teaching the discipline at hand. Our "realistic" social scientist, however, would suggest that a student's self-regard (or future orientation) is a precondition for his achievement of both cognitive or affective ends and thus should be a primary task for teaching. Even so, the profession continues with its specialisms, separating the task of generating self-confidence from the task of formal teaching, with predictable results.

It is clear that there is much dysfunctional and ineffective in the existing educational system upon which fair-minded teachers, as well as social science researchers, can agree. The catalogue of sins

above is only suggestive, but it is a beginning. It is enough to provide a sense of where teacher education might go beyond the
scholarly and craft training represented in *Teachers for the Real
World* and in the James report.

Teacher education should do more than prepare a professional for a classroom, important though that is. A true professional
must look beyond the expectations of his public and of his corporate
constituency. He must understand not only the inherited traditions
of the craft through apprenticeship (which is, of course, what
teacher complexes and teacher centers are all about); but he must
also visualize the practical implications for the learning of youngsters both of his own common sense and of theoretical reformulation
based on new scientific evidence. A correctly trained teacher should
be a critic of compulsory education as presently practiced, as it is a
system which assumes that human beings learn in the same way at
the same rates at the same time. He must understand the whipsaw
of prejudice and opinion and recognize his own ideologies as well
as the need to prepare youngsters both to develop their own and to
criticize all of them. In a word, he must learn not to be deluded by
outmoded traditions of the past, by recollections of his own education, or by dysfunctional convention.

Teacher education in the 1980s? If the foregoing are to be
more than brave words, teacher education must be forwarded on
two fronts simultaneously. On one, the sensible incremental improvements suggested for American and British education since the
1950s by Conant, Koerner, James, and the rest should be implemented: increasing the quality of scholarly preparation in the teaching and vocational fields and sharpening the professional training of
teachers through "clinical" apprenticeship in well-supervised, imaginative teacher complexes or centers. How one accomplishes each of
these will vary considerably from district to district and country to
country, but the outlines of what needs to be done have been well
argued now for over twenty years. One needs merely to get on with
them, with a minimum of wordy nit-picking.

The second is more difficult and less familiar for educators.
One essential is research, and if teacher educators, schools of education, do not promote it assiduously, the needed inquiry will
languish. A firm basis for teaching practice is needed, and only

systematic and sustained inquiry can provide it. Shared anecdotes of able teachers can help, but, given the likely fundamental flaws in current school organization, the collective best experience of professionals will not provide the understanding that is required. Since no academic institution save the school of education now exists to champion such work, it is up to the teacher education fraternity to see that it happens.

Equally important will be the creation of an "invisible college" of educators devoted to the reformulation of formal education. Few social reforms, at least of the magnitude of that needed in education, have succeeded without a sound scholarly base and a corps of scholars and activists devoted to its promotion. In the natural sciences, the importance of "invisible colleges" has long been recognized. It has been almost completely ignored by those concerned with educational reform, who have concentrated on the externals of scientific research in making hopeful analogies, on laboratories, budgeting systems, and the like. The low-profile community of scholars that forms the center of sustained inquiry is notable for its absence in education. Our professional organizations look far more like labor unions than the Royal Society or Benjamin Franklin's Junto (Price, 1963). What is needed is a group of experienced educators who are willing to consider the education of children (a far larger topic than schools) and the means by which the youngsters' interests could be forwarded. Such a group is unlikely to be an association or anything with boards of directors, letterheads, or the other familiar institutional bric-a-brac. It will be a group of people brought together, in person or through its writings, by ideas or scientific approaches. A small such group now exists around Lawrence Cremin on historical studies in education. Some social scientists who were principally brought together by common interests in the famed equal educational opportunity study —James Coleman, Samuel Bowles, Henry Levin, Christopher Jencks, Daniel Patrick Moynihan, Thomas Pettigrew, among others —are in touch, and their published work (often contentiously) constitutes a coherent debate on an important aspect of educational policy. The group made up of John Holt, Jonathan Kozol, Ivan Illich, and others also operates. Yet each of these informal, and largely happenstance, groupings is yet too narrow, too devoted to a single line of concern. A group in education with the breadth (if not the precise focus) of the scientific group which staffed the President's Science Advisory Committee in the late 1950s and 1960s is needed.

How to create it? It will require a focus—a Coleman report or a PSAC—or a devoted individual who works at it, such as Cremin has done in his field. It could be provoked by a foundation, simply by giving an individual a line of credit to bring people together, to try to get the "chemistry" going. From the work of individuals in such a group, from their discussion, inquiry, and experiment, a comprehensive approach to education could emerge, and the issue of children's learning addressed from a broader perspective than formal classrooms. A network of colleagues could be the cell from which public understanding of the need for a broader, more realistic conception of education can grow.

Thus teacher education must proceed both toward incremental reform, through strong disciplinary training and professional preparation and continual retraining in teacher centers and complexes, and toward comprehensive reform, through systematic inquiry into teaching and learning and through a network of devoted schoolmen and scholars who can create the conditions for fundamental change in the education of children.

Chapter 4

Improving Teacher Education Through Exposures to Reality

Harold Howe II

No one, teachers of teachers included, presumes that undergraduate or graduate concentration in education courses is the prime requisite for turning out effective educators. Every evidence is that much, even most, of what makes the able teacher or the able administrator effective he learns on the job by doing it. Consider the analogy of learning how to play tennis. (It could just as well be golf, or cooking, or speaking French, or music. The incomparable blues singer B. B. King once tried to explain to an interviewer how he reached his preeminence: After a respectful salute to the values of formal education, he credited twenty-five solid years of "majoring, minoring in the blues, living the blues.")

53

But returning to tennis, where I can adduce firsthand experience. The only way to learn tennis is to play with someone better than you who can provide what psychologists call immediate feedback. Few rewards, if any, come to the would-be player from reading about tennis, watching other people play tennis, seeing tennis on film or television, or from mastering the technical details of how to build tennis courts, string tennis rackets, and put the fur on tennis balls. One technological refinement might help: seeing your own game on television (even as "microteaching" can help the teaching novice by allowing him to see himself on the small screen and to join in appraising his performance with his peers and elders). Tennis demands judgment of the actions of others, a capacity to anticipate, a set of physical skills, and endless practice. You can talk about tennis all you want, seek out tennis players at parties, and pay high prices for seats in the front row at Forest Hills or Wimbledon without improving your tennis game very much, even though you may improve your tennis conversation.

To be sure, teaching takes place within an intellectual context, as tennis does not, and requires a mastery of subject matter and an understanding of the peculiarities of human beings who teach and learn. Teaching also includes, however, a large component of what some call methodology, others call art, and what I regard largely as a complex of skills. These skills are based on the ability to size up individuals, to judge their responses, and to make your responses reflect theirs, to diagnose each one's special needs and problems, to present ideas and activities in ways that will motivate interest in learning, to coordinate varied materials into their most effective impact, to sense the nuances of individual and group attitudes and feelings, and to balance all these variables in a kaleidoscopic drama featuring players with different rates of learning, different backgrounds, and totally different feelings.

The human equation of teaching is infinitely varied, and whoever learns to solve it does so not by reading about the solutions of others past or present, or by attending lectures on how others have approached the problem, or even by watching movies of good teachers at work. However valuable the good teacher's academic preparation may have been, he only emerges as a good teacher and comes somewhere near solving his multifaceted problem by getting into a classroom, contending with reality, and getting immediate feedback on his performance from someone more skillful than he is, someone who can tell him how he might perform a given task better, why one activity or another seems more or less productive, and which alternative approaches might yield better results.

If this observation is true for teachers, it is even more true for school leaders. Certainly there are management practices and systems techniques applicable to education and its leadership to be learned, together with aspects of economics, psychology, history, and other fields. The large fact still remains, however: An effective school principal, or an outstanding superintendent, or someone capable of the balancing act a state commissioner of education must perform needs political skills, emotional poise and personal confidence, and the ability to deal calmly with crisis, all qualities that are best learned by practice.

To emphasize experience is not to demean the university. If an educator is to be highly competent, he must have an excellent academic preparation. But the best educators, whether teachers or administrators or specialists, are those who combine this background with the capacity to assimilate and profit from experience.

Universities have long recognized the importance of direct experience in the preparation of teachers and administrators. Practice-teaching, internships, special research assignments in the schools, and related programs are integral elements of formal teacher preparation and inservice training. In theory, at least, the conventional wisdom recognizes that learning by doing must complement the purely academic education of the educator. In practice, however, this essential element of training teachers and administrators is all too often neglected.

One reason for this neglect is human enough: Professors in schools of education are more comfortable in schools of education than they are in schools. They and their institutions tend to be insulated from the realities of the schools and of teaching young people. Their research and writing is frequently oriented to bookish problems rather than practical ones. Course work is too frequently a well-packaged academic exercise instead of a confrontation with the disturbing reality of a rapidly changing world in which the needs of children have outstripped capacity of the schools for response.

To avoid charges of oversimplification and unfairness, it is only right to add that teacher training is better than it used to be. In New York State, for instance, notable for its unusually strong and enlightened state education policies and leadership, basing permanent certification on competency on the job instead of on successful completion of traditional and often mediocre graduate courses has been official policy for some time. And the teachers college has gone the way of the normal school, even though the transformation may be only name-deep. Progress has been made in deeper ways, too, for example, the development of the degree of master of arts in education and other efforts to integrate undergraduate teacher preparation more closely into the whole university fabric and to replace the old time, often unproductive, practice-teaching with more responsible internships. Yet progress has been too slow. New problems and challenges (or old ones long ignored) keep cropping up, the special needs of children from the slums, for instance, or the boredom and rebellion of bright high school students, or the competition and opportunity presented by modern telecommunications.

All over the country educators are making efforts to improve learning in the schools through the use of new and imaginative approaches that break down lockstep routines. The key word in the new reforms is *open,* and let us hope that it escapes the debasement into a stylish catchword without substance that has happened to many a promising idea in the past. It is not just in a few selected New York City schools that the open classroom, adapted largely from the British experience, is being tried. It is attracting widespread interest: For one notable example, the open classroom idea underlies the plan of North Dakota to reform its entire educational system.

But even assuming good will and conviction on the part of educators in trying out such reforms, it is obviously easier to say "Open, classroom!" than it is to do it. For teachers and administrators alike, running effective open programs means breaking hard, unfamiliar ground, where the signals are changed and the signposts are nonexistent. They need all the help they can get. The Ford Foundation, for instance, is increasing its emphasis on helping centers that are training or retraining teachers as well as assisting programs that try to open up the learning process, pursue and apply pertinent research, and relate school and community more closely. Two recent foundation grants assisted centers organized to develop leadership among practicing urban educators. In Boston, the Institute for Learning and Teaching of the University of Massachusetts is training teachers for the new open schools, exposing teachers of Spanish-speaking children to Puerto Rican culture, and making it possible for community residents to earn bachelor's degrees and full certification through working in the schools. The Community Resources Institute, an affiliate of the City University of New York, conducts workshops in pilot schools for teachers, aides, parents, and principals and trains advisors who can help teachers make the new approach work well. The Ford Foundation plans to assist a number of other programs designed to assemble teachers to learn how to use new materials, media, and pedagogy. Backed up by advisors, teachers themselves run centers where they can exchange ideas, study, perhaps develop new curricula and materials, and extend their repertoire of ways to reach children and ease learning. In these and other foundation-assisted programs, the focus is on retraining educators rather than on training for entry to the profession. But there are already indications of the salutary effect that greater use of the classroom for inservice training can have on preservice training.

Indeed, if a well-disposed critic were allowed only one suggestion for improving the preservice and inservice training programs of teachers and administrators in the United States, it would be to center a higher proportion of the process in the schools rather than in the university. This is by no means the same as urging the abolition of schools of education or the reduction of their staffs in significance or size. It is shifting a good proportion of those staffs from the universities into the schools. Surely one of the great untapped resources for the education of educators is that small band of extremely skillful and gifted teachers and administrators who grace our schools.

Excellence by definition is rare. The term *master teacher* understandably raises hackles in some quarters; the idea it implies has been a controversial aspect of team teaching. Besides that, one hardly wants to invoke echoes of the medieval master and apprentice. Unwarranted prejudice aside, however, superior teachers are everywhere, in schools large and small, urban and rural, rich and poor: the man or woman particularly talented in reaching eight-year-olds, for instance, or making the school library a popular resource, or matching guidance service to pupil, or, as principal, orchestrating the entire school program, or, as superintendent, setting the tone for the complex set of relations between school and community. An effective way to reorganize a school of education would be to compose perhaps half the staff of such practicing experts, organizing their schedules so that they have time to work with preservice and inservice trainees who are trying to become real educators.

The staff of my ideal school of education would also include people seldom found in such institutions, many of whom could not meet the usual requirements for being professors, associate professors, assistant professors, or instructors. Sympathetic officers from the police department who are regularly in contact with young people, social workers who are in and out of the homes that produce the toughest problems of schools, court officers and probation agents of various categories who deal with juveniles in problem situations, workers from the recreation department of the city and the parks department, businessmen who operate establishments where young people congregate or who are potential employers, and a variety of other people from the community whose work or avocation as well as outlook and temperament can engage the interests of the young —all are candidates. So are painters, poets, musicians, actors, television producers, lawyers, doctors, politicians, craftsmen of all kinds. The list is endless.

Enlightened school systems across the country are involving outsiders such as these in the work of education, bringing them into the school and, what is even more effective, bringing schoolchildren out to their workplaces. Not long ago a New York City meeting that was convened to devise better bridges among ethnic groups heard an Italian-American high school boy say: "I know Michelangelo was a great guy, but I find it hard to relate to him. If I go into the community, I can relate to a lawyer or a garbage man." Schools of education could learn from this and other such examples.

Young people spend most of their lives out of school and are more influenced by what happens out of school than what happens in it. (Think of the familiar statistics on time spent watching television.) Schools must understand this reality and ally themselves with positive outside forces while they work constructively against negative forces. Teacher-training conducted in substantial isolation from the realities of the community does not prepare teachers or administrators to deal with real children and their world. One thing is certain: Neither the school nor the school of education can beat the community. They must join it. If schools and schools of education try to preserve their privileged sanctity, act as if the community were not there, and assume that the five hours of daily leverage which the school exerts on the pupil can offset the ten or twelve hours that the pupil spends in the community, they are clearly wrong.

Perhaps proposing to appoint as much as half the staff of the schools of education from atypical resources is going too far. I have no doubt, however, that education of teachers and administrators could profit immeasurably from using the schools themselves and the communities as a major training ground.

To reemphasize an earlier point, a considerable proportion of the inservice and preservice training of educators belongs in the university. But on campus much greater efforts are needed to broaden the contact of the education student with the university and to breach the too-restrictive walls of the school of education.

In the law school, in the schools of social work, public health, and public administration, in the graduate departments of the arts and sciences (particularly the social sciences), and in urban institutes and other special centers, research and teaching are going on that could enrich the intellectual background and understanding of those who would serve the schools. A number of universities are moving to make available to the students of education some of the resources that could help them develop the understandings they need to be successful educators, but too many students are still behind too many fences.

To place major responsibility for this situation on the schools of education would be both unfair and fallacious. More often than not, the fences were built long ago and assiduously maintained by the rest of the university to keep the school of education in its place. Campus snobbishness of this sort is particularly true of the academic departments, which are primarily interested in turning out academicians and experts in specialties and lack enthusiasm for helping students with other goals in life. As a result, the courses that economists, for example, design and the research they pursue are not always appropriate for prospective educators.

So the schools of education try to develop their own sociology, economics, and other departments, sometimes tenuously linked to the major university departments. Perhaps if the link were stronger, a school of education could continue this pattern productively. But the basic need persists: to open up the total institution in the cause of education. Helping to educate the people who will help educate the young is a high mission. And although it is unlikely that the economists will ever rank it higher than developing more and better economists, a growing number appear to be willing to give time and thought to the contributions their discipline can make. Economics is not necessarily the most significant discipline for educators, but the example is pertinent because a fair number of economists have changed their aloof posture and are applying their tools to the problems of education and to training future educators.

As to ways, then, to make the school of education respond to current needs, let me recapitulate three possibilities. First, schools of education must make much more effective use of the schools themselves. Second, they must enlist community resources as well as school resources in the training process. Finally, within universities schools of education must stop fencing themselves in and seek access to other schools and departments on behalf of a set of students whose learning and understanding require the full resources of the university.

The observations on needed reforms in preservice training apply equally to inservice training. The role of the school of education in this all-important activity requires more critical attention than it usually gets even though it engages a substantial part of the time and talents of the educators of educators. The quality of inservice training has improved since, say, the early 1950s, but without question further and more radical improvement is needed.

Again the most promising avenue lies close to the real world of schoolchildren. Along the lines mentioned earlier, a major proportion of inservice training should take place away from the university, within the schools and their surrounding communities. What is wrong with having a school of education give semester hours of credit, whether for salary increments or for more exalted reasons, for a variety of activities that teachers or administrators might undertake right within their own schools? Whenever anyone takes the responsibility for doing something new and different, with an important end in view, he is learning, and this should be the name of the game. If he does well, he adds to his resources and becomes a more valuable educator.

The teaching and tennis analogy is apposite here. Schools of education could devise systems that would allow teachers and administrators to work together in the schools, analyse and criticize each other's work, grow in understanding and expertise—and receive credits from the university for the process. Just as the way to become a better tennis player is to get on a court with a superior player, one of the ways to become a better teacher is to be exposed in the classroom to the more experienced, confident, and successful teacher who will help with working out problems and weak spots. For either experience to pay off, the novice must take responsibility, for swinging his own tennis racket in the first instance, for teaching the children himself in the second. Spectatorship will not help in either instance.

Inservice education may well be the most important role of the school of education in the years immediately ahead. For the first time since the Great Depression, there is a vast oversupply of teachers. The universities are adding to the surplus every year. Moreover, although school staffs will still shift to some degree, rising salaries are making teaching jobs ever more popular. A high proportion of the teachers in the schools now will still be there in five or ten years. Recent estimates indicate that about 75 percent of the teaching force will be stable in the 1970s, with the balance in constant change. It is thus more important than ever to enhance the quality and reach of inservice training. It must bypass the old road that leads only from credentials to salary increments and substantively help practitioners become increasingly effective in serving young people.

Many of the federal resources available to school systems for retraining teachers are not being used. In particular, Title I of the Elementary and Secondary Education Act, now funded at the rate of one and one-half billion dollars a year, has never been adequately tapped for this purpose. Instead, school systems buy special materials or hire additional staff to help youngsters with special needs. A much more significant way to use these considerable funds would be to strengthen the teachers in the school system, its capital structure, by developing their deeper understanding of the problems of living and learning that young people meet and at the same time developing their greater expertise in the teaching process itself.

Every time the word *teacher* appears in these pages, the word *administrator* could be substituted, but a special note on training administrators is needed. During the 1970s some fifty major cities in America will enroll more than 50 percent of their pupils from minority groups. The demand for well-trained black and Spanish-speaking school leaders is already great, far greater than the supply, and will continue to grow. In their fellowship awards and selection procedures, schools of education bear a profound responsibility for determining whether that demand will continue to be frustrated or whether it will be more effectively met.

Administrators in schools of education and state departments of education should be aware that the design of internship opportunities requires careful and immediate attention. Many internships are of dubious value because they give no responsibility to the novice. The analogy of the medical intern, however overworked by educators, is valid. The intern should know that it is up to him to diagnose, to prescribe, and to see what result his decisions produce, short, shall we say, of allowing the patient to die. With the expansion of the American school system and the growing attraction of administrative salaries, the more able and ambitious teachers (especially the men) sought to advance themselves to the role of principal and beyond. The net effect, from which the school system still suffers, was doubly unfortunate: Good teachers no longer taught, and men and women with no particular gifts or training for administration became administrators.

Programs are underway, some assisted by the Ford Foundation, to reverse this trend. Individuals already equipped to cope with real children and their needs are being trained to be administrators. The job is a complex one, involving coping with parents, teachers, and students and at the same time providing leadership in the classroom. The title *principal*, after all, derives from *principal teacher*. The superintendency is even more demanding because political and fiscal responsibilities are added to the role of educator. The new breed of principal and superintendent is committed to the ultimate consumer, the child, and to helping teachers learn and progress in their jobs.

Among foundation-assisted programs toward this end is a seven-university consortium that offers a doctoral program in educational administration. The program is designed to attract imaginative people from government, business, and other careers as well as from education. It consists of universitywide study tailored to individual talents rather than to homogenized credit requirements. Another is the new Institute for Educational Leadership at George Washington University, which provides varied internships to from fifteen to twenty young potential leaders annually.

If the need for overall educational leadership is great, the need for minority-group leaders is acute. Both programs cited above recognize this need; a high percentage of participants in both consortium and institute come from minority groups. Similarly, with foundation assistance, a program run by the Council of Great Cities Schools is making fellowships available to blacks and Spanish-speaking Americans so that they can get the credentials needed for central administrative posts in urban school systems. The Foundation's Leadership Development Program, begun in 1967, has made awards to nearly two hundred young men and women. Well over half of these potential leaders, from small towns and poor rural areas all over America, have been black, Chicano, or native Americans, the rest chiefly from white ethnic groups, French Canadians from the Northeast, for example. The criteria for selection emphasizes, not the usual academic credentials, but a strong personal commitment to the candidate's own region and background and to a career of educational leadership.

I have suggested a few of the efforts required to breathe life into the education of educators. Some can be spurred by public funding, some by private philanthropy, and some by the schools. It is patent, however, that the heaviest burden must be assumed by the chief purveyors of teacher education, the schools of education and the universities they inhabit. Any school of education undertaking the kinds of reforms the times and our children demand will become a different institution. Much of the faculty will be working in the schools and in the community rather than in the university, and so will many of the students. Their work in the university will reflect their exposure to reality; the philosophical, psychological, historical, economic, and sociological studies the university must provide if educators are to acquire deep understanding about teaching and learning processes will have new, direct, and immediate meaning. Studying theory unconnected with reality has characterized the training process; so has exposing the education student to reality without the genuine responsibility that alone makes the experience meaningful. Too often practice teaching and internships have stressed observation rather than participation. Perhaps the American passion for watching TV and sports has bulwarked the notion that watching education is the way to learn about it. The facts are otherwise, as results have demonstrated. The training that is needed combines a more thorough exposure to a new reality with the irreplaceable functions of the university in advancing knowledge and understanding.

But what about research? Most important and useful research in education will be done in close touch with reality. There are exceptions, of course. Historical research, for example, may best develop in the traditional scholarly atmosphere. But even that will be arid unless the researcher brings to it an immediate sense of how things are in the schools, to provide a mental mirror that will heighten his sense of how things used to be. Important areas of research need greater emphasis and financing in schools of education, without question, but they need the same firm base in the reality of home, school, and community that teaching does.

Will needed reforms in the education of educators come to

pass? I believe that the momentum for change is growing and is all but irreversible. The forces demanding reform are basically three: the students, the parents, and the teachers. Neither parents nor students think the schools are doing a good job. So far they have directed their protests toward the schools rather than the departments of education. But it is likely that these institutions will soon be next. Teachers and administrators deplore their lack of preparation for the problems that confront them, particularly in the cities, and look to their educators for new and helpful resources.

Underlying these discontents are deeper forces at work. The college generation has articulated many. The insistent cry for relevance in education is a symptom of more fundamental concerns. The roster is all too familiar:

The goal of individual affluence has turned out to be inadequate for many Americans, either in aspiration or achievement. Can education help provide more meaningful goals?

Citizenship in a nation that monopolizes the wealth of the world but does not share it equitably with its own have-nots and with those abroad is deeply disturbing to many Americans both old and young. What might the schools do about this?

Educational, governmental, and other institutions have not countered the effects of rapid technological change on jobs, leisure, and urbanization with constructive and rapid adjustment. How can teachers and school leaders be helped to understand and respond to these momentous changes?

The list of problems and pressures could obviously be extended. The point here is that schools of education must confront these concerns. The slow-moving machinery of education must accelerate its tempo. And schools and departments of education must assume the significant role which should be theirs in forging the America that will soon enter the twenty-first century.

Chapter 5

New Weapons in an Old War

Robert W. Blanchard

To invite the comments of a superintendent of schools on the general state of teacher preparation is risky at best. Since he is faced with union conflict, local funding failures, a deteriorating urban environment, and significant public hostility to the role of the schools, the invitation invites projection. His response is likely to resemble the natural reaction of a high school teacher to a review of achievement test data. The high school teacher eventually gets around to commenting on the sad state of elementary education.

Despite the builtin bias of the administrator's perspective, it should be made clear at the outset that although generalizations concerning teacher preparation institutions are automatically misleading because of the wide differences among them, the quality of teacher preparation nationally has never been better. The vitality, courage, and skill of teacher institution graduates committed to serving in a city school system is in remarkable positive contrast to that of even a decade ago. Although training institutions can be improved, they need not be destroyed in order to sustain or develop healthy schools or a healthy society. I do not suggest that America set about the deschooling of its society or the dismantling of the preparation institutions that serve these schools, but I strongly believe there is a need for urgent and rapid change within teacher education.

Changing Conditions

Change is a given, and the rate of change in society is obviously continuing to accelerate. This fact conflicts with the tendency of established institutions to resist change; hence, efforts must be made to influence, not the fact of social change, but the perception of these changes by established teacher preparation institutions. An outline of the agenda from a recent meeting of the Portland, Oregon, Board of Education gives an example of these changes and may throw light on my feelings of urgency that programs of preparation of future teachers be adapted to meet the needs of the changing conditions of American education.

First, the president of Mothers for Children made a twenty-five-minute presentation on the twelve-month school year, an issue not before the board. This woman is opposed to year-round schooling. She claims that the moral fiber of American society and its families will be drained if year-round operation of schools is adopted. She seems to feel that any move in this direction reflects a conspiratorial plot on the part of federal and state governments to take over the role of the family and to diminish the patriotic spirit of the nation.

In response, an equally committed citizen suggested the immediate adoption of a year-round plan of education to resolve the budget crisis. Her thesis was that young people could be educated more rapidly and at substantial savings because with the plan employees of the school system could work fifty weeks for the same salary they received for thirty-eight weeks.

Second, a representative of the American Federation of

Teachers eloquently criticized the board of education for having reduced the number of employees in the school system because of a recent tax-base defeat. The reduction, totaling 508 full- and part-time employees of which 140 were teachers was, in his view, wholly unnecessary. He suggested that the approximately nine-million-dollar gap between resources and required expenditures, which had also forced the shortening of the school year by one month, could have been eliminated through an exercise of alternative priorities (unstated).

Third, a citizens' committee from a decentralized area of the school district asked the board to authorize a special dress code for Vocational Village, an alternative high school for dropouts. The proposed dress and grooming code, more rigid than the citywide board policy, was felt to be necessary to make the Village students employable. Sitting at the meeting were a number of school administrators whose hair was in obvious violation of the suggested code. The change was rejected.

Fourth, another decentralized area proposed that the board remove Rose Festival princess selection from the high schools. The Rose Festival, an annual citywide event, has involved the selection of princesses from each high school and eventually a Rose Festival Queen for the city. This selection process was viewed by the protestors as inappropriate, degrading, and an abuse of women's rights. The board rejected this contention and approved continued cooperation with the Rose Festival but recommended a broadened advisory committee for this event.

Fifth and finally, before the board of education was a recommendation that a sixty-four-year-old technical high school restricted to male enrollment admit women. One board member moved to approve such admission and direct the superintendent to provide a plan for doing so at the next public meeting. The superintendent allowed that what had taken sixty-four years to create might require somewhat more than two weeks to organize along alternative lines. The issue was tabled until the next meeting of the board of education, thus preventing a vote on the original motion.

This agenda is in some respects peculiar to one city, but parallels can be found in the agendas of boards of other city school districts, matters ranging from the effects of a reduced number of middle-class residents in urban environments to the growth of security forces employed by the school system. They illustrate a social scene dramatically different from that of even five years ago and demonstrate the need for changes in the preparation of teachers who serve city youth.

Specialization and Diversification

The need for specialization is one message for teacher preparation institutions that seems indicated by this example. Enormous differences between the kinds of problems encountered in rural and urban America require substantially different teacher preparation.

A second message involves diversification of roles. Both rural and urban schools require an increased variety of personnel, possessing varying levels of skill and proficiency. This development stems in part from the realization that public need for education is rapidly outstripping its willingness to provide resources for education. Thus, just as the public health physician must increasingly use assistants with less training if he is to carry on the practice of public medicine, so public schools must engage the services of personnel with less training in such positions as teacher aide, library assistant, and equipment operator. It may be in time that basic skill development will be left exclusively in the hands of teacher assistants with a personal disposition and preference for working with children. Although professionals may protest, school administrators may be forced to move in this direction.

Of enormous importance in anticipating future roles is a more accurate reading on teacher needs. We now know that the oversupply of teachers in the early 1970s was predictable as early as the mid-1960s. The data were available but were largely ignored, and control of the number of people preparing to teach was left to chance.

One immediate recommendation, then, to teacher education institutions is to quit preparing teachers *en masse*. A more long-range solution will stem from the elimination of undergraduate and graduate schools of education as they now exist.

Because of urbanization and the need for broader planning

of larger geopolitical units, public services are likely to become more integrated. Relationships between education, housing, welfare, health, and employment are growing closer, and further cooperation between divisions of public service seems inevitable.

To accommodate this development, it may be necessary to merge existing divisions and departments of universities that prepare personnel for these public services. This merger may help answer the problem of far more teachers being prepared than are required by public and private elementary and secondary education. If one factor in attracting young men and women to undergraduate schools of education is their personal preference for public service, the combining of education with other programs with similar goals may well lead many of them into a much wider range of service opportunities.

The time has passed when any individual of normal intelligence could, with perseverance, be certified for teaching. Reorganized schools of education, social work, public administration, and other public services should present a wide range of options and guide students at key performance checkpoints into community service roles dependent upon a careful evaluation of their abilities.

Under such a program, public education might well be the exclusive testing ground for potential educators. The internship would take the place of what we now recognize as student-teaching and provide greater breadth and depth in classroom experience. Together with similar field experience in other governmental agencies it would satisfy students' interest in exploring several public service roles appropriate to their individual aptitudes, abilities, and goals.

One suspects that a "go, no go" assessment of students planning on a teaching career at the end of two years of college will be essential. Those who did not pass this assessment could select an alternate goal and participate in some other service internship. Those sufficiently qualified could spend an additional two years of preparation exclusively on campus followed by a one-year internship in a school at a beginner's salary rate. The decision regarding certification could be made at the end of that year by the preparational institution and the school system in which the internship occurred.

A similar practice could be followed for those opting for public service in other fields of local government.

Tolerance of Ambiguity and Improved Role Definition

Two other suggestions regarding teacher education can be directed by the public school administrator to his professional colleagues in higher education.

The first relates to orthodoxy and toleration. School administrators are constantly faced by dedicated proponents of some educational practice or other that will remake the schools. They are sure that if their formula is adopted, the success of the educational enterprise will be assured.

The ferocious contest between the devotees of oral communication for deaf children and the devotees of sign communication is illustrative, but countless examples of militant advocacy can be found in every field of education. Indeed, an entire high school or elementary school can become committed to this or that methodology on the assumption that all children will respond equally effectively to a great educational idea if only enough resources are provided and enough people of the same commitment are employed.

To some extent the tendency to overcommit to a monolithic idea can be traced to the way in which faculty members of teacher preparation institutions are recruited. Frequently, they have had exceptional success in a particular discipline or methodology, so they spend the remainder of their careers capitalizing on it by teaching teachers to teach by their particular formula.

The school administrator can only plead for a greater tolerance of ambiguity within the field of education and for providing new teachers with a diversity of tools with which to respond to constantly changing educational demands.

Finally, it would be helpful if specific courses in role definition and decision-making were included somewhere in the already crowded undergraduate curriculum. The unification of departments devoted to the several public services might make this more possible.

The warfare between management and employee organizations within the public services must diminish in intensity. When this conflict is pressed to its ultimate conclusion, one suspects that both management and employee groups will wind up fighting bitterly for advantage, and the public will be the loser.

Only through more appropriate role definition can a healthier relationship between management and staff be created. School administrators who attempt to decide curricular issues to the exclusion of the more capable professional staff who should be making these decisions will inevitably generate conflict, just as will teacher organizations that leave all such determinations to the bargaining table, which is the antithesis of the widespread participation in decision-making that they advocate.

Educators enjoy different roles and responsibilities. Once these roles are defined, individuals in them must be held accountable for their responsibilities. Management must be held exclusively responsible for some decisions. Other decisions require maximum advice and input from every location in the organization. And in some decisions management should have absolutely no voice: Here choices must be left to the discretion of others more capable who must at the same time be held accountable for the results.

These facts about division of labor are not unique to education as a profession. However, education has been especially tardy in realizing the need to systematically analyze its decision-making in light of these facts. Earlier it was remiss in acknowledging the right of the public, within the framework of law, to determine the directions in which schools will move as they serve the public and the children in the schools. Now that the right of the public to representation is better understood, teacher preparation institutions can help forestall internal conflict within the schools through clearer conceptions of complementary roles in the education profession. Differentiation of roles in education seems inevitable. It need not be inimical to colleagueship. Indeed, only through better understanding of these facts and improved preparation of teachers and administrators can colleagueship be achieved.

Chapter 6

Governmental Roles

J. Myron Atkin

It is unlikely that a chapter in a book on teacher education would have been devoted to governmental roles before 1960. Only since that date have both state and federal activity in teacher education become intrusive and highly visible. Before then, teacher education was almost entirely in the hands of the universities. Although major responsibility still resides there, this state of affairs is increasingly subject to challenge and modification.

It is the central contention of this chapter that the changing roles of state and federal governments have been a result of three basic factors: the increasing attraction of large-scale social planning in the United States; the close coupling of that planning to evolving managerial styles in the government; and the increased assertion of executive prerogative, largely through the budgetary process, in the federal government and the individual states.

The 1960s reflected a new height in optimism that social problems are tractable if only one is wise enough to identify the

73

significant factors and powerful enough to address them. During the administrations of Presidents Kennedy, Johnson, and Nixon, outstanding social scientists were brought into key positions in the government and had the opportunity to implement plans that were judged to attack the root causes of national failures in health, education, poverty, housing, and other fields that directly affected the lives of the people. For example, it was widely agreed that programs designed to alleviate poverty had failed. The prevailing explanation was that these programs suffered from excessive professionalism bordering on paternalism. The poor themselves were not adequately involved in the decisions that touched their lives. A comprehensive federal attack on poverty was instituted through the Office of Economic Opportunity on the assumption that the poor knew best how to address their own problems. A condition of federal support in many poverty programs was strong participation by the "target groups."

Federal visions of desirable social policy became more than affirmations of conviction and subsequent dollar appropriation. Management mechanisms were developed to guarantee the implementation of declared policy. Individuals with training in management and in economics in particular were brought into the federal government to assure that the wishes of the executive branch were carried out. The president's staff grew severalfold in size to accommodate the new missions.

The social policy failures of the 1960s are becoming apparent. Educational programs, programs for the poor, health programs, housing programs, and transportation programs were subjected basically to similar approaches, and many of the effects not only are still with us but they are also growing, regardless of the fact that some scholars and politicians are beginning to take sobering second looks at the results. We are beginning to hear about federal and state housing plans and expenditures that destroyed a sense of community, about educational policies and dollars that did little to raise learning levels of children, about expenditures to alleviate poverty that kept the poor at the bottom of the socioeconomic ladder, and about health programs that did little but increase the income of physicians. While the apparent failures of American social policy are receiving growing attention, there is a residue in the 1970s of procedures and assumptions that flowered during the 1960's. It is still important to identify and describe some of these practices.

What happened during the 1960s? Robert McNamara's administration of the Department of Defense is correctly credited with impressing President Johnson with the possibility of exercising control over experts, in this case military experts, through the budgetary process. Until McNamara, the president of the United States watched a defense budget grow dramatically and seemingly uncontrollably. He was totally reliant on the advice of admirals and generals in exercising his authority as commander in chief. McNamara demonstrated that it was possible to move toward civilian exercise of major decisions. He demanded cost estimates. He pressed for analysis of total military systems and development of alternatives much more vigorously than had any of his predecessors. He asked about purposes of various military components and whether the purposes were best achieved by the techniques advocated by the military officers. Instead of solely questioning how many battleships might be needed, the McNamara style was to identify the purposes for which battleships might be used, then ask if there were methods of achieving these purposes that might be either less costly or more effective or both. Military experts were often seen as defending a possibly outmoded status quo. An aggressive manager, not necessarily conversant with technical details of the enterprise, was seen not only as a useful addition in decision-making but also as a necessary one.

In 1965 President Johnson ordered that all executive departments follow the managerial lead of the Department of Defense, including those agencies responsible for social programs in the Department of Health, Education, and Welfare, the Department of Housing and Urban Development, the Department of Labor, and the Department of Justice. And he added to the staff and power of the Bureau of the Budget, an arm of the White House to make sure the new management procedures were implemented.

The fifty governors learned a powerful lesson from the president. The managerial styles and budgetary control that served to strengthen the position of the executive, although developed initially at the federal level, were copied assiduously in the states.

As the president strengthened the Bureau of the Budget (the name of which was changed in 1970 to the Office of Management and Budget!), the governors began to strengthen theirs if they had one. If not, they established one. They staffed these agencies with individuals similar in background and training to those who worked in the federal budgetary planning units: overwhelmingly from management, from engineering, from business, and from economics.

With this increased executive capability, the governors found that they could rationalize their budgetary projections in a more sophisticated fashion than that usually available to the state legislatures. They had an ability not only to propose but also to monitor. Executive staffs increased ten and twentyfold.

At the same time that the various governors, particularly those in populous states, were increasing their planning and monitoring capability and therefore their control (especially in comparison with the power available to the various legislatures), concern about the cost and the direction of higher education was growing. Universities were multiplying and expanding rapidly in the 1950s and 1960s, often with little apparent coordination and occasionally with little regard to any factors beyond local pride. Higher education coordinating agencies began to be established to offer advice or to decide directions for higher education expansion. The prime motive usually was an economic one since there was a growing impression of waste and duplication, but the establishment of higher education coordinating boards, although related to the general press for rationalization of social programs, was initially separate from the budget bureaus, perhaps because there was not so clear a federal pattern for the states to copy in the case of higher education as in the case of other social programs.

Since a large number of the students enrolled in public universities matriculate in teacher education programs, such programs began to receive special scrutiny by coordinating boards, usually in terms of scale and unit costs. However, with their increasing influence over dollar allocations to publicly supported universities, it seems likely that these agencies will increase their attention to matters of program.

The net effect of strengthening the statewide coordinating boards and the planning and budgeting function of the governors was to diminish the influence of the governing boards of the major state-supported universities. Usually the governing boards of the state universities had been able to exert control through their direct contact with the state legislatures. This power began to erode in the late 1960s. On the other hand, the many state universities that began as teacher colleges often were strengthened with the ascendancy of more centralized state control, but in almost every case the strengthening was for programs other than teacher education. The increased dollars were appropriated to enable these institutions to broaden their mission beyond teacher education.

Inasmuch as higher education no longer enjoys the kind of unquestioned support it may once have received, these moves toward shifting major decision-making away from the campus and toward the executive branch of state government have not been questioned seriously by the public. The new controls are instituted in the name of economy and rationalization, two attributes highly valued by the people.

At the state level, the major direct influence on teacher education until the 1960s had been through the teacher certification process, the provision of considerable financial support through the legislature to the public universities (usually with few strings attached), and the mandating of certain curricular requirements (such as health education) in the curriculum of elementary or secondary schools. In almost every one of the fifty states, however, state influence on teacher education was usually soft, indirect, and minimal.

Federal influences on teacher education are different. Since the federal government does not have the responsibility for basic support because it does not operate universities, and the dollars the federal government spends in education are minimal compared to the states, the focus in Washington has been on providing leadership for major changes in directions that it sees as desirable. The mission has been one of showing others how to spend money for teacher education more effectively. The federal focus has been on exemplary efforts, demonstrations, and some research.

In several significant aspects, the federal government played a role similar to that of private foundations as it moved more aggressively into the field of education. Like the foundations, the

Office of Education has seemed a source of pressure to respond to the popular vision of what may be required to improve American education. Federal administrators have felt the need to appear current, even voguish. There was no well-established and accepted base from which Washington agencies might operate in education. Lack of precedent allowed considerable flexibility.

In addition, the Office of Education attempted faithfully to adopt the managerial procedures developed in the Department of Defense. There has been a strong demand from Office of Education personnel upon contractors and grantees to operationalize programs in highly prespecified form. Budgeting and management tied to objectives has been a particularly salient feature of Office of Education administration since 1965. Thus, currency as reflected in the influential media (emphasis on accountability, or excellence, or careers, or reading) has been coupled with management by objectives (PERT charts, program-planning–budgeting systems, behavioral objectives).

Constituents and the Congress have often been dazzled and perhaps even confused by the aggressiveness with which the new managerial look in the Office of Education surfaced, but allegedly the office was responding to the increasing control over all federal programs being exerted by the Office of Management and Budget.

It is revealing that the National Science Foundation, an agency that became involved in teacher education in science and mathematics in the late 1950s largely through special institutes both summer and year-long for teachers in service, did not find it necessary to develop the managerial styles in evidence in the Office of Education, at least not to the same degree. True, science education supported by the National Science Foundation did not flourish in the late 1960s, and the role of the foundation in education was eclipsed gradually by the Office of Education. However, there was broad agreement among constituents of federal programs that the quality of those efforts supported by the National Science Foundation continued to be the top-priority criterion in their decisions, rather than managerial elegance.

The Office of Education is held in particularly low repute in Washington, both in the executive branch and in the Congress. The creation of the National Institute of Education to promote research and development activities confirmed the fact that neither the executive branch nor the Congress had much confidence in the ability of the Office of Education to mount quality efforts. Individuals who staff the Office of Education are seen as being less imaginative than those who staff most of the other Washington bureaus. There surely are several important reasons for this state of affairs, including the facts that the Office of Education has few top-level positions as well as little direct authority. But one result has been a visible commissioner of education who points periodically to critical educational problems but who does not have the capability in dollars, personnel, or authority to ameliorate them. One commissioner speaks about the right of every American to read and suggests federal programs to blanket the country. Another commissioner speaks about the importance of improving education for careers. A third commissioner speaks of improvement of education in ghettos. Usually the executive branch and the Congress respond by appropriating some funds to support the commissioner's efforts, but the funds turn out to be modest, and the commissioner's rhetoric turns out to have promised more change than is realistic.

It often seems as if the Office of Education does not recognize what it takes to modify American education. The result has been one disappointment after another for Congress and the executive branch. The constant quest after a solution to the most recently recognized deficiency in American education has seemed a poor substitute for addressing fundamental problems, including problems in teacher education.

Perhaps each commissioner has seen no alternative. The managerial styles he feels he must use, the support he has received, and the talent at his disposal may foreclose other courses. In teacher education a major effort of the Office of Education in the late 1960s was directed toward the development of models for undergraduate education of prospective elementary school teachers. A "Request for Proposals" was distributed to the higher education community indicating that the Office of Education was allocating funds for the establishment of several exemplary programs. Although variety was sought so that programs ultimately funded might be compared one to the other, the RFP (incidentally, a procurement procedure copied directly from the Department of Defense), carried definite restrictions about the basic orientation that ultimately would receive support. Each of the proposals had to delineate in highly operational form, usually the intended behaviors of the college students, exactly what the output of the program was intended to be.

The procedure is quite similar to one the military establishment uses. A device is needed that has certain clearly specified characteristics. How fast must the plane fly? What is the desired payload? What is the necessary range? Economy and efficiency are judged by matching product with objectives and noting costs. Those who staff the Office of Education bureaucracy have been little inclined to examine the assumptions under which funding programs are undertaken. Thus the RFP mentality and its disheartening effect on potential grant recipients who recognize that research and development activities require greater flexibility is a point the Office of Education does not seem to appreciate or even acknowledge. In the example of support of undergraduate teacher education programs in elementary education, programs that did not embody highly operationalized prespecified objectives were ruled out, presumably because these output characteristics were required for evaluation.

The poor ability of Office of Education personnel to distinguish between procedure and substance has bedeviled the organization severely as it has become more aggressive in attempting to modify the schools. As a result the quality of the work the agency has supported often appears questionable to those who have the basic legal responsibility for sustaining the educational system.

To many observers the Office of Education support activities lack consistency and vision beyond the short term. The office is viewed as an agency with some money to spend but with unimaginative approaches to its responsibilities. Underlying issues in teacher education are addressed minimally: continuing education, the education that is effective and at what levels in the development of a teacher, the characteristics of those who choose early to enter teaching as contrasted with those who enter the field later in life and the implications of resulting staffing patterns. Federal administrators may not think that some of the longer-term problems are dramatic enough to capture the interest of the Congress, but most Office of

Education critics in the Congress and elsewhere agree that the types of short-term perspectives revealed so far in the agency may well represent a waste of dollars.

The Congress, perhaps recognizing some of the shortcomings in the Office of Education and acting on the initiative of President Nixon, established in 1972 the National Institute of Education. This agency may well carve a different role for the federal government in American education, including teacher education. Strong attempts have been made to protect the new entity by not staffing it heavily with individuals from the old Office of Education. The new agency also can hire more people at top levels of the federal pay scale than the Office of Education has been able to. Over the long term its future may be bright.

At the moment, however, teacher education is basically in the hands of the universities, although public schools are taking increasing responsibility. In any event, it is a state and local matter. Potent financial investments are unlikely to come from the federal treasury directly, and the federal role may well continue to be largely a prodding and symbolic type of activity, again not significantly different in scale or intent from the total efforts of the private foundations.

Such activities in the past seem to have been designed to jar rather than reform the educational system. A particular vision of attractive schooling is featured in the popular media. The government provides some money to establish exemplary programs. School people begin to feel uncomfortable, even guilty, about the criticisms, and they respond.

One of the problems with this pattern is that the visions of desirable education change with startling rapidity. In the late 1950s, the school systems were castigated for not producing enough talented scientists and mathematicians. Professors were funded to build new programs. By the early 1960s, poverty and racial discrimination captured the attention of the public, and schools were singled out both as being contributors to an indefensible condition and as necessary vehicles for the solution. By the late 1960s, the problem in the schools was identified as joylessness.

With each move of the spotlight to a different problem, foundations and the government try to support new activities to change the schools. These agencies seem to believe that a system employing well over two million teachers, employed by more than seventeen thousand separate governing boards, can respond quickly and effectively with infusions of bright visions from intelligent people. Although there have been some changes here and there as a result of governmental activity, the results have more often been confusing and disruptive rather than constructive.

A tremendous level of guilt surfaced within the teaching profession. Teachers and those in teacher education suffer a marked loss of self-esteem when their perspectives are most of the time featured as unworthy. Guilt turns to defensiveness. Ultimately this stress turns to aggressiveness. Teachers began to feel undervalued, and this fact strengthened their resolve to accent collective action. Teachers would speak for themselves, and forcefully, if no one else would speak for them.

A more constructive, although a less dramatic, approach that the government and the foundations might take is an evolutionary one. Governmental officials might try bending the system rather than attacking it or suggesting alternative visions. Attractive modifications are always surfacing within the schools. Strategies for change might capitalize on these influences. How can some of the energies presently directed toward organizing the professions be turned toward curriculum reform, including reform in teacher education? How can excellent practice be nurtured? Perhaps real change in education looks prosaic, particularly over short periods of time.

Perhaps greater distinctions can be drawn between a role for the foundations and a role for the government. The foundations might remain more visionary, even radical, in their approach to reform, highlighting possibilities that seem attractive, fresh, and risky. The government might look for more fundamental and longer-term perspectives. We might be entering into a period politically wherein our growing suspicion of social action programs will enable us to assume a softer stance.

Regardless, during the next decade major governmental effect on teacher education is likely to be observed at the state level. If the various state legislatures do not mount planning and monitoring capabilities to match those of the various governors, then statewide centralization is likely to accelerate. Predicting the future is hardly a science, but it is my view that legislative leaders in the states will begin to gain some ground in their competition with the state governors for power. The deficiencies of social planning and centralized management are beginning to be discussed widely. The future of teacher education will more than likely be determined by negotiation of competing interests among university groups, the organized profession, and the public, with executive-level governmental roles less intrusive than they were in the late 1960s. The legislatures are more sensitive to such pressures than governors.

Chapter 7

Role of State Department of Education

William H. Drummond

In using metaphors to describe or assign character to organizations they observe, people often like to use animal referents, usually sleeping animals; for example, sleeping dogs, sleeping camels, and sleeping lions. I would like to suggest that state departments of education are like sleeping whales. Anyone in the water recognizes their potential power, but seldom worries about being eaten. After all, whales eat only very little things in very large gulps. Few people notice the size of whales unless they are dead or beached, or unless someone has to do something about them.

The inclusion of a chapter on the role of state departments of education in a volume on new directions in teacher education is indicative of change, change either in what state departments of education have been doing or a recognition of a growing threat of what they might do. This chapter will: examine the changing role of state government in education, especially as this affects teacher education and certification; describe recent moves made by state departments of education in the certification of teachers and the approval of teacher preparation programs; raise philosophical and political issues pertinent to the role of these state agencies and the future of American education; and suggest ideas for action.

Changing the Role of State Government

Education is a state responsibilty. Since the Constitution does not mention education, the Tenth Amendment obtains: "The powers not delegated to the United States by the Constitution, nor prohibited by it to the states, are reserved to the states respectively, or to the people." All the states, as a consequence, have provided for education in their state constitutions, usually placing responsibility for the governance of schools in a state board of education and a chief state school officer. The coordination of public colleges and universities may be accomplished through a separate board or commission of higher education, but teacher education and the certification of teachers is usually administered by the chief state school officer guided by the policies of a state board or commission for the common schools.

State boards of education responsible for the common schools have been interested and involved in the specialized and general preparation requirements for teachers and interested in the effects of teacher education on the common schools; typically commissions of higher education have not been. Whether the governance of higher education is under the same state administrator who oversees the common schools is an interesting issue for those interested in the organization and operation of state teacher education activities. Even in states where higher education and common school education are under the same state administrator, activities concerning the approval of preparation programs and the certification of teachers are not usually organizationally placed with the bureau or division of higher education.

An important distinction must be drawn between accreditation and state approval of programs. Accreditation is a review and approval of an institution by other institutions or associations of institutions, for example, National Council for Accreditation of Teacher Education and Northwest Association of Secondary and Higher Schools. State approval, which may include similar visitation and evaluation procedures, is a review and approval by the state authority. In some states accreditation and state approval are combined. Although the procedures are similar, the interests of the state and the concerns of higher institutions may be different.

As states have moved to coordinate higher education through higher-education councils or combined boards, little or no attention has been focused on teacher education primarily because those who desire coordination are interested almost exclusively in the financing of higher institutions. Coordinating councils or boards have focused on standardized accounting systems, program-planning, budgeting, and evaluation systems, and elimination of duplicate programs, rather than on common school educational needs and educational program development. Current concerns of higher-education councils regarding teacher education are focused on the establishment of quotas for persons entering teacher education, again primarily for economic reasons.

The pressure to consolidate planning and budgeting statewide is probably best viewed by looking at what happens when legislative budget committees wrestle with recommendations made by their state governors. Legislators call for justification of requests, initiate their own studies or reports about programs and expenditures, and spend much of their energy practicing one-upmanship with the executive branch of government, especially if the governor happens to be of the opposition party. To parry political maneuvering and to justify to the voting public his budgetary requests, the typical governor consolidates his planning and budgeting efforts into a single office under a person whom he trusts, a person who is close to him politically and organizationally.

This shift toward the centralization of planning and budgeting has been made possible by the advent of the computer and the development of professional planners, persons trained to analyze tasks into component activities and subactivities for organizational operations in a manner much like the computer programmers who provide sets of instructions to data processing systems. To achieve coordinated planning and budgeting for a state requires an elaborate data collection and processing system; it requires access to information about the everyday operations of state agencies; it requires honest reporting of events by those who are carrying out the work of state agencies.

One possibility should be noted. Sometimes a small bureau provides a central agency with data about operations with the faith that the central agent will use the data to further the welfare of the bureau, only to find later that the central agent has used the information to thwart it. When this occurs, a subtle reluctance to be accurate in reporting begins and the centralized data bank gradually becomes polluted. In other words, the centralization of information can be seen as a centralization of power, which can result in corruption of the system. This facet of centralized program planning, budgeting, and evaluation systems is only beginning to be realized.

As education has become a major expenditure for local and state government, it has become embroiled in political activity. A local taxpayers' revolt, decisions by state supreme courts about the inequities of local property taxation, the frustration of local boards with collective bargaining (because they do not have the legal authority to provide adequate financing), the organization of political-action groups by professional associations and unions, all merge in the expectation that state legislatures will act. The action that most legislators consider, however, in effect increases state government initiative and power and reduces local authority. Local and state boards of education become less responsible for improvement because they have less control of the means for improvement. Thus, at both state and national levels, education has become a prime issue for conflict between the executive branch of government with its centralized information-services power and the responsibility to administer programs and the legislative branch with its logrolling and appropriations-control power and the need to be responsive to the voters and the financial supporters of particular interests.

In this context state departments of education characteristically do what they are required to do by law, often do what they are authorized to do by law, and may do, in rare instances, what they are not prohibited from doing by law. It follows that department leaders can focus upon any one or more of three courses of action: They can try to change the legal authority of state boards of education, either by working with the legislature or by working with groups of citizens who can change or influence the legislature; they can extend or reinterpret existing authority; and they can try out new or different strategies that are not explicitly authorized or prohibited.

Moves by State Departments of Education

"The major role of state education agencies in teacher education has been administering teacher certification and the approval of teacher education programs" (Daniel and Crenshaw, 1971). This statement is accurate, but the moves that state departments of education are making and the context of forces in which these moves are occurring indicate that the nature of their work is changing rapidly.

State departments of education are beginning to substitute approval of programs for the evaluation of individual transcripts. Frinks reported in his recent study that forty-two states now use the program-approval approach (Frinks, 1970). This means that instead of checking individual transcripts of those persons seeking state certification against a list of approved course titles and credits, state department of education personnel can merely check to see if the candidate has been recommended for certification by an approved institution. In effect, the state department of education delegates the appraisal of transcripts and records to institutions and focuses more of its time and energy on visitation and review of institutions that prepare personnel. State approval of programs may be based upon regional or professional accreditation, upon state visitation and review, or both.

State departments of education are now making a move toward basing interstate reciprocity on state approval rather than on accreditation. Both the efforts of the Interstate Reciprocity Compact (The University of the State of New York, The State Education Department, undated) and the committee on standards of National Association of State Directors of Teacher Education and Certification (1971) emphasize a means of interstate licensure based primarily on state approval of programs rather than on accreditation by regional or national associations of institutions. The Interstate Reciprocity Compact calls for the legislatures of participating states to pass identical legislation authorizing chief state school officers to enter into certification contracts. Once contracts are signed between states, persons can prepare for teaching in one state of the compact and apply for and receive without question certification in another. The new National Association of State Directors of Teacher Education and Certification Standards Bulletin (formerly known as Bulletin 351) asks participating states to approve institutional programs on the basis of specific subject-matter programs. Once approved by the state, other states that recognize state approval under the standards of the association would issue appropriate certificates automatically. Moves are being made to recognize the involvement of professional associations in accreditation and certification. In recent years a number of attempts have been made by teachers' organizations to become more influential in accreditation. The controversy generated by the development of the National Council for Accreditation of Teacher Education (NCATE) is dealt with elsewhere in this volume. It is enough here to quote Mayor (Mayor and Swartz, 1965): "The strongest supporters of NCATE and national accreditation of teacher education are organizations affiliated with the National Education Association, the state teachers associations, and the professors of education in colleges and universities. The philosophy of these groups, so far as they enjoy a common philosophy, is predominant in the standards and procedures of NCATE. The teachers in the schools have supported these groups because they believed them to be the ones who were interested in them as teachers and in the schools. Now that the academicians in the colleges and universities have displayed new interest in education in the schools, in teachers, and in teacher education the loyalty of some of the profession is tending to shift."

When the history of the National Commission on Teacher Education and Professional Standards of the National Education Association is written, it will show a gradual shift in emphasis from attempts at changing teacher education through persuasion and open dialogue among diverse groups to the changing of teacher education through political action and collective bargaining (Lindsey, 1961). As associations and unions have become more active politically, they have attempted to control or govern more of teacher education. Professional standards and practices commissions have been established in several states with dubious success (National Commission on Teacher Education and Professional Standards, 1970). These commissions have usually had less authority than professional-association advocates hoped. Conflict has occurred between commissions and state boards and between associations and unions. As unions and associations merge and as the supply of teachers continues to be greater than the demand, pressures by teacher organizations to control preparation and licensure will undoubtedly increase.

A variety of pressures has caused state departments of education to accept and promote management by objectives. The federal government has provided funds for massive training of department personnel in the techniques of management by objectives. Professional planners and evaluators funded by the federal government have been placed on state department staffs. Training linkages have been made between business and industrial managers and school administrators. The need for tax reform and the alleviation of the inequities involved with local property taxation, and the public outcry for accountability have forced executives in government to require detailed priority planning and budgeting. The development of planning procedures that can be computerized and monitored by "objective" electronic machines has seemed attractive.

In teacher education and staff development two major changes seem to be occurring either as a result of management by objectives or concomitantly with it: state approval of elementary and secondary schools, based upon specific school objectives and subsequent achievement; and the introduction of performance-based teacher preparation. Some states have dropped uniform requirements for graduation from high school and have indicated to local education agencies that they must establish measurable objectives for schooling consistent with state-established goals; in these cases, continued state approval of local education-agency programs is to be predicated upon their achievement of objectives.

Colorado, perhaps, has gone as far as any state. It has proposed to base state financial support of local education agencies partially on the performance achievement of pupils in the district, such achievement to be consonant with district objectives and given state goals. Using pupil achievement of objectives as the criterion for further funding places a tremendous burden of anxiety on school personnel.

Several states have taken steps to develop performance-based teacher education (PBTE). Elam summarizes (1971): "PBTE has five essential elements: 1)' Teaching competencies to be demonstrated are role-derived, specified in behavioral terms, and made public; 2) assessment criteria are competency-based, specify mastery levels, and made public; 3) assessment requires performance as prime evidence and takes student (person preparing to teach) knowledge into account; 4) the student's rate of progress depends on demonstrated competency; 5) the instructional program facilitates development and evaluation of specific competencies."

The federal government has supported the move to performance-based teacher education in several ways: direct support to states interested in developing new regulations, for example, Washington (Andrews, 1971), Texas, and Rhode Island; encouragement and recognition to states that have moved to performance-based teacher education, Florida, and Minnesota, for example; development contracts with teacher corps; and a nine-state communication consortium among states that have declared their intention to move to performance-based teacher education. State approval of common schools based upon specified objectives and the adoption of performance-based teacher education have forced the staffs of state departments of education to change their patterns of operation, refocus their energies, and adopt different strategies. For example, they now spend an inordinate amount of time on broadening the base of participation in planning, decision-making, and monitoring. They also are much more heavily involved in the analysis and development of programs and materials. Coalitions or consortia of institutions, agencies and organizations are brought together for program development. In approving programs, more attention is placed on program integrity, internal consistency, and process/planning steps rather than reacting to individual cases using some universal set of external criteria. More attention is placed on packaged protocol and training materials—materials that help provide situation-specific, focused experiences to achieve a given objective.

State departments of education that are committed to change have also had to make heavy investments in staff retraining in such areas as needs assessment, objective writing, group-process skills, evaluation, and organizational feedback—all competency elements of a systematic approach to teacher education and curriculum development.

Again quoting Elam (1971):

> *The impact of the PBTE movement already ranges through teacher education institutions, state departments of education, the professional organizations, and into the communities these serve. It facilitates a sharing of decision-making power and redefinition of the roles of these institutions. Yet PBTE's development has been to date scattered, sporadic, and tentative.*
>
> *Many unanswered questions still plague PBTE programs. Establishing valid criteria for evaluating their effectiveness is particularly difficult. Pupil learning is the appropriate criterion for assessing the effectiveness of teacher trainers and training programs; but until relationships between teacher behavior and pupil learning can be more firmly established through research and improved measurement, judgments will have to be made on a priori grounds. There is a danger that competencies that are easy to describe and evaluate will dominate PBTE, hence a special effort will be needed to broaden the concept and to emphasize more divergent, creative, and personal experiences. Also, important political and management problems are associated with PBTE.*

Philosophical or Political Issues

Given the types of roles that state departments of education can play, the political, social, and economic pressures brought to bear upon them, and the changes that are under way in teacher education, what are the issues that face leaders in state departments of education? Assuming that the state will provide more and more of the financial support for education (with less coming from local property taxation) and assuming that the state will begin to administer more of the business aspects of education (with each state a school district, like Hawaii), what questions need to be asked and answered by educational leaders and lay citizens?

Who is the client? This may seem like a funny question, but it is a necessary one. Answering it requires that the people to whom and for whom the services of the public school are intended be made explicit. Some leaders in state departments of education apparently think that state legislators are the clients ("Whoever pays the piper calls the tune"). Some see the electorate or the power figures in the community as the clients. Some see the teachers or principals as clients. Some see the children in schools as the clients. Others view both children of school age and their parents as clients. Assuming that the state department of education is a service agency, where should such services be felt? By whom should services be evaluated?

It is good for state department of education personnel and others interested in educational organization to remember that schools have been created to help parents and the society with the education of the young. Even though schools may be asked from time to time to take on other more expansive tasks such as community or societal reform, the central purpose of the school remains: to provide educational opportunities for children that will lead them to become happy, productive, full-fledged citizens. In other words, the students and their parents (as long as they have responsibility for and influence on the students) are the clients of the school system. The effectiveness or worth of an educational system, from the state commissioner for education down to a janitor in a local building, must be judged on the basis of the goods and services provided to children in school and the effects of these goods and services on the lives of children and their parents.

How should decisions about education be made? Often in educational circles, people say that those who know the most or those who have the most information should make the decisions. In computer language this idea might be stated: Only those "on line" are capable of making decisions. Modern management theory indicates that decisions should be made at the lowest possible organizational level consonant with the ability to accept the consequences of decisions. Are the common people able to make wise choices if they have the truth?

Should curriculum decisions be decentralized? Should they be more centralized? If children and their parents are the clients, should they make most educational decisions? Can state departments of education trust parents, children, and teachers to make wise choices? What are the dangers of localism in education? Can the financial support of schools be separated from operational control? If financing for education is centralized, will curriculum decisions become centralized, too? Should we (can we) expect individual teachers to become more professionally autonomous? What alternatives do we have?

Education is a sharing of power. As a person becomes more skillful and knowledgeable, more self-directive, he can (and should) use his energies and talents to achieve his own and shared goals. It is sometimes difficult for school officials to remember that the school should not be designed solely for the social control of the young; rather it should be designed to foster the enlightened self-interest that will help the young take on responsible freedom. Schools should provide the intrinsic motivation necessary to maintain a sense of order and justice in a democratic society.

To promote these goals, new organizational structures and norms should be institutionalized. Among these, educational decisions (what will be taught to whom when, using what materials and methods) should be made closer to the clients of the system, at the building level if possible, by teachers, students, parents, and principals working together. The decisions so made should be known to those affected and open to feedback and evaluation.

Open and available parent-teacher–child-care cooperatives for all children ages three to five and their parents will also help promote these goals. The cooperatives should include both child care—nursery school, medical-health services, and so forth—and parental education. Appropriate liaisons among home, school, and community social services can be developed through these cooperatives.

The size of schools should be limited. Each student should

be known by at least three members of the faculty and be recognized by all members.

Communities or geographical regions should encourage the development of schools that provide different styles of instruction or different learning environments.

More technical teacher preparation should be designed for and done at the school site and in such a way that teachers have time for and access to nonthreatening–staff-development opportunities.

Further, school building personnel should have immediate access to state and national information systems. Each school building should have an electronic data processing terminal tied into the state information system and should be on line for closed- and open-circuit educational television and facsimile equipment. Preparation and staff development can then be related to the information systems as well as to the materials available and the goals of the school.

The climate of the school should not be neglected either. As much as possible the school should model the good society, with the interests and talents of students and faculty combining to create a warm, psychologically supportive atmosphere.

Should the state department of education take initiative in promoting change? Should it attend primarily to regulation and the collection and sharing of information? What should be the role of state departments of education in teacher education? How much time should be devoted to development? To monitoring or evaluation? To needs assessment? How should the staffs of state departments of education work with preparation agencies? How should teacher preparation and the curriculum offerings in schools be related?

State departments of education must take the initiative in promoting change in teacher education. To do so, they themselves must change in a number of ways. They will have to earmark funds and resources for preparation and staff development. This includes funds for pilot projects and studies involving testing and evaluating materials, techniques, and organizational arrangements. Earmarking funds has several advantages from the point of view of state departments of education. It helps guarantee that funds will be spent as intended, it allows legislators to receive recognition for their resource allocations, and it focuses adversary collective-bargaining relationships at the state rather than at the local level. These points may make it easier for state departments of education to make changes in their financial role.

State departments of education will also have to change their approach to curriculum. Instead of organizing and writing state-wide curriculum guides, personnel will have to provide technical assistance to individual school faculties. They will have to design and field test several kinds of materials—materials for training teachers and administrators, alternative protocol and teaching materials that teachers and administrators can use in working with students and parents to achieve specified objectives, and materials for assessment and diagnosis of learning difficulties. To make sure that the ideas and programs that are developed are disseminated, they can be fed into a statewide data processing and retrieval system, which can relay them to individual schools as well as to professional workers at all levels.

A statewide information system is not the only way to bring together the resources of higher institutions, school organizations, professional associations and unions, and administrators to improve preservice and inservice preparation and staff development. Meetings, workshops, and conferences held for the purpose of sharing knowledge, skills, and methods can also contribute to the improvement of professional practice.

Leadership in establishing appropriate public policy and regulations is another important ingredient in the changing role of state departments of education. Policies should be directed toward defining the distinction between professional and lay concerns in education. Other policy matters include establishing a better system of recognizing and motivating professional service, improving the evaluation of school programs in relation to pupil outcomes, and promoting a more open educational system—a system that is sensitive to internal and external feedback.

State departments of education should also extend their services to communities and parents by having on their staffs persons who can help local school personnel, parents, and students establish new coalitions. When problems arise, these persons should be available to help. State departments of education should specifically acknowledge the role of parents in the schools by designing and conducting training programs that will encourage and help them to participate effectively in school affairs.

Who should be the gatekeepers? If professional practitioners are to be judged on the adequacy of the professional practice they provide (as in the medical model) rather than on the effects of their professional services on the lives of their clients, who should judge practice? What factors in preparation or practice are appropriate for clients to judge, for lay citizens, for professional colleagues, for other professional experts?

New arrangements for preparation and certification of professional personnel will have to be invented once it is agreed that education decisions are to be decentralized and that the interest of the state in certification is to be focused on basic competence. Such new arrangements should include the delegation of gatekeeping—the control of who eventually is awarded full-fledged professional status—to those who have a stake in who is allowed to enter teaching and to those who have the qualifications to assess performance and who are at the same time in a position to see teaching competence demonstrated. This means that once the state has specified the goals of education, once it has guaranteed that individuals, agencies, and organizations which have a stake in preparation are involved (have an opportunity to be involved) on an equitable or parity basis, then it can delegate gatekeeping to a local consortium of organizations: colleges and universities, school organizations, professional associations and unions, students in preparation, and community citizens. Gatekeeping decisions need to be made where teaching is going on and where the training of teachers actually occurs, that is, at the school site. How decisions are made with respect to individual candidates for teaching can and should be delegated by the state if a broad spectrum of interests are involved at the policy level in the beginning (Office of the State Superintendent of Public Instruction, State of Washington, 1971).

Have we gone too far in developing a credentialed society? Should the state allow anyone who can perform satisfactorily as a teacher to have a license to practice as a teacher? Does the same apply to medical doctors? Does credentialing really protect the client from malpractice? Or do credentials serve to protect the practitioner from job competition? Do credentials keep services away from those who need them?

The state has already gone too far in developing a credentialed society. Over the years, legislators and members of state school boards have responded to two forces—citizens who are searching for certainty and assurance of goodness in professional services and practicing professionals who want job security and protection from "unqualified" competition. More regulations are passed, more specialized groups want certificates, and access to professional status is more and more difficult. As a result, many school districts and practicing professionals use certificates in ways they probably should not be used: for job placement, for restricting role mobility, for forcing practitioners who are bored with their current assignment to return to the university before they can try different roles or assignments.

The state should distinguish between certification and professional career development. The interest of the state in certification should be limited to the issuance of general licenses to practice, certificates allowing educators to work "with status" in schools. Beyond this basic certificate, the paper proof apparently needed for discriminating between counselors, principals, social studies teachers and others should be left to professional associations, unions, or societies. The posture of the state should be one of encouraging career-long learning, rather than one of forcing further schooling. In dealing with professional career development, the state may wish to consolidate the personnel record-keeping now done in individual buildings and districts and establish electronic means for maintaining an up-to-date vita on each practicing professional that lists assignments held, competencies mastered, career goals, and so forth. This file, of course, should be open to the practicing professional at all times; it could also be available to all schools who are seeking personnel within or outside of the state. Records needed by the state for parceling funds, for planning, for responding to legislators and state school-board members might as well be kept by the state rather than by all the local schools, . . . as long as, and this is an important point, the local school has immediate and direct access to the information system.

The conclusions reached in this chapter can be summarized briefly. In an educational system decisions about schooling should be made as close as possible to the clients of the system. Most of the decisions now being made at the school district level should be either decentralized and given to the staff and faculty of the individual building and their clients or centralized and coordinated by the state department of education. State government should establish enlightened public policy and an appropriate management system for public education. In addition it must provide the financial resources and the technical assistance that the local schools need to do their job. The major thesis of this chapter is that the state must allow and encourage the local school professional staff and their clients to create and carry out their own educational program. If this is to be done, state departments of education must play very different roles from what they have in the past, especially in the areas of curriculum and personnel development.

Dead whales are not too bad if you are in the blubber-rendering business, and the carcasses are near the pot. If this is not the situation, however, the wiser course might be to entice sick or sleeping whales into deeper, more salubrious, waters. Whales respond to care and kindness, and most of all to positive reinforcement. I am told that most whales do not know how much potential power they have. I, for one, would just as soon not tell them even when we wake them up.

Chapter 8

Governance of
Teacher Education

James D. Koerner

Let me state at once my fear that no genuinely new directions are possible in teacher education. For as long as I can remember, the teacher education industry itself has been talking about change. Monographs by professors of education and by administrators, chapters in books, articles by the hundreds in journals, reports by the committees of a dozen professional bodies, panel discussions without number—all have been addressed these many years to reform in teacher education, to breakthroughs, sweeping changes, and, indeed, to revolutions. It is all nonsense.

No industry as monolithic and monopolistic as teacher education can change itself in any but the most routine and innocuous ways. At least it can not change itself for the better. Change at glacial speed is what happens in teacher education. Unfortunately, even then change is not necessarily progress; it may be retrogression.

Either way, the mills grind slowly. The problem for anybody interested in improving teacher education is how to speed up the mills just a little and keep them turning in the right direction.

One of the ways to do this is to recognize that improvement is preeminently a political problem. The problem is not one of shuffling certification regulations, tinkering with course requirements, or creating a new accreditation body (which will merely substitute new rigidities for old ones). Changing the minds of those in power is obviously no easier in teacher education than in any other field, especially if the proposed changes will diminish their authority. But this is what one must try to do first of all in teacher education.

To illustrate both the difficulty and the feasibility of improvement of teacher education at the political level, I am going to record a case history in which I had a role. I do so, not for prideful or self-serving reasons, but for the sake of introducing concreteness and specificity into what would otherwise be a somewhat generalized argument.

My little case history begins with a proposal I made in 1968 as a member of a statewide study committee in Massachusetts. The proposal grew out of my conviction that change in teacher education can not take place on a scale that means anything as long as control of the industry is predominately in the hands of people who call themselves professional educators. I felt that some means of introducing representative government into teacher education and certification had to be found before any other improvements were possible.

I therefore proposed that the study committee build its report around a plan for reconstructing the political apparatus through which school personnel are prepared and licensed for their jobs. I did not regard my proposal as the ideal answer to the problems in Massachusetts, only as the best answer that might be hoped for, given the political realities. Had I wanted to propose an ideal solution, I would have proposed the complete abolition of state licensing. I am persuaded that we have now reached the point in our educational development when school authorities ought to have complete freedom in staffing their schools or at least freedom from the state. Although many school authorities would doubtless abuse that freedom, so many others would profit from it that its advantages far outweigh its liabilities.

But it would have been futile to make this proposal to the study committee, which was heavily weighted, as such committees always seem to be, on the side of administrators and professional educators. They would have greeted such a proposition with shock and disbelief, maybe even paralysis as would those persons and organizations that have a vested interest in the present cartel through which both teachers and administrators are readied for their jobs.

Since the idea was not politically feasible, I contented my-self with a proposal I thought embodied a much more reasonable, practicable reform. I proposed that a new kind of authority be established to carry out the obligations of the state in the licensing of teachers and administrators. For want of a better name I called it the Commission on the Education and Licensing of School Per-sonnel, and conceived of it as an autonomous body appointed by the governor from nominations by scholarly and professional as-sociations and other groups. The rationale for the commission was simple: The education and licensing of teachers and administrators is a large and complex enterprise that requires, but does not receive, continuous attention and regulation by a state body representing the public interest. No state board of education in any of the fifty states can give more than cursory attention to this enterprise and, too often, it relinquishes its authority to the industry itself. My assump-tion in proposing the state commission was that no amount of fiddling with the existing machinery of licensing in Massachusetts (or any other state) would be adequate to our needs. A new kind of instrumentality was required. Although licensing officials in state departments of education would not share this assumption, I thought the idea might be acceptable to enough of the other inter-ests involved to have a chance of adoption.

The commission, as originally proposed, was to be indepen-dent of both the state board of education and the state department of education and was to be given full authority to carry out the responsibilities of the state. It was to bring a new and greatly broad-ened control to teacher education and certification. The new com-mission was to enfranchise those groups that have always had a major stake in how teachers and administrators are prepared and licensed, but have had no voice in it—classroom teachers themselves, scholars and representatives of the arts and sciences, and the taxpayers.

For the first time, instead of being controlled by the old oligarchy, the industry of teacher education and certification in at least one state would be put into the hands of something like representative government. That step seemed to point the way in turn for many other kinds of changes that simply can not be effected in most states today because the power to change anything is pretty well concentrated in the hands of people whose natural inclination is to sustain the status quo.

To avoid opposition from vested interests, certain modifications in the proposal were made even before it was incorporated into the report of our study committee. The most important change was to make the commission an integral unit of the state department of education. This step seriously compromised the idea of creating a balanced body that had real freedom to act, but even in this debilitated condition, the commission might have been effective if it had had an independent spirit and a stubborn determination. Certainly it promised, even as a division of the state department of education, to be an improvement on the present system of control in Massachusetts.

To the surprise of many people, the board of directors of the Massachusetts Teachers Association (the state affiliate of the National Education Association) endorsed the idea of the commission and offered the services of its lawyer in drafting legislation that would make the commission a reality. Some people felt that the Massachusetts Teachers Association was taking an enlightened position but for the wrong reasons: It could control the commission, or the commission would offer a chance for teachers to assume exclusive authority over licensing. The leadership of the association, however asserted that it saw the commission as an important means for the advancement of education in the state and as an instrument that would give teachers at least a voice in training and licensing. In any case, a legislative bill was prepared and introduced into the Massachusetts Senate in January 1969.

As filed, the bill created a fifteen-member Commission for

Certification and Preparation of Educational Personnel, to be appointed by the state board of education and to be responsible to it. The commission would also fall within the state department of education. It was to be composed of seven persons from the public schools, including at least five teachers, five faculty members from colleges and universities, including at least three engaged in teaching, one superintendent of schools, and two laymen. The bill would empower the commission to develop standards and procedures for licensing teachers and administrators and to provide general leadership to teacher education in the state. It carried an ample number of grandfather clauses to protect all licensed personnel then in the schools and everybody then in training.

There was quick and vociferous opposition to the bill. The Massachusetts Federation of Teachers (the state affiliate of the American Federation of Teachers), which I expected to support the bill, immediately announced its opposition. It was not clear whether the federation did so simply for partisan purposes (to be on record as against whatever its rival, the Massachusetts Teachers Association, was for) or out of genuine disagreement with the bill. Massachusetts at that time was the only state in which at the state level serious discussions about merger were going forward between the National Education Association and the American Federation of Teachers, but their respective attitudes towards this bill did not exactly forward the establishment of cordial relations.

Strenuous opposition also came, predictably, from the state department of education, both from the state commissioner, Owen Kiernan, who later departed the state to join the national office of the National Education Association, and from others in the department. Kiernan's successor, Neil Sullivan, came on the scene from Berkeley in February 1969, reversed the stand of the department and supported the bill, but did not manage to silence its natural enemies within the department.

To everybody's surprise, ferocious opposition came also from a tiny insurgent group of teachers within the Massachusetts Teachers Association itself. They called themselves the MACE Action Committee, MACE being the unfortunate initials of the Massachusetts Advisory Council on Education, which sponsored our study committee and published our report. The MACE Action Committee mounted what can only be described as a holy war against the bill. They gave truculent speeches against it, circulated inflammatory broadsides on a wide scale, wrote letters to editors, lobbied the legislature, and sounded the klaxon of fear among the teachers of the state.

Passage of the bill, said the MACE Action Committee in one of its documents, would bring disaster to Massachusetts teachers: "Your profession will become a NONENTITY. . . . COLLEC- TIVE BARGAINING will be seriously infringed upon . . . TEN- URE CONTRACTS WILL BE IN JEOPARDY. . . . YOUR DEGREE STATUS will be destroyed . . . Local control of our schools will be seriously hampered. . . . UNLESS YOU'D LIKE TO BE PART OF AN EDUCATIONAL MEDICAID, CON- TACT LEGISLATORS NOW" [Emphasis in the original].

Sinister suggestions were bandied about, for example, the bill would allow large numbers of foreigners to come into the schools of Massachusetts and drive the present teachers out. There would also be "the possibility of espionage in those cases." In one of its broadsides to teachers, the MACE Action Committee declared that noncitizens "will be allowed to become certified teachers in Massachusetts despite the stern warnings of the FBI as to the vast infiltration of subversives in our country." Writing to a local news- paper, a member of the MACE Action Committee alleged that the bill would "set up an enormous state bureaucracy costing the tax- payers a fortune and producing nothing . . . it will send state examiners into our schools as is done in France and Russia."

Contrary to some of these allegations, the bill clearly and specifically protected all tenure contracts and made no mention of the other matters that seemed to induce hysteria in its opponents. The bill did nothing but establish a commission to consider reforms and to give teachers, for the first time, a direct voice in such re- forms. Far from being a threat to teachers, it was an opportunity for them to exercise some power over their own fate. Nor was there any assurance that the commission, once established, would adopt all or any of other recommendations of the study committee.

In all conscience, the commission, constituted as it was in the bill, would not have been able to promote anything radical. It would obviously have had to settle for exceedingly modest reforms and then only after prolonged deliberations and a full expression of views from the field.

The opponents of the bill played on the fears of enough teachers to neutralize the work staff of the Massachusetts Teachers Association and to discourage whatever support the bill had in the Massachusetts Senate. The association offered a thousand reassurances to those of its members who had been taken in by the campaign of the MACE Action Committee. It also organized meetings throughout the state, lobbied extensively in the Senate, and otherwise tried to refute the misrepresentations of the bill, but its efforts were not enough. The bill reached the Senate Ways and Means Committee in an aura of doubt, distortion, and declamation. "I never anticipated," said Kevin Harrington, then the majority floor leader in the Senate, "the tremendous amount of pressure that a very small group of teachers could bring among the teaching profession. The present posture of teachers who seem to want no change in the present indefensible certification system has not exactly bolstered my confidence in the quality of Massachusetts education." The bill died in the Ways and Means Committee, a victim of fear. It is doubtful that the idea of a balanced state commission to govern teacher education and licensing can ever be resuscitated in Massachusetts.

While the fight in Massachusetts was going on, a related story was unfolding on the West Coast, where a bill based on my proposal for Massachusetts had been introduced into the California Legislature. The fate of this bill further illustrates the professional and political limitations that always operate on reform proposals in teacher education. The story begins in 1961 when the California Legislature, after prolonged debate, passed a famous and bitterly contested piece of legislature known as the Fisher Act. Just about everybody in the state supported this legislation except the education establishment. In the eyes of the state board of education, then composed of appointees of Governor Pat Brown in whose office the Fisher Act had been written, in the eyes of the legislature itself, and in the eyes of the general public so far as one can judge, the Fisher Act was one of the major reforms that people frequently talk about in the education and licensing of teachers and administrators.

But developments since 1961 attest eloquently to the ability of the education establishment to dilute and delay such reforms. The history is a complicated one; it is sufficient here to say that the intent of the Fisher Act has been systematically undermined by the people and groups for whom it was always anathema. Moreover, great numbers of the new teachers, perhaps half, who are licensed each year in California, and probably 90 percent of the administrators, continue today to be certified under pre-Fisher standards. They come in under grandfather clauses that have been repeatedly extended and are still being extended—twelve years later! People so licensed do not have to worry, ever, about meeting the requirements of the Fisher Act even in their diluted form.

Since 1961, California has therefore had two separate and distinct systems for licensing school personnel. Five years ago, an educational subcommittee of the California Assembly (the lower house) put the matter this way in one of its reports: "Seldom in the history of California has a public mandate of such a proportion [as the Fisher Act], heavily supported by both parties, been subjected to so much bureaucratic frustration. We think it is incumbent on the State Department of Education and the persons responsible for teacher education to accept the public demand and do their duty."

In 1967, the California legislature appointed still another educational committee, the Joint Committee on Teacher Licensing and Public School Employment, to look into the question of what had gone wrong with the implementation of the Fisher Act and to propose further legislation. The joint committee was headed by a former teacher, Assemblyman Leo Ryan, a Democrat from South San Francisco. In its first year of work, the committee found great dissatisfaction around the state with the licensing system for both teachers and administrators, but did not garner many promising ideas from educators in California or elsewhere about corrective action. Then a member of the state board of education called the Massachusetts plan to the attention of Assemblyman Ryan and his staff. For them it was catalytic. They took up the proposal that had been made in Massachusetts, adapted the main idea to conditions in California, and in March 1969 filed a bill that would create a new state authority, a fifteen-member broadly representative body called the Commission for Teacher Preparation and Licensing.

The California bill departed from the Massachusetts bill in

several vital respects that raised professional eyebrows and tempera-
tures all over that large state. The California bill kept the commission under the state board of education but placed it outside the
state department of education, a provision that sorely irked State
Superintendent Max Rafferty and others in the department. The
bill required that members of the commission be appointed by the
governor with the advice and consent of the Senate, thus making
such appointments subject to public scrutiny and debate.

Further, and more important, the bill made written qualify-
ing examinations mandatory for both teachers and administrators,
a change that really was radical. Further still, it prohibited training
institutions from requiring more than nine semester hours of course
work in pedagogy and professional subjects before practice-teaching,
the intent being to restrict professional training to a total of one
semester out of a four-year undergraduate program. And that was
pretty radical, too.

The bill also eliminated the awkward distinction between
academic and nonacademic majors that was one of the well-meant
but administratively sticky problems in the implementation of the
Fisher Act by the state board. But the bill was careful to retain
provisions that would prevent people with either an undergraduate
or graduate major in education from being licensed as teachers or
administrators. And it spelled out in considerable detail the additional responsibilities of the commission, most of them admirable
improvements, in my opinion, over the existing standards and
practices.

Professional opposition to the idea of mandatory exams was
immediate, widespread, and thunderous. Opposition from the
California deans of education to the nine-hour limit on education
courses was also immediate and hysterical. School administrators of
California, who have always resented insistence of the Fisher Act
on academic majors for administrative licenses, lobbied against the
bill. They especially disliked compulsory exams for either teachers
or administrators, and they resented the denigration of majors in
education implicit in the bill. As I have mentioned, most newly
licensed administrators in California are not actually affected by
the Fisher Act. They come in under pre-Fisher options, meaning
that they can come in with majors in education rather than in

academic subjects. The bill, although it eliminated the academic requirement as such, specifically prohibited administrative licenses to persons with majors in education and was therefore just as objectionable to administrators as the Fisher Act was. The bill in its initial form was also opposed by the California Teachers Association (the state National Education Association affiliate) (unlike in Massachusetts). The California Teachers Association is the largest state teachers association (175,000 members) and has a lot of influence in the legislature.

Other groups took varying positions on the bill. Just as in Massachusetts before Sullivan, the state superintendent (Rafferty) and the state department of education fought the whole bill with every weapon they could command, although they seemed to command fewer than they once did. The California School Boards Association disliked the bill because it felt it transferred too much authority from the state board of education to the new commission. It also felt that more laymen were needed on the commission, just as teachers thought that more teachers were needed on the commission, administrators more administrators, and so on. The state board of education itself, now a wholly Reagan-appointed board as its predecessor had been a wholly Brown-appointed board, opposed the bill on a number of grounds. Board members felt that the bill weakened the power of the state board and that the commission, if there was any need for one, ought to be under the state department of education, not outside of it.

Major amendments and compromises were unavoidable in view of this widespread opposition, and Assemblyman Ryan and the other sponsors of the bill made many. The most fundamental change came, as one would expect, in the matter of compulsory examinations. The bill was amended so that compulsory examinations for the graduates of training programs approved by the new commission were waived, a change that converted the nuclear bomb of the bill into a conventional hand grenade. The control of the state board over the commission was strengthened, and numerous technical amendents were incorporated into the final draft.

In August of 1969, the bill passed both houses of the legislature with large majorities, only to be vetoed by Governor Reagan at the urging of Superintendent Rafferty, the state board, and others. The veto message, however, was a reasonable one, reflecting the fears and uncertainties of the opponents of the bill and leaving the door open for its sponsors to continue developing the idea of a commission and to reintroduce the proposal at the next session. In the meantime, a statewide educational reform commission appointed in 1969 by Governor Reagan himself filed a preliminary report in which it strongly endorsed the basic idea of the bill and urged the governor to support the establishment of such a commission on teacher education and licensing.

Assemblyman Ryan and the joint committee continued to refine the bill, mend fences, and gather support. In January 1970, the bill was filed anew. Further and prolonged debate took place in the legislature, and additional amendments were promoted by the education lobby. Ultimately the bill passed both houses and this time was signed into law by the governor.

Hence, for the last two years California has been going through the painful process of implementing a piece of legislation that in theory represents a new direction in teacher education. Actually, no particular breakthrough has occurred. The teacher education industry is now busily undermining the intent of the legislature, as it quite successfully did with the Fisher Act. The new commission will mount no revolutions, depose no monarchs, shake no foundations. It will, however, for the first time introduce a measure of representative government into teacher education. If it is able to resist professional pressures, it may over time effect some modest improvements in the preparation and licensing of school personnel.

The stormy odyssey of these bills in Massachusetts and California tells us something about the politics of reform in teacher education. That there probably are no really new directions that can be taken in the industry, least of all by the industry itself, is demonstrated once again. External pressures in the future may possibly produce greater change than has occurred in the past. The idea of accountability, the formation of a single national union for teachers (a dismal prospect), the exigencies of the marketplace as they affect the supply and demand of school personnel, and the desperate search of legislatures and school boards for ways of reducing the unit costs of education—it is possible that such forces may change teacher education more than anything the industry itself will do; but even so I look for no fundamental reform. At worst, we may have reaction that parades as reform; at best, a mild meliorism is all that the politics of the situation will permit for the foreseeable future.

Chapter 9

National Accrediting

Lindley J. Stiles
Jack A. Bils

Nothing is more controversial in teacher education, perhaps, than its system of national accrediting. The conflict was born with the movement itself. Despite determined efforts to establish confidence in accrediting procedures and decisions, criticisms promise to continue indefinitely. So persistent is the controversy and so divisive its impact that leaders of the movement are beginning to doubt whether national accrediting of teacher education will ever become a viable operation (Edelfelt, 1970; Stinnett, 1970).

Controversy about accrediting, of course, is not indigenous to teacher education; it prevails wherever educational or professional programs are evaluated. Disagreements relate to whether accrediting is necessary and, if so, who should do it. Concerns are expressed, also, about the standards used as well as the validity of judgments made. Decisions not to accredit almost always are criticized by those affected. Professional accrediting, particularly, generates many differences of opinion. Yet, with teacher education, accrediting seems to arouse deeper internal antagonisms with greater public visibility than prevail in other fields. A unique characteristic of the criticisms related to the accrediting of teacher education is the source: The criticisms tend to come from better rather than weaker institutions. Furthermore, the rank and file of practicing professionals in elementary and secondary schools, unlike professionals in other fields, give little support to accrediting. Then, too, academic scholars in colleges and universities, who typically support general and professional accrediting, show little confidence in accrediting of teacher education (Conant, 1963; Forman, 1971).

Clearly, part of the trouble in accrediting teacher education programs stems from trying to apply national standards in a field that has yet to define itself precisely or to validate adequately its processes. Also, institutional and regional differences in the academic achievement of future teachers have fostered divergence in the quality of teachers produced. The professionalization of teaching is in an embryonic stage; it is to be expected that teacher education would be trying to find its way. With so little research to give direction, dogma and tradition compete for acceptance, and experimental programs, which are growing in number, challenge both. Accrediting is caught in the crosscurrents of these struggles to establish viable patterns for teacher education. More significantly, it runs head-on into another pressure—a widespread popular rejection of the idea that teachers should be prepared through the study of education courses.

Over and beyond such obvious sources of conflict about national accrediting of teacher education are problems that are generated from the goals, standards, and procedures followed as well as from the politics of control that characterize the entire operation. The teacher education establishment (deans and professors of education in colleges and universities, state certification officers, and key bureaucrats in the National Education Association, the American Association of Colleges for Teacher Education, and the National Council for Accreditation of Teacher Education) has not been able to agree on what accrediting is supposed to do. As a consequence, goals and standards tend to be stated in general, nonassessable terms. With no generally accepted norms established, it is to be expected that evaluations are shaded by individual biases and prevailing professional opinion. Undermining the entire process are political efforts to use accrediting to keep control of teacher education "in our hands," as one dean of education put it.

National accrediting of teacher education may be failing simply because it is an impossible task. It is one thing to administer nationally approved standards to 85 medical education programs, 143 law schools, or to 298 engineering schools (National Center for Educational Statistics, 1971), but quite a different challenge to try to accredit 1246 teacher education programs in which as much as one-half to two-thirds of the professional sequence involves supervised clinical experiences in thousands more elementary and secondary schools. The contrast is further reflected by the number of professionals produced. In 1968–1969, the number of degrees awarded in different fields were: medicine, 8082, law, 17,308, engineering, 60,173, and education, 229,500 (National Center for Educational Statistics, 1971). Regulations require that each program of teacher education be reaccredited every ten years, which means that about 125 institutions, not to mention the cooperating schools that provide clinical training, must be examined annually. To date, NCATE (the National Council for Accreditation of Teacher Education) has been able to provide accrediting services to only about 470 colleges and universities. From 1955 through 1969, the council has been able to add to its lists, on the average, only thirteen new institutions a year (Stinnett, 1969). If this average continues to hold, all teacher education programs will not be examined until the year 2030. All these considerations raise the key question: Can accrediting procedures be conducted on this massive scale and still maintain necessary validity?

To answer the question about whether national accrediting of teacher education can be successful, it might be helpful to determine whether alternative systems could be implemented that might be more effective than national accrediting. If not, ways to overcome deficiencies in national accrediting must be developed. The purpose of this chapter is to help bring perspective to these and related questions. A brief review of the historical background and the contemporary operations of the movement will help us understand the current problems faced in national accrediting.

Historical Background

The intent of accrediting is to certify that a school or college meets prescribed academic standards. The objective is to assure that all graduates will have achieved an acceptable level of academic or professional competence. Self-accrediting by educational institutions originated in the United States. It evolved in a vacuum of failure by states to regulate the quality of schools and colleges, despite the fact that one state, New York, had legally accredited colleges as early as 1787. Self-accrediting was predated in the 1870s by the practice of the state university certifying the acceptability of high school programs as preparation for college (borrowed from German universities by the University of Michigan). Later, some state departments of education assumed this function. Toward the end of the century, colleges and universities, following a pattern pioneered in the New England states, joined in regional associations to accredit secondary schools for college admission. Likewise, institutions of higher learning began to accredit themselves to attest qualification of their graduates for entry into graduate and professional schools. Throughout, the accrediting process followed the pattern of a group of strong institutions setting the standards that others had to reach if they wanted accreditation.

As professional schools developed, national self-accrediting became the means of maintaining acceptable standards of professional preparation. Beginning with medicine, various professional and specialized fields, for example, chemistry, art, and home economics, established their own accrediting associations. Sometimes several accrediting associations competed. The numbers grew so much that by the 1940s a university might be dealing with 100 or more different accrediting agencies, each of which made visits to the campus, prescribed standards to be met, and assessed a fee for its services. The proliferation finally provoked rebellion. In 1949, led by the Association of College and Land Grant Universities, the National Commission on Accrediting was formed to regulate accrediting agencies. It gained its authority from the commitment of its membership, individual institutions and associations of colleges and universities, to deal only with accrediting bodies approved by the commission (Mayor and Swartz, 1965).

It is significant that accrediting of teacher education programs was initiated by the American Association of Teachers Colleges. Its lists of accredited institutions, first published in 1928, included only teachers colleges and normal schools. Standards established were those considered appropriate to such institutions. Not until 1948 did universities and liberal arts colleges become involved in accrediting. That year, the American Association of Teachers Colleges, the National Association of Colleges and Departments of Education, and the National Association of Teacher Education Institutions in Metropolitan Districts united to form AACTE (the American Association of Colleges for Teacher Education). The new agency expanded the accrediting lists to include all members of the association and form what was the first national accrediting program for teacher education.

Accrediting of teacher education programs was not initially approved, however, by the National Commission on Accrediting. One reason was that the AACTE combined membership and accrediting, a practice not endorsed by the commission. Another was that the commission "may have doubted at that time whether teaching was well enough recognized as a profession to have an accrediting body" (Mayor and Swartz, 1965, p. 52). To qualify originally for consideration by the National Commission on Accrediting, the AACTE organized NCATE (the present National Council for Accreditation of Teacher Education) in 1952. Other sponsoring groups were: the National Association of State Directors of Teacher Education and Certification, the National Commission on Teacher Education and Professional Standards, and the National School Boards Association. All institutions on the AACTE accrediting lists were included in the new NCATE, which also adopted the AACTE standards. With the new organization and its broadened sponsorship, the long struggle to gain recognition from the National Commission on Accrediting was undertaken, a goal that was not fully achieved until 1966. In 1963, John R. Mayor, director of education for the American Association for the Advancement of Science, was commissioned by the National Commission on Accrediting to assess the viability of national accrediting in teacher education and the strengths and weaknesses of NCATE. His report, already cited, was a key factor in persuading the commission to recognize NCATE as an accrediting body.

From its inception national accrediting of teacher education has generated intensive controversy. A key source was the historic conflict between professors of liberal arts and education concerning the need for professional preparation of teachers, which centered on the practice of separately accrediting the professional-sequence segment—from 15 to 30 percent—of the teacher's preparation. The continuing conflict had the effect of making accrediting of teacher education a symbol of professionalism for teachers. Proponents of the movement became extremely aggressive in their efforts to protect and expand its influence. Challenges to accrediting procedures and practices, even friendly ones, were equated with efforts to deny teaching its professional status.

Once NCATE was provisionally recognized by the National Commission on Accrediting as the official accrediting agency for teacher education (1956), it moved rapidly to establish its control over programs. Legal and political power were exercised to force teacher education institutions to seek accrediting and to follow the prescriptions for teacher education made by the council. By 1963, about half of the states had been persuaded to grant automatic initial licensure to graduates of institutions approved by NCATE. Reciprocity in awarding licenses between these states was linked, also, to accrediting. High schools were urged to advise prospective teachers to attend only accredited colleges and universities. School boards, similarly, were placed under pressures to employ only teachers and other educational personnel who had "NCATE Approved" stamped on their diplomas. Schools and departments of education were urged to employ professors with doctorates from NCATE-accredited graduate programs. Such pressures to cooperate with NCATE were the gospel of the educational establishment during the late 1950s and early 1960s.

By 1960, many leaders in teacher education had become apprehensive about the prescriptions of NCATE for teacher education. They were powerless to change the organization, however, since the agencies that had created NCATE had made no provision for accountability of that body back to its sponsors. NCATE had autonomous authority to prescribe what teacher education should be, and there was no due-process procedure by which policies and decisions could be challenged. One by one colleges and universities preparing teachers were being forced to comply with mandates of the council.

A crisis in the quest of NCATE for power came with the refusal of two institutions, a distinguished private liberal arts college and a world-renowned state university, to accept its mandates. First, in 1962 Carleton College objected when NCATE criticized an English professor of long, successful experience who taught methods courses for prospective English teachers for not having studied education courses as preparation for the assignment. Before the Carleton "rebellion" was completely resolved, the University of Wisconsin, in 1963, refused to accept the prescriptions of the council for its teacher education program. NCATE, applying its restricted image of teacher education and functioning as a power arm to keep control in the hands of educationists, had raised questions about Wisconsin's interdisciplinary faculty for teacher education and its alternate patterns of preparation for prospective teachers in particular subject fields. The University of Wisconsin faculty decided that to make the changes NCATE prescribed would violate fundamental traditions within the university, negate experimental programs, and bring too much regimentation into patterns of preparation for teaching; it decided to withdraw its application for accrediting.

NCATE responded to this action by generating nationwide pressures in the education establishment against Wisconsin, with the object of forcing it into compliance. The attacks boomeranged: The restricted image that NCATE had of teacher education and the power tactics it was willing and able to employ to force its prescriptions on local institutions and agencies were broadly exposed. That NCATE had become a "quasi-legal body with tremendous national power" was further documented by Conant (1963). As the picture became clear and widely disseminated, NCATE was forced onto the defensive. The result was that the accrediting body rather than the University of Wisconsin was forced to change. The mandate came from the National Commission on Accrediting, which had not yet given full approval of NCATE as an accrediting agency. The commission ultimately gained support from the sponsors and financial backers of NCATE who, despite their strong support of the council against Wisconsin, had realized that professionalism really was not the issue. Instead what was involved were the standards and prescriptions NCATE maintained, the fact that the council was not broadly representative of all groups concerned with teacher education, and the larger issue of due-process control over the accrediting operation. Behind the ultimatum to NCATE, and a key factor in the actions of its sponsoring agencies and the national commission, was the widespread expression of dissatisfaction among the general public, teachers and administrators in elementary and secondary schools, academic scholars in colleges and universities, about half of the state departments of public instruction, and many professional educationists, as well. A crystallizing factor was the 1963 publication of Conant's scathing criticisms of the operations of NCATE.

NCATE Today

Since the Wisconsin confrontation in 1963, NCATE has been going through a process of reorganization and regrouping. Some changes it has made are fundamental; others represent only minor adjustments intended to give the illusion of change without altering the actual power structure or procedures. Of significance is a provision in the new (1967) constitution for NCATE that permits constituent sponsoring organizations to share responsibility for council policies and procedures. The vehicle for achieving such due-process accountability is the Coordinating Board, composed of thirteen voting members who have power to review and approve policies and procedures of the council. In addition, the American Association of Colleges for Teacher Education is now responsible for developing standards. A new set of these descriptive statements (National Council for Accreditation of Teacher Education, 1970), which includes an introduction setting forth the purposes of accrediting, was adopted by NCATE in January 1970 and made mandatory in the fall of 1971.

The reorganized NCATE carefully preserves control of accrediting in the hands of professional educationists in preparing institutions. Merrill states: "Both sets of standards (meaning the new as well as the old) assume that national accreditation of teacher education should be carried on primarily by the higher education community but in close cooperation with the profession, professional organizations, and state departments of education" (1970, pp. 102–103). The method of maintaining control on the Coordinating Board and council is to prescribe that representation should come from the sponsoring agencies—all but two of which (the learned societies and the School Boards Association, which have only token representation) form the corps of the teacher education establishment. The learned societies are not represented on the Coordinating Board.

Of the total of sixteen members on the 1970–1971 Coordinating Board (four of which are liaison representatives to the board from constituent organizations, that is, executive secretaries of such groups) only three, a token number, could be considered to approach accrediting of teacher education as noneducationists. Missing from the board is adequate representation from the academic and school (classroom teachers) communities. Neither is provision made for representation of various kinds of key educational practitioners, such as school administrators, supervisors, counselors, or other educational specializations (National Council for Accreditation of Teacher Education, 1971, pp. 1–2).

The 1970–1971 NCATE council, which is responsible for interpreting and applying the standards and for making judgments about individual institutions has only seven (out of twenty-two) representatives who by their background and position might be expected to view teacher education from benchmarks other than those of the professional educationists. Clearly it is the intent of NCATE to maintain narrow control of teacher education programs. Its new Standard 1.5 specifically states: "The design, approval, and continuous evaluation and development of teacher education programs are the primary responsibility of an officially designated unit; the majority of the membership of this unit is composed of faculty and/or staff members who are significantly involved in teacher education" (National Council for Accreditation of Teacher Education, 1970, p. 7). That professors of education should make policy for the academic and specialized, as well as the pedagogical segments, of the teacher's preparation is clearly documented by the fact that the standards provide for evaluations to be made of the program of liberal studies and subject-field specialization.

In developing its new standards for the accreditation of teacher education to be transmitted to NCATE, the committee of the AACTE sought advice from representatives engaged in teacher education, learned societies, professional associations, state departments of education, the teaching profession, and students preparing for teaching. Before adoption, the new standards were tested in eight colleges and universities after which final revisions were made. Yet the standards are viewed as evolutionary; the new NCATE constitution requires that they be under continuous review and evaluation, a responsibility that AACTE has assumed. The standards proclaim that accrediting is a voluntary process and theorize that accrediting should reflect changing conditions in higher education generally and in teacher education in particular (National Council for Accreditation of Teacher Education, 1970). Experimentation and innovation in teacher education are specifically encouraged to the point of making special provisions for the evaluation of programs that do not conform to the usual standards.

The purposes of national accrediting of teacher education as stated by the new standards include the following: to assure that particular institutions—those named in the *Annual List*—offer programs for the preparation of teachers and other professional school personnel that meet national standards of quality; to ensure that children and youth are served by well-prepared school personnel; to advance the teaching profession through the improvement of preparation programs; and to provide a practical basis for reciprocity among the states in certifying professional school personnel.

Standards are provided for all basic programs (including five-year programs and programs leading to the Master of Arts in Teaching degree) for the initial preparation of teachers for nursery through high schools and all programs for educational personnel beyond the baccalaureate. Both sets of standards include questions about: curriculum, including general and specialized subject courses as well as the professional sequence, faculty qualifications, student characteristics, resources and facilities for the programs, such as library, instructional media, equipment, and buildings, and provisions made for evaluation. Standards for graduate programs ask questions about these areas and include a section on research as well. To be eligible for NCATE accrediting, an institution must offer four years of work, be approved by the state department of education in the categories for which accrediting is sought, be accredited by its regional accrediting association, and have graduated students from its teacher education programs. An institution may request accrediting only in specified programs, but it must present to NCATE for review information on all programs offered.

Accrediting procedures followed by NCATE remain substantially unchanged. An institution requesting to be accredited is required to undertake self-study of its operations along prescribed guidelines and to prepare a comprehensive "Institutional Report." Subsequently, an NCATE visiting team, whose members are approved by the dean of education as well as the accrediting body, visits the institution for a few days to verify information submitted. The team then makes its report (strictly factual without recommendations) to the Visitation and Appraisal Committee of NCATE, which in turn makes its own report and recommendations to the council. In most cases, a member of the visiting team meets with the Visitation and Appraisal Committee.

As it now functions, NCATE is primarily an instrument of AACTE, which is composed primarily of deans and presidents of teacher education institutions. The association provides ten of the twenty-two members on the council and most of its financial support. Just recently, the National Education Association cancelled its annual contribution (forty thousand dollars) to NCATE but indicated a desire to continue as a constituent member. The AACTE board of directors set up a contingency fund to keep NCATE operating and initiated a study of the future of accrediting (American Association of Colleges for Teacher Education, 1972, p. 1). Nevertheless, advocates of national accrediting of teacher education still hold high hopes that the recent reorganization of NCATE and its newly adopted standards will reduce the controversy related to the process. Such apparently is not a realistic anticipation. The problems with national accrediting in general and with NCATE in particular are still with us despite the contributions that NCATE has made to teacher education.

Contributions of NCATE

After an extensive study of NCATE, Mayor and Swartz observed that persons who have some knowledge of accrediting in higher education tend to fall into three categories: those who refuse to admit that accrediting has been a constructive force in higher education; those who believe accrediting has made a contribution but is losing its usefulness; and those who feel accrediting will continue to be a constructive force. Their own bias is that "accreditation has become an integral part of the American educational fabric, and is in a way symbolic of the American way of life" (Mayor and Swartz, 1965, p. 218). They feel that national accrediting has contributed to teacher education in a number of ways. It has forced institutions to give teacher education its own separate department and leadership. It has forced reorganizations in teacher education curriculums to achieve a balance between general, specialized, and professional; provide better sequences for education courses; expand provisions for laboratory experiences; and designate one "path" for certification. Further, because of its influence, institutions have increased the numbers of full-time specialists in education on their faculties, improved the selection, counseling, and graduation requirements of students preparing for teaching, and increased financial support to and expanded resources and facilities of teacher education. NCATE has also caused institutions to consider alternate routes to teacher certification as experimental.

A more recent study by Maul (1970, pp. 47–52), which relies exclusively on responses from individuals representing 149 institutions that were accredited or reaccredited from 1965 to 1968, suggests that the function of national accrediting is now established but that considerable disagreements prevail over how it should be operated. Eighty percent of those polled feel that NCATE accreditation procedures actively stimulate improvements in teacher education; 89 percent believe that NCATE accreditation strengthens the status of the department of education; 76 percent think that accredited status improves relationships with other institutions engaged in teacher education; and 88 percent think accrediting helps to clarify problems in teacher education and to relate needs to sources of support. Overall, 94 percent favor continuing a national system of accrediting with only 24 percent indicating that they think a regional accrediting agency can do the job.

Since the central purpose of accrediting is to force institutions to maintain prescribed standards and procedures, the test is how well an accrediting body is able to enforce its mandates. Maul considers this to be an unanswered question. He points out, as "perhaps the single most meaningful item in the entire study" the fact that 72 percent of the institutions queried indicated that without NCATE intervention they probably would not engage in institution wide self-analysis of their programs of teacher education.

Facilitating teacher certification, and particularly reciprocity of licensing between states, is often cited as a contribution of national accrediting. Twenty-eight states now automatically grant initial teaching licenses to graduates of "NCATE Approved" programs. Differences of opinion prevail, however, as to whether such practices are desirable. What is clear is that to make accrediting and certification synonymous, based on a judgment of an institution rather than on professional qualifications of individuals, in effect, nullifies the certification process. Some states are unwilling to base reciprocity agreements on accrediting standards because so many weak institutions have been able to gain NCATE endorsement. Then, too, accrediting judgments do not guarantee individual professional performance.

Another contribution of NCATE is the stimulation given to state departments of public instruction to move into the field of accrediting teacher education programs. Self-accrediting, as a procedure, came about because state departments had not exercised its responsibility in this area. As NCATE negotiated with state departments for cooperation in accrediting, they were forced to examine their responsibility for protecting the quality of teacher education in their states. Recently, some states have moved toward accrediting teacher education programs because they are unwilling to accept the ratings made by NCATE. Usually such states feel that the NCATE standards are too low or are too meaningless to guarantee quality in teachers produced. Whatever the attitude a state may have toward the accreditation that NCATE provides, one must believe that its pioneer efforts done on the national level have played a role in motivating states to accept responsibility for judging the quality of teacher education programs.

Individual institutions can point to specific contributions that NCATE prescriptions have made for them. These may include such gains as improved curriculums, higher standards, expanded faculties, budget increases, or new buildings. The establishment of a separate organization for teacher education, which NCATE mandates, is considered by many to be an advantage in that it fixes responsibility and authority for teacher education programs. Others claim general contributions, such as some that Mayor lists (for example, designating one "path" for certification), generate disagreements even within the teacher education establishment. When the opinions of academic scholars and practicing school personnel are sought, the controversy is widened. As a result, several alternatives to national accrediting have been considered.

Alternatives to National Accrediting

Differences of opinion prevail among supporters of NCATE about whether national accrediting of teacher education can ever become a viable operation. Edelfelt speaks for many educators when he says: "If accreditation in teaching education is nothing more than a procedure to go through in order to gain a seal of approval, it will lose its impact and importance in American higher education" (1970, p. 68). Even so, he holds hopes that if NCATE can achieve the participation of educators broadly representative of the profession, it may be able to provide fair and equitable, yet firm, judgments about the quality of teacher education institutions.

More pessimistic views are expressed by Stinnett, one of the founders of NCATE, who has now changed his views about the possible national role of NCATE and suggests that state accrediting programs will likely take over this work in the future. Stinnett reasons that NCATE has achieved what it was created to do, namely, placing a quality floor under teacher education programs, and likely will be reduced to some sort of advisory role in the future. His predictions stem from the fact that a number of states have established their own standards and procedures for accrediting institutions for teacher education and more are moving in this direction. Forty-six states now use the approved-programs approach in certification, which means that they have to examine the quality of teacher education programs. An even stronger force that Stinnett identifies as working against NCATE is the increasing demands of teachers to participate in, or to control, programs of accrediting and certification. Thus NCATE risks extinction by continuing as it is at present to be dominated by deans of education and associated educationist bureaucrats and by coming under the domination of practicing professionals, which Stinnett foresees.

Associations of teachers in different subject matters, English, history, business education, and physical education, for example, may assume greater roles in accrediting teacher education in the future. Such groups are now critical of the failure of NCATE to relate accrediting decisions to the quality of programs for producing teachers with their specializations. Many such bodies have developed criteria for judging professional competence in their fields and are actively seeking to influence accrediting and certification decisions. As of 1971, the National Science Teachers Association, Modern Language Association of America, Music Educators National Conference, American Speech and Hearing Association, National Council for the Social Studies, and the American Home Economics Association have developed policies and standards for certification of new members. Likewise, the Modern Language Association of America, Music Educators National Conference, American Speech and Hearing Association, and the American Home Economics Association have recommended policies and standards to the various states as guides to certification practices for teachers in their fields. In general, the effort of each organization is directed nationally toward achieving minimum levels of performance for all personnel prepared and licensed. A possibility is that such bodies will move toward making their own ratings of institutions, as is being done in some specialized fields that give national examinations. If this practice spreads and the number of specialized accrediting agencies proliferates, accrediting in teacher education will be retracing its own history—a trend that the National Commission on Accrediting is committed to counteract. Nevertheless, it is possible that such specialized groups may begin to publish lists of institutions that measure up to prescribed standards in their fields.

Accrediting could become regional if existing regional associations assume such responsibility, a not very likely possibility, or if groups such as the Education Commission of the States take a greater interest in approving programs in an effort to move beyond the norm of national practice in educational operations. If the states join together to improve schools, it is natural that they will become concerned with the preparation of educational personnel. Reciprocity in licensing is one type of agreement that is likely to emerge. If it does, it may be related in some way to quality of programs of preparation.

Another alternative to national accrediting is the possibility that states and institutions with common concerns, similarities, and standards of quality may join together to form their own lists of approved institutions. Already, some states such as New York reach beyond their own boundaries in endorsing programs of teacher education. States now moving toward the use of performance-based judgments of teaching competence could develop their own plans of reciprocity in accrediting and licensing. Another example is the field of correspondence education, which has its own accrediting association. Proprietary schools may well move in the same direction since regional associations refuse to accredit them and the courts have sustained their parochialism. Liberal arts colleges, which are always under pressure from NCATE to assume the teachers-college image, may be forced to develop their own standards for teacher education. Comprehensive universities could do the same thing. Outstanding experimental programs of teacher education could be forced to associate as a protection against status quoism and poor quality in programs approved by NCATE. School- and community-based programs to prepare educational personnel might be forced to do the same thing. Such responses would give expression to the basic motivation in accrediting, which is to differentiate between types and quality of programs.

An alternative to NCATE, but not to national accrediting, is the possibility that the U.S. Office of Education might become the official accrediting agency for teacher education. Already that body has shown its interest in the area by appointing groups to study standards and procedures. It specifies that institutions receiving certain federal grants must be accredited. Should NCATE continue in its failure to be broadly representative of the various groups concerned with teacher education, the Office of Education will be under strong political and professional pressures to use accrediting lists that have broader public support. These pressures could force the office to develop its own classifications of institutions. To the extent that accrediting becomes a legal or quasi-legal operation, governmental agencies will increase their responsibility for it. Increasing financial support for education is coming from the federal government, and we can anticipate that controls will be generated along with the financial support.

An alternative to national accrediting that must be recognized is the possibility of dispensing with accrediting altogether. Many favor this alternative. They believe accrediting has outlived its usefulness, that quality in education must come from within an institution rather than being imposed from without. Accrediting of any kind is seen as a threat to faculty autonomy and an unnecessary intrusion on institutional priorities and programs. Should accrediting be discontinued, quality would be maintained by natural pressures, primarily competition in the marketplace for well-prepared graduates. A college or university would gain prestige by the performance of its products rather than by placing "NCATE Approved" in its catalogs and on diplomas.

In our opinion, the most likely alternative to national accrediting of teacher education is state approval of teacher education programs, as Stinnett predicts. This approach caters to the desires of people for local control and can be more responsive to differences that prevail among institutions. States have the capability, too, of examining all colleges and universities and can include in their assessments of programs the contributions to clinical training that school systems make. In addition, states have the power to enforce their judgments. State accrediting plans may be more representative of all groups concerned with teacher education, academic scholars and practicing professionals as well as professors of education and state bureaucrats. On the other hand, they may be more susceptible to political pressures. A question related to state accreditation concerns its capability of including nonpublic institutions. Then, too, without national standards, such as are now being developed by the AACTE for NCATE, state plans are likely to employ multiple definitions of adequacy in teacher education programs.

If states take responsibility for accrediting operations, it is likely that the NCATE will continue to function as an advisory body that projects national standards and criteria for judging teaching competence. It is even possible that state systems for accrediting individual institutions could be approved by NCATE to assure that national standards are maintained. This distribution of responsibilities would be manageable and at the same time maintain the advantages of both state and national systems of accrediting. We suggest that this may be the way of the future for accrediting of teacher education.

Improvement of National Accrediting

The possibility that one or more of the suggested alternatives actually will replace the NCATE is remote. Accrediting associations cling to life with remarkable tenacity. Survival of national accrediting of teacher education, either in its present form or under an alternative arrangement such as we propose, however, will require finding solutions to a number of complex problems that now undermine its effectiveness. Some difficulties stem from resistance to the idea itself; others grow out of confusion over what comprises teacher education and the vested controls that are maintained. Many difficulties result from the failure of NCATE to define and delimit its mission: to focus on stated objectives, to develop effective operational procedures, and to adapt to the changes taking place in teacher education. The problem of enforcement has still not been solved. To understand why national accrediting is so enmeshed in controversy, and what needs to be done to improve it, one must examine the matrix of problems it faces.

Typical criticisms of NCATE are summarized in Table 1. This list is not all-inclusive and does not indicate the depth of the criticisms. Checks indicate only that each person made or reported the observation. It should be noted that many of the same criticisms arose both before and after the new NCATE standards were adopted in 1970. Even though many of the observations are quite specific, they do point to several larger problems in national accrediting that must be resolved before it can become a truly positive, effective force in teacher education.

Resistance. The American public and many professionals resist the idea of national accrediting in any field. People are suspicious of attempts to impose any type of uniform standard on a nationwide basis. Loyalties to local and state control easily come into conflict with efforts to apply national standards. Thus, each state maintains its own system of judging qualifications for practice in most professional fields, and states are increasingly developing their own systems for accrediting programs for professional preparation.

In the field of education, local autonomy is almost a religion; people defend it with deepest dedication. In addition, differences in the quality of educational programs, including those to prepare teachers, are so great from one state or region to another that the strict application of minimum quality standards would result in many institutions in some localities being disqualified. Were NCATE really to refuse accreditation to weak institutions, as it purports to do, it might soon be out of business. People would reject the accrediting agency rather than admit that their own institutions are weak. Thus national accrediting may confront an unresolvable dilemma: If it is true to its mission, it may destroy itself. Even so, NCATE must be willing to take the chance. Were it to turn the accrediting of individual institutions over to state departments, as recommended under proposed alternatives, it might be able to disperse the political pressures that now limit its effectiveness.

Definition and Control. Failure to define clearly the components of teacher education and to relate control in such manner that all who share responsibilities for preparing teachers have a voice in policy-making continues to plague NCATE. Educationists argue that the professionalization of teaching is generated from the professional sequence, the from 15 to 25 percent of the prospective teacher's undergraduate program that must be taken to obtain a teaching license in all states. From this premise, it is argued that professors of education who teach education courses, and who presumably know more about what is going on in schools, should

Table 1. REPRESENTATIVE CRITICISMS OF NCATE BEFORE AND AFTER ADOPTION OF NEW STANDARDS (1970)

	Conant 1963	Mayor 1965	Stinnett 1970	Edelfelt 1970	Maul 1970	Forman 1970
STRUCTURE						
Responsible to no definite constituency	✓	✓			✓	
Need more representation from:	✓	✓				
scholarly disciplines		✓				
learned societies		✓				
teaching profession	✓	✓	✓	✓		✓
lay public	✓	✓	✓			
Control by "teacher education establishment"	✓	✓	✓	✓		
Three levels of NCATE structure too complex		✓			✓	
STANDARDS						
Quality of graduates not assessed	✓	✓				✓
Standards not directly related to educational process	✓	✓		✓		✓
Vague and ambiguous statements	✓	✓		✓		✓
"Rubber ruler" (standards vary from school to school)	✓	✓		✓	✓	✓
Narrow view of teacher education:						
undue uniformity; promotion of status quo	✓	✓		✓		✓
No provision for different types of students (future teachers)				✓	✓	✓
PROCEDURES						
Time involved with self-study report too great	✓	✓		✓	✓	
Strongest people not selected for visiting teams		✓		✓	✓	
Poor communication between NCATE and institutions		✓		✓	✓	
Little emphasis on stimulating improvement		✓				
GENERAL						
Little help with reciprocity	✓		✓			
Universal accreditation not achieved			✓			

be in control of teacher education programs and accrediting. When this kind of reasoning is advanced, it is argued that the regional accrediting associations accredit the liberal and specialized subject-field courses that prospective teachers study. The adopted standards, however, make clear that NCATE will judge an institution by the nature of the "general studies component" and the "content of teaching specialties." They prescribe, further, that decisions about the work that prospective teachers will take in these areas must be made by faculty members in the department or school of education. And, as has been shown, accrediting is in similar hands.

Were NCATE to define its task as simply the accrediting of the professional sequence and really leave to the regional associations judgments about other aspects of the prospective teacher's program (as we believe it should), there would be little objection to professors of education being in control of this work or of the accrediting operation. Since it has consistently and deliberately refused to delimit its reach, NCATE must expect continuing controversy over who controls both teacher education and accrediting. Conscientious professors of liberal arts and of other university schools who help to prepare teachers deeply resent being accorded second-class, nonvoting status in the area of teacher education. They will not be content with the token representation that NCATE and most schools of education extend as appeasement as long as their contributions are being evaluated as part of the accrediting process.

Establishing Objectives. A deficiency in NCATE has been its inability to establish specific and measurable objectives. Those responsible for the accrediting process have never been willing, for example, to limit its contribution simply to judging whether an institution has achieved defined minimum standards; the insistence is that prescriptions must be made to improve all programs, even the most outstanding ones. As a consequence, the council falls into the practice of using the "rubber ruler" with no defined level of adequacy.

Another weakness in the accrediting process that needs correcting is the focus on quantity rather than quality. The tendency is to assume that the size of budgets, faculties, and course offerings and the number of library volumes are what is important. Mere existence of programs, form of organization, extent of faculty involvement, plans underway, and operational procedures are other considerations that weigh heavily in accrediting judgments. Little attention is paid to actual quality of the teachers produced by an institution, despite lipservice given to the goal in the new standards.

Worse still, NCATE standards are not stated in terms that permit precise assessment. For example, consider the standard relating to admission of students, Standard 3.1: "The institution applies specific criteria for admission to teacher education programs; these criteria require the use of both objective and subjective data" (National Council for Accreditation of Teacher Education, 1970, p. 9). Subquestions are raised about the requirements of an institution for admission, evidence that they have been met, numbers applying and actions taken, extent to which objective data and national norms are considered, provision for remediation for substandard admittees, and characteristics of students admitted. In no place do the standards suggest a minimum standard for admission; hence, the council has no criteria to rule that any institution disqualifies because it admits weak students. Conant found that the best students admitted in some "NCATE Approved" institutions would not qualify even for admission in others. There is no reason to believe that conditions have changed with the use of the new standards.

NCATE standards have been criticized not only for being vague but also for being misleading. Forman points out that standards for the library ask such questions as whether in developing the library, serious consideration is given to the recommendations of appropriate national professional organizations and learned societies. But when he checked with the five organizations that NCATE named to set standards, he found that none made recommendations (1971, p. 520). Thus specific, measurable, understandable objectives should be developed and implemented.

Guaranteeing Quality. The major purpose of national accrediting, as stated in the new standards, is to ensure that children and youth are served by well-prepared school personnel. One must ask, then, how NCATE gives such guarantees. In judging an institution, it ascertains whether it maintains a "well-defined plan for evaluating the teachers it prepares" (National Council for Accreditation of Teacher Education, 1970, p. 12), but it provides no criteria for judging the quality of the product. Nor is quality of product given a high priority when accrediting judgments are made.

In spite of this, NCATE has so much confidence that its accreditation of an institution assures that all graduates will be successful teachers that it encourages states to certify automatically graduates of "NCATE Approved" institutions. NCATE grants a general rating for an institution that has no reliability when applied to the quality of teachers produced in particular fields or for elementary or high school teaching. An approved institution may produce poor teachers in one area and good ones in others. If its counts of books, budgets, and courses are adequate and if its organizational pattern, procedures, and controls are in order, it can win approval. To claim that accrediting protects children and youth is, as Forman charges, "professional irresponsibility" and "malfeasance in office." NCATE can improve this aspect of its operation by distinguishing between the accreditation of institutions and the certification of competence of individual teachers. The latter function should be left to state certification boards.

Developing Standards. Present standards do not differentiate between weak and adequate institutions. One reason is that NCATE has not made this a prior objective. Another is its failure to focus on quality. A third, mentioned above, is that no norms have been set in the various categories in which judgments about accrediting are made. All three activities are needed.

NCATE standards and accrediting procedures are validated by a majority vote rather than by research. Much is made of the fact that the opinions of academic scholars, practicing professionals, and even students were sought when the new standards were being developed. Ultimately, however, the standards came from the majority decisions of a corps of professional educationists. As an example, Maul's study depends on the votes of heads of teacher education programs in institutions undergoing accrediting or reaccrediting to verify NCATE procedures. Because its constituents can not agree on norms and cutoff points, NCATE is trapped with standards that are so vague that they are almost meaningless. To win widespread respect, NCATE standards must distinguish between adequate and inadequate programs of teacher preparation.

Adapting to Differences. Institutions that prepare teachers are vastly different—in size, general purposes, approaches to teacher education, clientele, and faculty composition. Whether national accrediting can adapt to the differences and still certify minimum quality remains to be proven. Size alone presents almost unsurmountable challenges in accrediting. To attempt to apply the same criteria to a small liberal arts college and a large comprehensive university requires distortions that defy objectivity.

To make matters more difficult, perceptions of teacher education are changing rapidly within institutions. The new experimental programs make the preparation of teachers for inner-city schools, to illustrate, more of an off-campus process, with community-action groups, schools, and teacher preparation institutions engaged in new kinds of partnerships to recruit and develop the kinds of teachers needed for different minority groups. Here NCATE faces a problem common to all accrediting bodies—how to keep abreast of change. One way is to keep standards flexible; another is to develop alternative standards for experimental types of programs. An even greater challenge is to train members of accrediting teams to look at new programs without being blinded by traditional images of teacher education.

Developing Operational Procedures. Maul's study of NCATE deals almost exclusively with how well it is functioning. As he concludes, many of the operational procedures need much improvement. A source of irritation among institutions accredited, to use one example, is the practice of having evaluations of an institution made by a partially misnamed Visitation and Appraisal Committee which, in actuality, does not visit a campus but does make recommendations to the council. In 17 percent of the institutions studied, no member of the visiting team, which did visit the campus, appeared before the Visitation and Appraisal Committee to help it interpret the data on the institution. Sixty percent of those polled do not favor the use of the Visitation and Appraisal Committee. Reactions to the operational procedures employed by the council, although not always overwhelming numerically, are sufficiently forceful that even though other problems related to national accrediting can be resolved, NCATE still has to learn how to function effectively.

Keeping Abreast of Change. The problem of keeping abreast

of change is one that torments all accrediting bodies. With standards generated from popular opinion among teacher education establishment leaders, as is the practice with NCATE, it is inevitable that the status quo is stressed. Yet changing social conditions are pressing for changes in the preparation of educational personnel so rapidly that accrediting guidelines quickly become obsolete. Accrediting can easily be an enemy to progress.

An example of change that is currently challenging accrediting standards in teacher education is the trend toward making clinical training a function of school systems rather than colleges and universities. NCATE standards prescribe that all aspects of the teacher's preparation must be under the jurisdiction of campus education faculties. Thus, practice and prescriptions come into conflict. Provisions must be made for these new programs.

Differentiating Between Accrediting and Licensing. A stated purpose of NCATE is to facilitate the licensing of educational personnel, particularly for reciprocity purposes between states. To accomplish this objective, efforts have been made to persuade state licensing boards to license graduates of "NCATE Approved" institutions almost automatically. As a consequence, accrediting and licensing have tended to become synonymous. The effect is to weaken rather than strengthen teacher education.

Accrediting and licensing serve two separate and distinct purposes. The former aims to assure that colleges and universities, as well as school systems when they are involved, provide the conditions and resources essential to maintaining acceptable quality in programs of preparation; the latter, licensing, functions to guarantee that individual candidates meet minimum qualifications for practice. Accrediting properly should take into account the quality of graduates produced as an indicator that an institution's program is functioning well. Of necessity, it must be realized, accrediting assessments of quality of graduates will deal with the typical— averages and ranges—rather than with specific candidates. Licensing, in contrast, must judge each individual's qualifications. As everyone knows, weak teacher candidates can graduate from strong programs of preparation and vice versa. To assume that a judgment about the program of an institution will guarantee that all its graduates are either eligible or ineligible for a teaching license is erroneous. This NCATE advocates or at least permits to persist. In doing so, it encourages abandonment of efforts to evaluate the effectiveness of teachers, which is a disservice to the profession.

Enforcing Accrediting Mandates. As Maul points out, it is not yet known whether NCATE will be able to enforce its decisions either on institutions applying for accrediting or on the teaching profession as a whole. To be effective, an accrediting body must enjoy the confidence of the various public and professional groups that it serves. When such is the case, as is true in the field of medicine, accredited status becomes a necessary prerequisite for programs to prepare professional personnel. Nonaccredited institutions soon go out of business. To the extent that confidence in accrediting is lacking, nonaccredited programs flourish.

NCATE clearly does not enjoy the public or professional confidence that would permit it to enforce its accrediting mandates. As it presently functions, it tries to persuade institutions to make changes that the council thinks will improve its program, but it really can not enforce its mandates with the kind of authority other professional accrediting bodies have. To achieve that support, national accrediting of educational personnel must resolve the problems it now confronts.

For national accrediting of teacher education to become more than merely a "procedure to go through in order to gain a seal of approval," as Edelfelt implies it is now, it must act now. Present vested control of NCATE by deans of education and state education bureaucrats must be broken. NCATE must become broadly representative of all groups concerned with the preparation and use of educational personnel. A way of measuring excellence in teaching must be found and applied to graduates of teacher education programs. Quality of graduates should ultimately be guaranteed by the standards adopted. Recommendations to individual institutions for improvements in programs must be enforced. Similarly, adapting to differences in institutions will require flexibility in evaluation but must still provide minimum standards of performance. NCATE can do much to improve its operational procedures. It can limit its efforts to defining and evaluating minimum qualifications for institutional accrediting and abandon its highly controversial improvement ambitions. If it revises its standards frequently enough and relates them to innovative programs, it can make its assessments more relevant. In addition, NCATE could make a distinction between accrediting and licensing, to the advantage of both operations and the quality of teachers developed. Public and professional confidence in NCATE must be developed so that it can have power to enforce its mandates. Only after many of these problems have been resolved can the flames of controversy be extinguished and a truly effective accrediting of teacher education take place.

Chapter 10

Effecting Reform in a College of Education

Luvern L. Cunningham

This chapter is essentially a case study report on our attempts within the College of Education at The Ohio State University to remake (rebuild or reform) programs of teacher education and to do so as rationally as possible in irrational times. We have experienced frustration, agony, pathos, disappointment, and some success.

This large College of Education has over the past decade produced hundreds of teachers, most of whom are employed in Ohio, many within a one-hundred-mile radius of Columbus. Teacher education programs—despite the size and cosmopolitan nature of the college—have evolved in a rather parochial setting. We have not been very successful with teacher education programs for blacks or in meeting the "urban crisis"; with a few notable exceptions we relate essentially to local educational constituencies.

The College of Education faculty numbers about 285, assistant professors or above. The college structure is typically atypical. In 1972 we certified well over 2000 teachers—in 1971 there were 1823. More than 1200 of the 1971 graduates wanted to enter teaching; the others selected marriage, graduate study, or other occupations. Of the 1200 who entered teaching, only 600 will remain in teaching two years later, if past attrition rates continue, and five years later fewer than 200 are expected to be in classrooms. (Our attrition history seems to parallel that of other training institutions.) With new dynamics operating in regard to teacher supply and demand and no new follow-up research available, it is hard to predict future attrition.

We have little placement data regarding 1972 graduates, but we suspect that the percent actually occupying teaching positions will be similar to that of 1971. It appears that the number of current graduates who would prefer to enter teaching is greater than it used to be; but the fiscal crunch has altered the views of graduates toward immediate entry into the field. Unemployed teachers-to-be are waiting in the wings, bringing pressure on the placement office to find them jobs. The shift in teacher supply and demand over a twenty-four–month period has been remarkable.

Report as an Instrument of Change

Our teacher education offerings remained essentially unchanged from 1940 through 1970. There have been tinkerings—course title changes; an hour added here, subtracted there—but before 1969–1970 the College's philosophy, program content, and general approach to the education of teachers had not changed substantially. Continuing criticism came from students, old and recent graduates, other departments and colleges within the university, the central administration, the State Department of Education, school districts, parents, relatives, friends of students—and ourselves. We were remote from practices in the schools, we had closed our laboratory school, our enrollments were growing, our resources were not. How does one begin a "revolution"?

Institutional reform is made exceedingly difficult by the fact that it must be accomplished while institutions continue to provide conventional services. Institutions do not have the luxury of dry dock. Most colleges and schools of education are on twelve-month programming cycles. There are seldom extended opportunities for faculty, administrators, or students to work on program reform over extended periods of time and in surroundings conducive to achievement.

We live with the myth that faculty members have extraordinary amounts of free time and should be able to give it generously to program change. Obviously they do not, at least not at our college. Quarter breaks are usually heavily committed to nonteaching university responsibilities, other professional duties, or personal matters.

Program planning is energy-draining and time-consuming, especially when large numbers of individuals and constituencies want to (and should) participate in reform. It would be so simple if change could be achieved through mandate, directive, edict, or executive order. Since it does not work that way we are left to locate our own, usually makeshift, ways of getting the job done. We chose to fall back on the practice of inviting some faculty members to double-up on teaching loads or research obligations, in order to free other faculty members part time for planning reforms.

In the early months of 1969 a major committee was formed within the College of Education to chart the future. The Teacher Education Study Committee, chaired by Elsie Alberty, functioned as a nucleus group of fifteen responsible for preparing a reform report. The committee worked with a number of satellite groups in an effort to solicit a wide range of ideas about teacher education reform. Participation extended beyond the boundaries of the college to other departments within the university, graduate and undergraduate students, teacher organizations, and representatives from school districts throughout Ohio.

As a prelude to the formation of the study committee, the dean's staff, along with interested faculty members and graduate students, toured Ohio meeting with alumni. The purpose was to sense the mood of the graduates and to seek their notions about reform. They were asked to reflect on their experience in the college as well as on their professional practice. These sessions generated many specific suggestions for program reform which seemed to make sense and were compatible with our own thoughts about the need for change. Included were recommendations for: much more work in schools during teacher training; revised methods courses; improved on-campus instruction (relevance); the firing of some of our professors; more teaching by major professors and less by teaching assistants, and vice-versa; better program counseling; and above all, genuine concern for the welfare of students in training. The contributions of field people solicited in this way provided the dean's staff with legitimation for a collegewide assault on teacher education. It also provided a data base, albeit soft and mushy, for the committee's work.

The Teacher Education Study Committee (as is the habit of such groups) produced several drafts of their report. Reviews were held with the college executive committee, the senate, and in one way or another with the faculties of the college and the School of Health Education, Physical Education and Recreation. Several drafts later it was approved by the senate and eventually by the college faculty as a whole. The result, which we now affectionately call our "bible," bears the title *The Future of Teacher Education in The Ohio State University.*

This report is a thorough document, providing not only specific recommendations for change but also step-by-step means to implement them by specific target dates. The principal recommendations were to achieve these eight goals: increased urban emphasis; reduced and limited enrollments; selective admissions; substantial early experience in schools; clinical emphases throughout programs; partnerships with cooperating schools; course reforms; and growth in faculty competence. It is essentially a direction-setting treatise aimed at collegewide changes rather than program-by-program content, structure, and goal appraisals.

A committee report may be a good or a bad means to achieve reform, but, as it was the strategy we selected, we were stuck with it. There were diverse reactions to the finished document from faculty, field people who knew of the report, and students who had participated in its development. Some people despaired that like most reports, it would be shelved. (It's a nice idea but we just won't be able to do it.) Others hoped that it would be shelved— quickly. Still others were mildly optimistic that at least some of its recommendations would become realities, and of course a few insisted that the complete report be implemented fully—now, not next month or next year.

Implementation

The 1970–1971 year opened with two preliminary administrative strategies, the first a two-and-a-half-day retreat involving the college's Executive Committee and the College of Education Senate and focusing wholly on implementation. The second was an implementation plan prepared under the leadership of Associate Dean D. Alexander Severino. It was a step-by-step implementation program, a PERT chart of sorts, to be our guide for the year. (The committee report itself contained what now appears to be a more adequate calendar for implementation.) This guide allowed us as administrators to keep the press on for implementation and has proven to be a remarkable aid, contributing to whatever success we have had thus far. Our activities were governed in large measure by its target dates and deadlines.

Faculty Involvement. Our reform attempts relied heavily on the faculty committee to develop a general pattern for change. After the committee's document was approved by the several decision mechanisms within the college, the administrative team went to work. Many of our steps were fairly clear and already endorsed by the faculty. Problems arose, however, as we proceeded through the year. Faculty recall about specific features of the reforms grew dim. New faculty and students arrived on the scene. Contact with people in the field grew infrequent.

During much of 1972 we were hard pressed to keep faculty and students informed about progress on implementation. The need for communication was especially evident in regard to establishing college enrollment limitations and selective admissions, two ideas imbedded deeply in our total reform design and essential to its success. Once again faculty either overlooked those changes, failed to take them seriously, or were making bets that we would not implement those features of our reform. Concern over these issues could escalate into real problems in the coming months. We have found it necessary to backstop administrative action at the dean's level with a special admissions committee chaired by an assistant dean. Committee members include the chairman of the faculty committee that prepared the reform design as well as graduate and undergraduate students and persons from other units of the university that have become involved in implementing selective admissions.

To summarize this discussion quickly: It is very difficult to separate faculty and administrative responsibilities for reform within a professional school. The widely held value of faculty control is only a part of the problem. An equally important feature is the need for sustained commitment to reform. Administrators who value getting the job done must retain enough patience to sustain the faculty participatory ethic through implementation phases.

Student Involvement. Our experience with student participation in relation to the Teacher Education Study Committee was rewarding, to say the least. We invited students to participate in several ways. Some took part because of their positions in student government; others were invited as leaders in student associations. In still other cases we simply identified persons randomly and asked them to be subcommittee members or assume other types of responsibilities. Student contributions were exceedingly fine; although the amount of involvement as well as quality varied, the overall input was excellent.

Field Representative Involvement. Teachers and administrators from nearby schools were likewise significant members of the administrative reform team. In fact, had their membership been overlooked our changes might have been less dramatic, less focused on the genuine needs of those who practice. It was difficult to achieve consistent participation on the part of these field representatives. We did not have resources to provide substitutes for classroom teachers who wanted to be on satellite committees, for example. Those who came made personal sacrifices in order to help out; they gave up evenings, Saturdays, and other off-duty time. Their only rewards were the satisfactions that came from a sense of contributing to the improvement of professional preparation.

As indicated earlier, when the implementation of reforms began, communication with those who had had a part in the design became less frequent and more difficult. During 1970–1971 the college administrative team was often challenged for not ensuring broad involvement in the initiation of reforms. The changes were viewed as administrator-sponsored and therefore narrowly conceived. Reminders that there had been substantial input from many sources helped quiet critics, but did not always satisfy them. Such reactions came frequently from blacks who saw selective admissions as a threat to the entry of minority students.

Role in Statewide Reform

The first object of teacher education reform is *program,* but campus reformers must keep in mind the interests of many institutions and individuals beyond campus boundaries. We discovered that our efforts to achieve change internally had to be linked forcefully with outside constituencies. The achievement of large-scale reform not only requires their participation and endorsement but depends on stimulating these parties to make changes.

It is worthwhile to discuss some of these constituencies. First there is the State Department of Education. The chief state school officer and his immediate associates constitute a critically important participant group. Within the department of Education, the Division of Certification is obviously important. Similarly, many other state agencies have departments of general teacher education as well as departments of vocational-technical, distributive, agricultural, and home economics education. In these there are sometimes state supervisors and program planners who hold appointments on college campuses. In addition to the state department, there are public school systems—especially those which have close working relationships with colleges of education. Similarly, state teachers associations or unions are increasingly cognizant of the relationship between programs of preparation and their own interests; they too must be involved in teacher education reform. State institutions of higher education as well as private institutions preparing professionals have a stake in what a major institution in their midst does in regard to changes in teacher education. In Ohio the chancellor of the State System of Higher Education is intensely concerned about teacher education reform.

The governor's office as well as the U.S. Office of Education could be added as significant centers of power and interest in regard to teacher education change. The accrediting bodies likewise are influential. In short, continuous communication with a variety of leaders throughout the state is needed.

The problem becomes how to achieve effective involvement; discover which of the constituencies are the more important; define the appropriate points at which involvement can be most significant; and distinguish involvement for the purpose of refining ideas from that of gaining legitimation and support.

Fortunately, in Ohio we have a reform-oriented certification division and teacher education group within the State Department of Public Instruction. They have worked faithfully and effectively to reform certification standards and to allow institutions freedom in developing their own teacher education programs. We have tried to keep department leaders involved in our changes and informed of what we intend to achieve in the future. We have incorporated many of their ideas in program change.

There also exists in the state an association of deans of colleges or schools of education from the twelve public-assisted universities. The deans' group meets at least once each month and often with the chancellor of the State System of Higher Education. These sessions, formerly devoted to details and trivialities of administration, now turn fundamentally on basic issues confronting teacher education institutions. Currently the deans are working on the development of a network of multiunit schools to be associated with public institutions across the state and on in-service programs for faculty members of public universities.

Governor's Request

Our plans for reform at Ohio State University received a substantial boost in January 1971 when Ohio's new governor, John Gilligan, requested suggestions for reforming and revitalizing Ohio's schools. This was a fortuitous request and without precedent. Three of the recommendations included in the resulting report to the governor if accepted would be central to achieving teacher education reform on our campus and would stimulate a statewide attack on teacher education deficiencies.* These recommendations and excerpts of their discussion are quoted as follows:

* The complete report contained thirteen recommendations. See Cunningham, 1971.

Improve Preservice Education via Subsidized Clinical Experience. *Confusion abounds in regard to preservice education of teachers and paraprofessionals. Teacher educators once thought that the preparation of teachers was rather straightforward. Programs were to include general education, subject field, and professional education components. But recently teacher education has been subjected to intensive scrutiny by citizens, teachers, and administrators in the field, students in preparation, as well as faculty members from other sectors of colleges and universities. . . . In response to such uncertainties, the federal government has allocated substantial amounts of federal resources to the analysis of teacher education, and the invention of new forms of teacher preparation.*

Considerable emphasis is being placed currently on clinical experience; i.e., teachers-to-be in schools working with students, teachers, and parents. Most professional schools have worried for decades about the so-called academic program-practice gap. Leaders in teacher education are now trying to locate an appropriate middle ground. Teacher education partnerships are being forged between school systems and universities. New roles are being created in the public schools for teacher educators. They will assume responsibility for some of the clinical features of the total sequence of professional education for teachers and paraprofessionals. Teacher educators are interested in relating preservice and inservice education with local school systems as laboratories. Colleges and universities are insisting that their professors and advanced graduate students spend more time in schools. Exchanges are being attempted between public school personnel and college and university faculty members. Classes once taught only on campus locations are now being taught in the schools. Membership in those offerings include both teachers-to-be as well as established practitioners. New formats for testing fresh university ideas in local schools are also being produced.

In Ohio a great deal has been discovered relative to the selection of teachers and administrators-to-be. Experiments with the placement of potential teachers for one quarter in school systems in their freshman or sophomore year are yielding interesting results. We are discovering that young people either elect to continue in teacher preparation or reject it as a consequence of one quarter's work in schools. We now believe that every professional-to-be should spend at least that amount of time in schools (working at defined tasks) in advance of his electing to come into the profession as a student, or his acceptance by a college or university into teacher preparation.

New costs accrue both on the part of the student, the university, and the public schools. Our proposal is that the State of Ohio support early school experience, as well as other clinical opportunities, through subsidization.

Create a Network of Laboratory Schools. *Costs are incurred by local school systems as a consequence of their participation in preservice education of professionals. For years practice teaching has been conducted in public and parochial schools. Laboratory schools no longer serve that need for many teachers-in-training. Similarly, local schools have been sites for observation, experimental teaching of a micro nature, and other forms of direct encounter with the problems of education. These have, with the possible exception of practice teaching, often been haphazard, poorly organized, intermittent, and generally of questionable value.*

We know now that we must invent new ways of providing for clinical experience in professional preparation involving more work with students, university faculty, and school district teacher education staff working together in schools. *It will require careful delineation of what is expected of each partner in the laboratory setting. It will call on faculty members and university administrators to be more skillful in supervision. It will force faculty members to sharpen their clinical capacities and extend their acquaintance with today's school problems.*

New Investments for Inservice Training. *Most of Ohio's present money for inservice education comes from federal sources. Federal programs are now either being curtailed or discontinued. Some districts budget small amounts of monies for seminars, workshops, outside consultants, and travel to professional meetings. Many give credit for inservice training on salary schedules. The magnitude of such support is considerably less than what is needed.*

The available options for inservice education are unimpressive, often impoverished. Traditionally we have looked to colleges and universities as places where new ideas could be located, and as sources of stimuli to better performance. But for the problems teachers are encountering, universities are found wanting. In many cases universities are plagued by the same questions and issues in the secondary schools: student aggressiveness, racism, understaffing, bureaucratic inefficiencies, poor morale, and irrelevancy. It is hardly useful for public school personnel to pile into a sinking lifeboat that already is overloaded.

The State Department of Education should be invited to create productive, useful new options for the utilization of inservice monies. We know that carefully designed inservice programs can make a difference. We should avoid spending money on approaches that are already known for their ineffectiveness. And we should find ways of crediting (for salary purposes) inservice education experiences other than those that have university credit attached.

There is an emerging recognition that problems can be best solved where they are located. Most schools' problems are at the building level. It is there where teachers confront the complexities that threaten and overwhelm. It is there where poor motivation resides. It is there where racism is most ugly. It is there where the limitations of a poorly prepared instructional staff is most telling. It is there where curriculum reform is paramount. It is there where youngsters arrive every day with mixed expectations in regard to their educational fortunes. It is there where diagnostic and prescriptive capabilities are most needed. It is there where supporting services should come to rest.

For these reasons, each school faculty, building-level administration, student body, and parent community should have primary responsibility for defining how they can strengthen themselves. They are privileged to know their problems best. They live with them every day. They know their own weak-

nesses as well as their strengths. They should be responsible for developing and perfecting their own problem-solving capabilities. They should select the on-site inservice education experience most conducive to that purpose. They should be expected to reach out for resources elsewhere if they can't be located internally, define their problems, and create frameworks within which solutions can be located.

Problems and Prospects

Acquiring Funds. Our work at implementation has produced substantial progress, but it has also revealed much that remains to be done. We have learned that it is extraordinarily difficult to achieve reform while doing the regular business of the establishment. We have encountered considerable fatigue, both personal and institutional, as a consequence of our hard press to achieve change. Only through faculty overload and commitments beyond the call of duty have we been able to move ahead. I have considerable doubt about how much more we can legitimately ask of our staff. Therefore, I think it is imperative that we acquire dollars to be used for program development. These dollars are legitimate costs of doing business in public universities and they should come from state funds. University authorities should allocate such monies for program development throughout the institution.

In the absence of such support, colleges have to appeal to foundations and other governments. Money available through the Office of Education, especially the Triple T Program, has been useful to some institutions. Similarly, federal support for the development of model training programs has assisted the several universities wise enough to construct proposals attracting those funds. Institutions must search for support from whatever outside source seems promising. A third option is to bootleg funds from programs already in operation, with the prospect of limiting program effectiveness. Such changes can be justified under the tenet that dollars applied for program restructuring are more important than dollars used to support deficient programs now in existence.

Faculty-by-Faculty Reforms. In the College of Education,

the various divisions possess unusual freedom and autonomy and are basically responsible for program change that has to do with the substantive content of their areas. Although there is collegewide monitoring, motivation for change comes essentially from the grass roots. In our judgment, fundamental change will come only if it is advanced by the people who must be responsible for its delivery and administration. Faculty members are those persons, and the processes of designing and planning reform will strengthen substantially those who must achieve it.

Grass roots responsibility has produced useful diversity in approaches to program change as well as in specific reforms. We have arrived at the point where faculties are watching and learning from one another; approaches tested within one domain are sometimes adopted or adapted in our programs. We have also witnessed differential pacing toward reform. In the language of innovation, we have "early achievers" and "late adopters." Science and mathematics education and industrial technology are out in front in achieving attractive new program changes, whereas vocational and technical education is lagging behind. Humanities education and foreign language education are proceeding slowly, not keeping pace with the frontrunners. Promising evidence of arousal exists within the faculty in early and middle childhood education and the faculty for exceptional children, evidence which should lead to improved programs.

There have been some unexpected dividends. Some of our experimental programs (especially those having to do with urban teacher preparation and the two-year "new careers" program) have produced insights that are now being incorporated into almost all our efforts. We are moving toward more extensive experience in the schools, refinement of partnerships, and faculty members working in schools with teachers-to-be.

General College Requirements. "The traditionals" are general courses expected of all persons to be certified. Educational psychology, history of education, philosophy of education, physical and health education, art and music education are examples. Negative student reactions bear most forcefully on our courses in educational psychology, with history and philosophy of education offerings running a close second. Students are turned off en masse by either

the content or the instruction; indeed we ourselves are hard pressed
to find evidence that the content of those courses contributes to
improved teaching. Historically we have held that knowledge of
learning theory provides a stable base from which pedagogy could
proceed. Similarly, we valued the history and philosophy of education as the cornerstones of civilization and professionalization. Now
that there is substantial reason to doubt the validity of those arguments, what is to be the future of such content?

We are also wrestling with the incorporation of "new content," giving thought to courses for all students on racism, to fresh
ways of presenting human relations issues, microteaching, sociology
and anthropology of education, sensitivity training, and new foci on
emerging educational problems. We either must *add* content to total
programs or *make* substitutions. When substitutions are proposed
faculty turf is threatened, and the resultant defensiveness either halts
or slows down program change.

Performance-Based Certification. We see performance-based
certification as fundamental to achieving some balance between
specialized work and general course offerings in our total program.
We must face straightforwardly the task of defining exit criteria,
literally spelling out those skills we expect our teachers to possess
when they seek certification. The need for close association with
other institutions as well as the State Department of Education goes
without saying, since performance criteria when incorporated into
certification will have to apply uniformly throughout Ohio. Unfortunately, at this time there is only modest interest and little action
in that direction.

Recruiting and Selecting Students. As indicated above, we
are at work on establishing admissions criteria. In the past, students
wishing to enter needed only to be reasonably healthy and have a
gradepoint average of 2.25 on a 4-point scale. Now, however, we
are exceedingly concerned about the quality of our product. The
special collegewide committee referred to earlier is identifying not
only criteria for selection but also ways of gathering unusual data
about freshmen and other transfer students who wish to enroll.

Currently thirty-five hundred freshmen and sophomore students have indicated an interest in going into teaching or educational occupations. From that number, approximately two thousand

will be invited to come into our college after they have completed ninety-seven quarter hours of work. One prominent criterion on which we are basing our selection is motivation. Students who wish to enroll must make a strong case for their admission. Conventional criteria, such as high school and college performance, as well as more subtle evidence of behavior that would appear to be important in teaching, will also be considered. We are concerned about students' creativity, experience, motivation, sympathy, and empathy for young people.

Needless to say, we are already receiving substantial static about applying selective admissions criteria. Negative reactions are coming from students, parents, other departments, the central administration, and a number of other quarters.

Minorities in Instructional Roles. Like most universities, we have been working vigorously to add minority representatives to our regular faculty. We have had some success along those lines, but like most institutions we still have a long, long way to go. Currently we are considering opportunities for "differentiated" staffing. The college is seeking representatives of minority groups—graduate students, undergraduate students, or even nonstudents (street people) —who can be employed as teachers of teachers-to-be. The New Careers Program has provided fresh insights into the contributions to be gained through thoughtful use of such resource people. We intend to include them as members of teaching teams, faculty aides, work-study people, even as full-fledged instructors with full responsibilities for teaching and advising.

Human Obsolescence. Traditionally, universities have relied on some form of sabbatical policy to give faculty members opportunities to regenerate themselves. However, valuable as these have been, they are no longer sufficient. The growth of knowledge in substantive areas is well known, and keeping pace grows more difficult day by day. Faculty in professional schools often try to keep current in several fields, an effort which multiplies the problem for them. For example, a specialist in reading may need to pursue research in reading, linguistics, language arts, psychology, measurement—even cultural anthropology. Professors with heavy teaching, research, development, and service obligations are hard pressed indeed to stay up to date.

In addition to keeping pace with knowledge growth, university personnel constantly encounter new attitudes, views, and perspectives, many of which strike harshly at their experience. Coping with change is a universal problem. Confrontation with aggressive students, many of whom may be black, Spanish-American, Indian, or Asiatic, can have a devastating impact. Universities, like public schools, need to allocate generous amounts for skillfully developed programs of faculty professional growth. Such efforts should have both a *content* focus and a *coping* focus. Talent for designing and conducting growth programs resides within our institutions, much of it in colleges of education.

Staff development programs offer only one of several approaches to obsolescence. Pioneering is in order in the direction of "sheltered" positions for ineffectives, partial and early retirements, and mid-career change. Some of our university personnel, though tenured, dedicated, and hard working, are not making it. Nor are the prospects bright that they ever will, even with promising staff development programs available. In the past, institutions have avoided the problem or swept it under the rug. They now may find it necessary to budget as much as 5 percent of their total resources for "sheltered" positions: nonacademic, nonmainstream positions jobs which yet retain some significance to universities. Persons acknowledged to be ineffective in their traditional roles (by themselves and others) would be shifted into such jobs. When available sheltered positions are filled, then partial or early retirements may be necessary. Institutions would in effect pay people to stay home. Individual and institutional contributions to retirement systems will have to be increased in order to carry the heavier burden.

A more promising practice would involve provisions for mid-career change. Programs should be designed to prepare professors, administrators, and other employees for new jobs outside the institution. In humanitarian terms, this alternative is superior to the others. Each approach to the obsolescence problem will require resources. When budget crises are severe, allocation of resources to this need may appear impossible; but when institutions are under attack for their deficiencies, it may be a priority area for investment.

Statewide Networks for Reform. Although experimentation should go forward within institutions, there must also be coordinated, statewide change. Certification is one focus for modification that produces such cross-state interest and response. (Over the years teacher education institutions have collaborated on certification and accreditation matters more effectively than anything else.) Getting together for other reforms is more difficult. Long-range planning at the state level for teacher education, for example, excites people temporarily but does not capture significant amounts of energy or resources—yet our courses on planning are saturated with rhetoric about its importance.

The rapid shift in demand for teachers caught most of us off guard: we were and remain tooled up to produce more and more teachers. Coordination and professional manpower planning are needed at the state level. We need better information about what future needs will be and must take such data into account—now. Most state departments or other agencies do not have enough manpower data to inform institutional leaders, let alone politicians.

Reformers should give attention to statewide networks of teacher education leaders. Although there are many organizations and associations of teacher educators, so far they have not been especially reform-oriented. New networks are needed that are action-minded and not essentially protectionist or concerned about turf. The networks should link into the political system sufficiently to carry reform messages to governors, legislators, and potential lay advocates for change.

Allocating Teacher Education Funds Directly to Schools. In an earlier section recommendations for reform made to the governor of Ohio were reported. One of these called for direct allocation of dollars to schools (not school districts) for their part in teacher education. I will not repeat all the supporting arguments here, but one warrants emphasis.

Schools will become genuine partners in teacher education relationships if it is clear that real benefits will accrue to them as a result. Improved education is the ultimate test of benefits. Short of such evidence, earmarked dollars are required to support staff, in-service education, travel, and consultants, or simply to deal with inconvenience introduced through the partnership. Such monies will be central to soliciting and maintaining the cooperation of schools in preservice teacher education.

Blending Preservice and Inservice Education. Teacher preparation has often involved preservice and inservice training simultaneously. Newcomers have benefited from (or tolerated) the "war stories" of the veteran teachers. Such contact has affected the socialization of inductees into teaching—positively and negatively. As a rule, these encounters have not been "designed" but result from attending the same courses or from student-teaching relationships. There are unrealized benefits available through richer, better-designed associations among veterans and neophytes.

Great advantage is anticipated from teacher education laboratories or off-campus centers. A school associated with a training program, designated as a lab or center, would have its own teacher educator (who may have a clinical professorship appointment) responsible for the school's part in the partnership. It would also be supported through state-allocated resources and enjoy the implied autonomy. To extend the impact of this idea, discussions have been held with representatives from several teacher-training institutions; hopefully, all will eventually adopt the laboratory centers.

Multiple Constituencies of Reform. Hosts of individuals and groups have stakes in teacher education reform. School systems, students, parents of students, parents of potential students, citizens, other colleges, the central administration of the university, professional associations, unions, and we ourselves are significant segments of those concerned.

We failed to anticipate the resistance of some members of our central administration to enrollment limits and selective admissions. Even though colleges of education have historically been treated with disdain and chided for the poor quality of this and that, our efforts to set the conditions for achieving quality were stoutly resisted. Apparently universities have sometimes found it useful to have catch-all colleges or departments—they appear to develop for fiscal and public relations reasons. In the past, schools of education have served that purpose, and thus some administrators are resisting their move toward independent and higher status.

Similarly, we were unprepared for the cooperative attitude of persons in the field in regard to teacher education partnerships. The idea encountered little resistance from teachers, principals, and superintendents; on the contrary, it received considerable applause. Some superintendents offered their support, as well as their communities' endorsement, for local district investment in their part of the teacher education partnership.

Focusing on Goals. Implementing reform produces side effects that are unpleasant. Unanticipated consequences of change occurred with enough frequency that serious doubts developed about the wisdom of reform in the first place. To illustrate: Incorporating places for minority group students in our plans for limited enrollments has been troublesome. What special admissions criteria are necessary to protect places for minorities—in our case essentially black students? Word about the prospect of applying selective admissions caused disquiet among black students and black faculty. The admission of black students is saturated with emotion; just to speak of the problem introduces difficult words such as *quota, double standards, discrimination,* and *institutional racism.* A special subcommittee of our admissions committee is now at work on criteria for admitting minorities, but at the moment those criteria remain unselected.

Investment of time and energy in such matters slows the pace of implementation. It seems diversionary until one realizes that solving such problems is consonant with the basic purposes of the reform itself: improved competence of the College of Education to meet urban imperatives and to prepare strong professionals for the future. In sum, maintaining a focus on the central goals of reform tests the merits of college leadership. There is pressure to abandon the effort and step back into the comfort of traditional and known ways of doing things; hence some tenaciousness is required to stay on target.

Fatigue, Uptightness, Momentum. Achieving change creates institutional as well as individual fatigue. Major reforms seriously threaten the energy levels of institutions and the people who have stakes in them—a consequence of maintaining conventional programs and responsibilities and simultaneously coping with the need to change. Such dual expectations drive many reformers to leave the "establishment" for alternative systems.

Organizational fatigue (the cumulative effect of individual fatigue) creates breakdowns in conventional services. Low morale results; tensions mount; despondency is common; doubts about leadership surface and grow. . . . Leaders not only must understand such phenomena but must be tolerant of their presence. They must not be traumatized when they recognize that their own credibility is questioned. There is also the danger that leaders will surround themselves with a cult of their own, limiting feedback and distorting their estimates of progress.

Uptightness and fatigue are parts of the same problem. Uptightness creates an energy drain on individuals and consequently the college. Direct work in schools by faculty members, incorporating early experience, building new clinical programs, dropping courses, changing requirements, and adding new content affect people in curious ways. Some persons experience substantial discomfort when challenging the past, whereas for others it is pure exhilaration. We have discovered that some of our articulate change advocates are quite protective of their own domains. They are affected psychologically by the prospect of losing control over aspects of their preparation programs, losing funds to support graduate students, loss of faculty, or performing under new conditions. Uptightness is infectious, spreading like fatigue, and deserves the direct attention of those in charge.

As fatigue, uptightness, and poor morale develop, the momentum for reform is reduced. The system becomes sluggish. Evidence of interest in abandoning direction and returning to an old stable state abounds. There appear to be few guidelines for administrators when this occurs. Return to the security of old harbors is hardly a happy prospect, but the chance of reaching a soft anchorage along uncharted shores, and finding a firm beach once there, often seem remote. Our only rule is to keep moving despite periodic slowdowns, attempting to redouble our energy and reaffirm our commitments to the worth of the ultimate objectives.

Summary

Leaders of colleges of education have often been preoccupied with changing education elsewhere; seldom have they examined themselves and how they engage in the reform of their own establishment. This chapter is essentially a self-report of one college's beginning efforts at reform. It is brief, incomplete, biased, and should be considered at best as preliminary and impressionistic. The report fails to communicate the anguish and pain of reform; also lacking is adequate description of the investment of hours and hours in debate. Missing too is appropriate representation of the tension and threat produced by change—threat for the advocates of change as well as others affected by reform. Concern over the lack of "hard data" upon which to base change is unreported. Large-scale modifications are drafted on slender evidence and often endorsed on feeling alone, plus the conviction that something new must be better than what we have now.

We have expanded our urban emphasis, even enlarged the number of faculty devoted to it. Limits have been placed on enrollments throughout the college; and selective admissions are being applied. Experiments with early experience programs are under way in nearby school districts, as more faculty members are trying to understand the meaning of clinical experience for them and their students. Course reforms appear to be occurring, but not so rapidly as students believe they should. Requests to identify cooperating schools as teacher education laboratories are coming in and a few leading practitioners now hold clinical professorships. It is encouraging from the administrator's perspective to note a steady growth in faculty confidence regarding our directions and a growing excitement about getting on with reform . . . yet there is a long, long way to go.

Chapter **11**

Developments in
England and Wales

William Taylor

Public and professional discussions of teacher education in England and Wales during the past twenty-five years have been dominated, first, by quantitative questions of recruitment and wastage, and second, by problems of organization, especially in relation to the overall pattern of postsecondary education. Only recently has serious consideration begun to be given to the content of teacher education and training, to the relationship between what is done and what can be done at the initial stages, to what should be done by means of inservice provision, and to ways in which the skill, knowledge, and attitudes developed in the course of personal and professional education can be related to the kinds of work that the teacher will be called upon to undertake in classroom and school.

  Emphases on numbers and on organization can be explained in part as a response to the chronic shortage of teachers that bedeviled educational planning for so many years after the end of World War II. But these emphases, and the relative neglect of consideration at the national level of what should go into the course and how it might best be taught, also reflect the tradition of curricular freedom that characterizes English education. Questions of syllabus and content are largely the responsibility of teachers themselves, whether in universities, colleges of education, or in primary and secondary schools. The creation in 1965 of the Schools Council for Curriculum and Examinations, itself a teacher-controlled body, followed by an increasing flow of advice on curricula, guides, and project materials, along with the greater interest being shown in systematic curriculum development in postsecondary education, have in no way diminished the importance of teacher- and institution-based decision-making concerning content and methods. This is one of the reasons why the 1972 report of the Committee of Enquiry into Teacher Training under the chairmanship of Lord James of Rusholme (1972), after whom the report is named, has rather little to say about the detailed content of teacher education, but a great deal to say about organization. Before examining the recommendations of the report and the discussions and decisions that followed and that will shape teacher education for a generation, it is necessary briefly to review how teachers are at present trained in England and Wales.

Existing System

At the end of World War II most teachers were prepared by means of two-year courses in what had been known for a century as Training Colleges. A minority, mainly specialist teachers in secondary schools, were university graduates who had either entered teaching directly from the university (which the possession of a degree entitled them to do) or had pursued one-year courses of professional training in university departments of education. Following the recommendations of the official McNair Committee in 1943, the training colleges were grouped around neighboring universities, forming consortia of teacher-training interests known as Area Training Organizations. In formal terms, the Area Training Organizations were groups of universities, colleges of education, local authorities and teacher interests that were recognized by the Department of Education and Science as bodies that award a certificate entitling the holder to qualified-teacher status. The academic authority exercised by the Area Training Organizations was in all cases but one (Cambridge) that of a university acting through its institute or school of education, and the qualifications awarded were those of a university.

During the 1950s and early 1960s there was a steady improvement in the qualifications of those entering the training colleges directly from school and, particularly in the second postwar decade, a very rapid growth in the numbers of students and of institutions in which they were trained. The normal training course was in 1960 lengthened to three years, which made it comparable with the period usually required to obtain a university degree. The 1963 report of the Committee on Higher Education under the chairmanship of Lord Robbins proposed that the colleges of education should move more closely into the university orbit and should be able to award degrees to a proportion of their students. The first of these proposals became caught up in government policy concerning the "binary system" of higher education, which put a brake on the numbers of postsecondary institutions aspiring to full university status. The suggestion that bachelor of education courses might be instituted for students in training colleges was taken up with varying enthusiasm both within the colleges and on the part of the universities that would award the degree, and by 1972 some 15 percent of students in colleges of education were following fourth-year–bachelor of education courses.

At the end of the 1960s, with the recognition that the pressure of numbers would slacken in the 1970s, with increasing student consciousness of the limitations of their courses and of the relatively poor status of teaching as a career, and with the growing interest of the teachers' organizations in professional upgrading, more attention began to be paid to the processes by means of which teachers were selected, educated, and trained. A select committee of the House of Commons took a mass of evidence on the problems, but failed to report due to the dissolution of Parliament in 1970. The Secretary of State for Education and Science (then Edward Short) asked that Area Training Organizations review their courses and organization and report to him on the changes and reforms that they considered necessary and desirable. But in 1970 a promise was made to the Conservative party's annual conference that if a Conservative government were elected, a national inquiry into teacher-training would be initiated. Thus, following the Conservative victory in 1971, the new Secretary of State, Margaret Thatcher, appointed a committee of enquiry with Lord James as chairman.

Lord James's committee was very different from many of the other committees and commissions that had at regular intervals examined different aspects of educational provision. It was given only a year in which to do its work. It operated on ground already tilled by a parliamentary select committee and by inquiries by the existing Area Training Organizations. It was set up partly as a response to criticisms of teacher education that were not new, that were not limited to one country, and that have in the past proved resistant to most of the remedies proposed for them.

But perhaps the chief difference between Lord James's committee and earlier inquiries was the extent to which the work of the committee had implications for aspects of educational policy much wider than its major terms of reference. At one and the same time, the James committee tried to provide a new structure for teacher education and to help solve the problems of postsecondary education in general, and its proposals for teacher education must be viewed in the light of this larger concern. In particular, the work of the committee was of great significance in indicating places where the burgeoning numbers of students wanting some kind of higher education by the end of the seventies might go and the kinds of courses they might follow.

Expansion of Postsecondary Education

There has been a massive expansion in postsecondary education in developed countries during the past ten years, and the numbers coming forward for such education are likely to go on increasing for the next ten years, if not at such a rapid rate. The reasons for this expansion are complex, but the phenomenon creates serious problems for democratic governments. In providing places for students most developed countries outside of eastern Europe have espoused policy of private demand. The Norwegian Ottosen committee (1969) stated this position very well in contending that "all who seek postsecondary education should be able to find a fully acceptable opportunity at the academic level for which they are qualified." This begs a lot of questions, but its implications are clear. The number of opportunities in postsecondary education should not be limited by the alleged demands of a society for particular kinds of highly qualified manpower or by any general economic advantage that the provision of such education might be shown to confer. But any government committed to meeting private demand faces very high costs. The current cost per student in universities or colleges of education in the United Kingdom is about ten times the cost per pupil in primary schools, and five or six times that for secondary pupils.

There are also political costs involved in not satisfying private demand. They are of a kind that make it worthwhile for politicians who want to get elected or to stay in office to do what they can to meet or to manipulate, but not to deny, the demand for postsecondary education. It is often suggested that we are moving from a system of elite higher education to one of mass postsecondary education. It may be a comforting vision for some, and a frightening spectre for others, but the term *mass* can not realistically be applied to the scale of development presently contemplated in England and Wales. The government White Paper on education announcing decisions on the James recommendations (*Education: A Framework for Expansion,* 1972) argues that by 1981 there should be places in full-time higher education for about 22 percent of eighteen-year-olds. Even if we add the large number of subdegree and part-time students and take into account the open university and other kinds of what the Europeans call permanent education, the applicability of the term *mass higher education* is still very questionable.

The costs of providing higher education, even on the scale at present contemplated, press upon the total of public expenditure at a time when a relatively slow rate of economic growth and, in some quarters, something of a political disenchantment with the benefits of such growth create a situation in which large-scale increases in public expenditure are more and more difficult to sustain. Further, an increasing number of people see the universities themselves not as a source of adolescent diversion or of long-term economic benefit, but as potentially dangerous, disruptive, and subversive institutions.

Broadly speaking, most countries have tried to meet the problems posed by the rapid expansion of postsecondary education in two main ways. They have either established a system of what can be called first tier colleges, which furnish shorter courses and are terminal for a number of students, but which for a substantial proportion lead on to further studies, or they have set up what has been called the alternative university, which provides courses of length and standard equivalent to those previously available only in universities themselves. The United States has followed the first path, the first tier college, as has Canada. In this country we have settled for the alternative university, in the shape of polytechnic schools and the creation of the degree-granting Council for National Academic Awards.

Short-cycle courses of the kind provided by both first tier colleges and alternative universities are open to two main criticisms. If their links with the traditional universities are too close, they soon cease to have an identity of their own and become screening devices for later academic programs. It has been suggested that something like this has happened in those countries where the first tier college is general.

The opposite risk is that if short-cycle courses are end-stopped and their qualifications terminal (so they do not provide much possibility for students to continue with full university studies), they fail to attract the best students and are labeled as lower-grade. In English terms, they become the secondary modern schools of higher education.

This dilemma is not easily resolved. It is perhaps hardest to overcome in countries like the United Kingdom, where what you study and where you have studied are both closely associated with occupational prospects, not simply in terms of technical competence, but because of status associations.

Proposals of James Committee

Turning to teacher education in particular, the James committee suggested that teachers be educated and trained within three related cycles. The first cycle was to be made up of either a traditional three-year university program, or a new, short-cycle–two-year course in a college of education or other institution leading to the award of a new Diploma of Higher Education. At the end of the first cycle, both graduates of three-year university programs and diploma holders would begin the second cycle with a one-year–full-time course in a college or university department of education, at the successful conclusion of which they would be granted the status of licensed teacher. Armed with this license, they would go on to the second year of the second cycle, which would be made up of school-based training under the supervision of a professional tutor specially selected and trained for this purpose. At the end of the second year of the second cycle, all teachers, irrespective of whether they held a university degree or a Diploma of Higher Education, would be granted a professional degree of Bachelor of Arts (Education). The Bachelor of Arts (Education) and the Master of Arts (Education) that might follow it would be awarded by a new body set up specifically for this purpose, the National Council for Teacher Education and Training, which would operate through a number of Regional Councils for Colleges and Departments of Education (RCCDEs) and replace the existing university based Area Training Organizations. The registered teacher, as part of what James calls the *third cycle,* would then be expected at various points in his career to engage in systematic inservice education and training.

The committee attached very great importance to its recommendations concerning the third cycle, which included opportunities for teachers to have study leave for one term, or its equivalent, every five or seven years. These recommendations for inservice education were generally welcomed. But the recommendations on the first and second cycle caused a furore, largely because these were so radically different from what had been proposed in the parliamentary select committee and through the large-scale Area Training Organization surveys of the previous year. The James committee explained, for example, that some holders of the new Diploma of Higher Education might move on to degree courses in universities, polytechnic schools, or within the college system, but for others the diploma course might be terminal. But critics soon latched on to the point that for the next few years at least the majority of diploma-holders would progress into the so-called second cycle of professional preparation for primary and lower secondary teaching. The committee made the ingenuous claim that a common professional course for diploma-holders and graduates alike must reduce divisiveness in the teaching profession and strenuously denied that the proposed diploma could be equated with the preparation of primary teachers. But the implications of what it recommended were clear. For some time to come, most primary teachers would be the products of short-cycle higher education, and most secondary, and a small but increasing proportion of primary teachers, would come from long-cycle courses in universities and polytechnic schools.

Despite these anxieties, there was sympathy for the concept of the Diploma in Higher Education, since it would not only offer an alternative form of higher education to a proportion of the very much enlarged body of applicants who would be coming forward in the next ten years, but, at a time when the demand for college-trained teachers was likely to be falling, it would also help to keep existing colleges of education in business.

There was also a broad measure of disagreement with certain of the James proposals for the second cycle. Very few people liked the idea of the proposed Bachelor of Arts (Education), and nobody had had a good word to say for the suggestion that the National Council for Teacher Education and Training and the Regional Councils for Colleges and Departments of Education should act, not only as bodies to validate professional qualifications and plan teacher-training in their areas, but also as academic bodies for the awarding of degrees. Further, the archetypal post-James student was seen as a person who would undertake his first-cycle work in the northeast of the country, the first year of his second cycle in the far southwest, and obtain a teaching post and pursue his school-based second-year–second-cycle studies in East Anglia, a sad wanderer within an anglicized system of *lernfreiheit*. In the face of the record-keeping that would be required to sustain such a system, the only people who seemed likely to benefit were the manufacturers of punched-card equipment and computers.

The James committee was also criticized for failing to take into account some of the difficulties in selecting individuals for training and in evaluating their performance. The report suggested that the increased numbers applying for entry into second-cycle courses would make it easier to select the right people and thus would reduce the chances of eventual failure. In 1960 the *Encyclopedia of Educational Research* concluded: "More than a half century of research effort has not yielded meaningful, measurable criteria around which the majority of educators can rally. No standards exist which are commonly agreed upon as the criteria of teacher effectiveness. . . . The dearth of adequate effectiveness criteria is largely responsible for our ignorance of the factors which account for success in teaching" (Mitzel, 1960).

Little has happened in the past ten years to improve our capacity to select and predict. As Broudy points out in a criticism of American performance-based teacher education, teaching performances are context- rather than rule-bound (1972, p. 12). The James report appeared to be almost entirely innocent of the difficulties that exist in selecting students and teachers and in establishing criteria for effective teaching.

Last, the James recommendations were criticized by many as antiintellectual and contemptuous of the contribution that universities have made and are capable of making to the improvement of teacher education. There is to be found in the report something of the tired old dichotomy between theory and practice in education, which ought to have been dead long ago. That it is not possibly reflects certain stubborn features of the English way of life— an insistence on being practical, a lack of trust in experts and intellectuals, a belief that if things are left alone, most will work out all right in the end. It can be argued that these are strengths, not weaknesses. But there is a point at which too great an emphasis on the practical, too marked a distaste for theory, can begin to be a disadvantage. This is especially so for teachers. Whether we like it or not, social, political, and educational theories have powerful effects on what goes on in classrooms and schools. The teacher who will not recognize this, or who does not understand it, is vulnerable to outside influences on matters about which he ought to be making up his own mind. Worse still, he is being irresponsible. At back of every practical action or decision the teacher takes in the classroom lie a whole series of complex theoretical assumptions about how children learn, about what kind of place a school should be, and about the kind of society in which we live. Not to be aware of these is to live the kind of unexamined life that may make little difference to the performance of some roles in society, but is certainly not appropriate to teaching. In spirit, if not in concrete recommendations, the James report went beyond the suggestion that students and teachers need some experience of life in a school before they can begin to understand what psychologists, sociologists, philosophers, and others have to say about the schooling process and appeared to many almost to encourage those teachers who deny the importance of theory. But denying the importance of theory amounts to a refusal to examine the basis of one's own practice and is to argue that one's assumptions about children, about society, about curriculum and teaching methods are not open to discussion or question and that what is true about teaching today was true yesterday and will be equally true tomorrow. Properly conceived, what the committee had to say about inservice provision, its third cycle of teacher education, could do much to insure that these out-of-date attitudes on the part of many teachers did not persist. Teaching is a demanding business, and few teachers have had enough opportunity to analyze their own practice or to study the contributions that psychologists, sociologists, philosophers, and others are making to the development of educational ideas. Change in this respect is dependent not only on better inservice opportunities but also on the existence of individual concern with professional upgrading and improvement. Such concern should grow as teaching becomes a more self-conscious activity and the standards of professional training rise. Unfortunately, many of the James recommendations concerning initial training were seen as unlikely to encourage such trends.

Proposals of White Paper

After a year of consultations and discussions, the government announced its decisions on the James proposals in a White Paper, which also provided a framework for educational developments for the next ten years. The Lord James tri-cycle, as it had been called, disappeared, but the desires of the committee to create a fully graduate entry to teaching, to improve the means by which the teacher is inducted into the classroom, and to expand opportunities for inservice education and training were all accepted.

The fully graduate entry into teaching is to be achieved by recruiting a larger proportion of teachers from first-degree programs (Bachelor of Arts and Bachelor of Science) in universities and polytechnic school into one-year professional courses in colleges of education and in university schools of education. University-entrance qualifications will be required for the reduced numbers entering colleges of education for three-year concurrent courses that lead to the ordinary degree of Bachelor of Education. The degrees will be awarded by the Council for National Academic Awards and by universities, not, as James proposed, by a new body set up for this purpose.

Practical difficulties inherent in the attempt of the James committee to integrate professional training and professional induction into a single cycle (second cycle), together with the objections of the teachers' organizations to having what they regarded as unqualified persons in charge of classes, have resulted in proposals for an improved probationary year following qualification. One of them is that regular provisions be made for continued education, and another is that specially trained professional tutors be introduced into the schools to help with student teaching and the induction of probationary teachers.

Large-scale increases in expenditure on inservice education and training are planned, and by the end of the decade some 3 percent of the half million strong teaching force will at any one time be out of the classroom attending courses and conferences of various kinds.

The White Paper proposes that the two-year Diploma of Higher Education be introduced in universities, polytechnic schools, and colleges of education and that it carry credit towards degree studies on an immediate or deferred basis. Again, the award of the diploma is to be a matter for the Council for National Academic Awards and the universities, not some special awarding body. Planning the improved arrangements for induction into teaching, coordinating the efforts of the local education authorities and other institutions in the inservice field, and undertaking the logistical functions (such as organizing student practice within an area, or interpreting at the local level national decisions on such matters as the proportion of teachers to be prepared for different age groups) are to become tasks of a new system of regional committees on which all the professional and teacher education interests are to be represented. The Area Training Organizations, as such, will disappear. Universities, if they wish, may continue to be awarding and academic coordinating bodies for those colleges of education that wish to be associated with them for this purpose. The alternative for the colleges is to approach the Council for National Academic Awards for accreditation of their courses, facilities, staff, and awards. Such accreditation is granted for particular programs for periods of five years at a time. It has the advantage of leaving the colleges free to get on with their own work during this period without academic surveillance of the kind that universities have previously provided in regard to the awarding of teachers' certificates and Bachelor of Education degrees, but it reduces opportunities for the continuation of relationships between colleges and universities that the post-McNair arrangements encouraged.

The recognition of degrees, diplomas, and certificates for purposes of qualified-teacher status (the whole process of what in the United States would be called certification) is to remain with the Secretary of State, at least until the question of setting up a National Teachers' Council is settled. Recognized-teacher status, as at present, will be good for employment anywhere in England and Wales.

The reception of all these proposals and plans has been mixed. Educators of teachers have had few regrets at the demise of the James cycles, the Bachelor of Arts (Education) degree, and the third awarding body. They have welcomed the commitment to a graduate profession and to the raising of entry qualifications, the improved arrangements for the induction of teachers, and the expansion of inservice education. But, although they recognize the case for change, they have expressed anxieties about the effects of changes in what were the responsibilities of Area Training Organizations on studies and research in education in universities.

Looking at what is still to be decided, the interpretations that have to be made (for example, where does coordination end and control begin) the number of colleges and other bodies that will be involved in the negotiations, and the scale of what is proposed (tens of thousands of probationers involved within five years in systematic induction programs of a kind that at present do not exist, a fourfold increase in inservice provision), it is obvious to teacher educators that there are some stiff tasks ahead.

Issues and Problems Raised by White Paper

One of the critical issues concerns the proposed three-year Bachelor of Education degree that will replace the existing three-year–teachers'-certificate courses in the colleges. A three-year Bachelor of Education degree, including professional training and school experience, has been viewed with much suspicion, especially on the part of those who believe that ultimately nothing less than a full four years of training for everybody will suffice. But in terms of present resources, it has been recognized that a three-year professional degree is the price of maintaining the possibility of close academic and professional relationships between the colleges and the universities. That teachers will be better able to improve and update their qualifications by means of recurrent education may compensate for the shortness of the initial course. Some universities have already gone some way towards agreeing to provide academic validations for three-year degrees in the colleges. Their final decisions, and the extent to which the rest of the university world is willing to follow suit and adopt a reasonably consistent pattern of courses and awards, is a crucial factor in the negotiations that will shape teacher education for the remainder of the 1970s.

It is possible that the Bachelor of Education degree itself will not present too many difficulties. The really awkward questions will be about how the new two-year diploma is related to that degree. Few colleges of education can be viable if they concentrate solely on concurrent three-year courses for the certificate in education, the ordinary Bachelor of Education degree, and four-year Bachelor of Education honors programs. The addition of inservice training may enable some colleges to remain as single-purpose–teacher-training institutions, but their numbers will not be large. To remain viable requires diversification. Equally, the present staffing patterns and professional orientations of the colleges mean that few will want to give up their stake in three- and four-year courses for teaching. Thus to fill their places, colleges will have to offer courses for the Diploma of Higher Education.

There is a strong vein of university opinion opposed to the diploma. To provide two-year courses within universities themselves is seen as a possible misuse of resources, especially if it leads to a reduction in the number of three-year degree places available at a time when the pressure for these is likely to be considerable. If the universities not only refuse to provide internal diploma courses for their own students but also refuse to validate diploma work in the colleges, the colleges will be forced to go to the Council for National Academic Awards. University rejection will not kill the diploma. For many colleges it will be the only way of keeping in business, and university attitudes are unlikely to dissuade college staffs from planning diploma courses. Nor, given the coming pressure for places in degree courses, are they likely to be short of students. Many colleges with diploma courses validated by the Council for National Academic Awards will be strongly tempted to approach the council for validation of their Bachelor of Education degrees, and one-year–professional-certificate work as well, especially if universities show themselves unwilling to grant full credit to diplomas awarded by the council. If this happens on any considerable scale, the real academic links between universities and the institutions in which the great majority of both primary and secondary teachers are trained would effectively be at an end. The new regional councils, lacking executive or financial responsibility for the services they are to coordinate, are unlikely to be a satisfactory substitute for the relationships that have been built up since McNair.

Academic and professional standards could suffer in the new arrangements. The question of standards is at the heart of the relationship between teacher-training and the universities. We have become so self-conscious concerning the inadequacies of our examining procedures, the difficulties of making comparisons between individuals and groups of students following different courses in different institutions, and the subjectivity that is involved in any assessment or evaluation that it sometimes seems that we can no longer speak about standards without embarrassment. In any subject or any activity, standards are difficult to define and agree upon.

They will not look after themselves, are hard to maintain, and easy to let slip. As student radicals have already sensed and sociologists of knowledge have tried to spell out, we may try to make the process of evaluation rational and explicit, but there is at its heart an element of judgment that can not be reduced to a formula or list of principles. Universities are not alone in recognizing the importance of standards or of having a commitment to their improvement. Where they are unique is in having on their staffs the largest concentration of those who are recognized as capable of setting standards in their respective fields. There have been many criticisms of the structure and content of the four-year Bachelor of Education degree (introduced following the Robbins proposals of 1963). Some of this criticism was justified. Yet a Bachelor of Education Science Syllabus Committee that requires eminent physicists to work alongside college-of-education tutors and enables both to learn something from each other to the benefit of their students and the children that the students will subsequently teach is not just sentimental imagery. It is an increasingly common reality that the existence of a university-awarded Bachelor of Education degree helped to bring about. Such a reality does not constitute the whole truth about the Bachelor of Education program, but it is just as much part of that truth as are the examples of academic domination that presumably had such an influence on the members of the James committee.

No one is going to pretend that every university in England and Wales has given adequate attention to its responsibilities in the field of teacher education or that there are not many cases where college staff have felt (with varying justification) that one or another university body is obstructing or refusing a desired course of action. One of the problems has been that the grants from the University Grants Committee earmarked for support of Area Training Organization activities were ended before all the organizations could establish themselves within their respective academic communities. Most of the Area Training Organizations that have been able to maintain a strong and meaningful relationship with the colleges, with teachers, with local authorities, and other teacher-training interests in their areas are those that for a variety of reasons managed to get off the ground well before the grants ended. What is worrisome about the arrangements now proposed is that they may represent a failure to adequately consider the need to maintain a proper balance of power between central government, the local authorities, the teachers' organizations, and the universities. It seems unlikely that a system of regional committees can be effective unless their activity is rooted in, and informed by the values of, the work of those academic institutions whose teaching they will coordinate. Whatever is done should recognize that the interests of the employing authorities should not be the only influence on initial and in-service education and training of teachers. The employing authorities have responsibilities for the children in their schools that require that their voices be heard on matters affecting such education and training. But the responsibilities involved in the process of training, as in the case of every kind of professional activity, transcend and may on occasion clash with those of any single employing authority. In most areas and at most times, the relationships between universities, colleges, local authorities, and the representatives of the central government Department of Education and Science have been fairly cordial and easy. But difficulties can and do arise. When they have, the fact that the directors of the Area Training Organizations and their colleagues held academic posts in an independent university meant that they could confront the chief education officer without any sense of career dependence, could argue with the Department of Education and Science knowing that, providing their case was well founded, they could count on the support of their own universities, and could face a diversity of teachers organizations without feeling threatened by the power of any one of them. The danger now is that the new regional committees will be largely rootless. The secretariat will be responsible to a committee so widely and carefully representative and balanced that it will have no sense of identity and will be incapable of developing a coherent policy.

There are many other questions that could be asked about the arrangements proposed in the White Paper. Throughout the arguments and exchanges of the past three years, agreement has been maintained that a substantial expansion of inservice provision is required. Now that agreement must be turned into reality. The danger here is that inservice work will be interpreted as more of the same. The sad fact is that at the moment we have very little idea of what kinds of inservice experience are most effective in promoting personal and professional growth and in improving the quality of what happens in classrooms. In relation to proposed expenditure of some £50m, the amount of research and inquiry so far undertaken is derisory.

There is much to be said for reconceptualizing the inservice task as staff development of the education service, for looking at it not simply as the provision of more courses and conferences, but as a much broader system of communication by means of which teachers, administrators, research workers, subject specialists, curriculum developers, advisors, and teacher-trainers keep in touch with one another and with developments in their respective fields. This involves consultancy arrangements, information services, and the development of a larger number of school-based programs.

The main focus of the White Paper is on the responsibilities of local authorities for providing inservice training. But it is highly undesirable for employers of teachers and institutions controlled by local authority to be the only providers of opportunities for staff development. The universities and the teachers' organizations will have an important part to play, the former not just with respect to advanced and award-bearing courses. Regional coordination must both permit and encourage pluralism of provision if the dangers of curricula and pedagogic orthodoxies in particular areas are to be avoided.

Some of the most awkward choices will have to be faced in the universities. Expansionist periods and liberal attitudes are mutually reinforcing; so are cutbacks and conservatism. Although universities will continue to grow during the next ten years, the growth will not be as rapid or as extensive as many have hoped, and staff-to-student ratios will worsen. Few additional resources will be available in this period to enable universities to manage the academic validation of the three-year degree and proposed Diploma of Higher Education. To require that universities control and oversee syllabuses, facilities, teaching and examining for three-year degrees and diplomas in the same way that they have for the existing four-year Bachelor of Education degree could be seen as imposing difficult burdens. Academics unsympathetic to the college connection will doubtless make much of this. Yet for universities to reject the three-year degree and the diploma is to risk losing their influence in an area of public and professional activity vitally important to the quality of their own work.

Some critics of the arrangements that have existed since McNair have argued that the involvement of the universities in initial teacher-training has distracted their attention from developing the kinds of higher-degree and research-and-development activities in education that they alone can provide. What will eventually be a fully graduate profession will generate a much greater demand for such high-level study opportunities. Universities in this country award now only a few hundred master's degrees and some fifty or so doctorates in education in any one year, compared with over forty thousand master's degrees and four thousand or so doctorates in the United States. Once again, resources are likely to be the key. After a tenfold increase during the 1960s in the money available to support educational research and development, there has been very little growth the last few years—in fact, a decline in real terms because of inflation—and there have been few new institutional initiatives. The new perspectives on initial training, induction, and inservice provision that the White Paper provides require that fresh attention be given to the future of the advanced study and research without which much of the effort at more basic levels is likely to be fruitless.

Once the present ferment of discussion concerning the organization and politics of teacher education dies down, there will be fresh opportunities to attend to the structure and content of courses and to the pedagogic practices and procedures of the institutions concerned. In a time of rapid social and educational change, it would be too much to hope for a period of peace and tranquillity in such a field as teacher education. But once the framework for future growth is settled, a greater proportion of activity and interest can be directed toward substantive educational issues. Change and reform in these promise continuing improvement in the quality of childrens' learning and experience in classroom and school.

Chapter 12

Curricular Developments

Margaret Lindsey

Few times have witnessed either the amount or the quality of search and research now going on in teacher education, and it is clear that the remainder of the 1970s will be characterized by unprecedented activity intended to improve both teacher education and education at large. Government agencies, the united profession, community groups, and other forces compelling the reform of education in general and teacher education in particular will neither become dormant nor fade in impact in the immediate future. More meetings will be held, more publicly and privately supported commissions will be appointed, new volumes will be printed, new nonprint materials will go to market, and greater numbers of researchers will be analyzing the education of the teachers of the nation.

Some of these efforts, as now, will focus on the selection, organization, management, and assessment of total teacher education programs or program components; others will be concerned with specific instruction and instructional materials. Brilliant scholars will advance conceptual models of teacher preparation; a few will move from conceptual schemes to operational proposals; teams of persons from diverse settings and with complementary specialities will continue to develop comprehensive systems for the education of teachers; and a few institutional groups will reconstruct their own teacher education programs, producing models that are unique to their own situations.

Of the current curricular models, the most popular are performance- or competency-based. They employ a major conception of teacher roles and from that conception derive specific behaviors (and sometimes knowledge and attitudes) assumed to be basic in performing those roles. Programs receiving greatest attention, besides being performance-based, are systemic in character. They establish behaviors as objectives, provide training in connection with those objectives, and use the specified objectives as criteria in assessing students' progress toward teaching competence.

The widespread acceptance and development of systemic, competency-based curricula will very likely mean that before this decade ends, taxonomies of teacher competencies, developed by collaborating groups, grounded in available knowledge, and field-tested, will be accessible to all who request them. Instructional modules with specified behavioral objectives, assessment instruments, suggested activities and materials, and self-recording and analyzing procedures will become available to those who choose to use them. Protocol materials will be retrievable on request. Computer programs for management of student records, materials, and environmental conditions will be common. And a number of new models developed by individual institutional groups, as well as the federally funded Elementary Education Models, will become readily accessible and widely used.

The impact of these curricular developments in teacher education will undoubtedly be positive in the improvement of both preparatory and inservice programs. However, concern about achieving the full benefit of current developments emanates from uncertainty about what responsible human beings will select as promising and how they will use what they select. Mindless adoption and installation of ready-made curricular models is not only possible but also, history and present events suggest, all too probable. In too many instances, these models will be adopted by single-handed power play, without involvement and preparation of those who must operate them. No curricular model, however good in one setting, can be transferred to a different setting and operated effectively by strangers who were not party to its development. Any comprehensive model requires modifications to fit the environment to which it is being adapted.

If program planners within an institution wish to start with an available curricular model, they should thoughtfully and deliberately select a model that has a conceptual base compatible with their own, one that accommodates many of their values and beliefs, fits most of the conditions in their setting, and provides for the processes they believe to be important. Then they should adapt the model by extension, elimination, and other kinds of modifications so that it responds to their own needs even more closely and conduct specific evaluations of the whole and its parts to assure that the adapted model fulfills the promise they thought it held. With wise and knowledgeable use, modifications, and evaluation, comprehensive curricular models hold much promise for the effective reform of present teacher education programs.

It is not the fully developed and complete models alone that hold promise. The principles and procedures used in constructing them are in many cases worth replication by other individuals and groups. The products that accompany them, such as taxonomies of teacher competencies, instruction modules, and assessment procedures and instruments, are useful to teacher educators in schools, universities, teacher centers, and government or private agencies. They also are promising for scholars and researchers of education. Yet, what promises to make significant and positive difference in the education of teachers is less the tangible products and more the dialogue precipitated by those products.

Conditions suggest that the dialogue will be more productive in the genuine improvement of teacher preparation than past discussions have been. Persons representing a wider scope of specialities are involved together in their deliberations, in contrast to the earlier separation of educationists from "others." The current atmosphere encourages honest recognition of unresolved problems and unanswered questions, promotes the dropping of defenses, and enhances openness to new ideas. Substantial support, including money, released time, and status rewards, is increasingly present. In short, discussions are now taking place in conditions that promote progress in reaching rational answers to questions made especially visible and critical by current curricular developments in teacher education.

Prominent among the questions being discussed are these: What kinds of knowledge shall serve as bases in designing teacher education curricula? How might reasonable balance in activities of both students and faculty in teacher education programs be protected? Who shall be involved in planning, conducting, and evaluating programs of teacher education? By what criteria shall progress of students in preparatory programs be determined? What shall be the relationship between preservice preparation, inservice education, and licensure of teachers?

Basis for Decisions in Designing Programs

The question of what knowledge shall serve as basis for selecting and organizing content and activities in the teacher education program is complex. How is knowledge to be defined by program planners? What sources of knowledge hold promise for providing help in structuring a preparatory program?

One evidence of the problem in defining knowledge as the base for curricular decisions is the repeated assertion that preparatory programs are based on inadequate knowledge. Yet if knowledge is defined as limited to fact or principle derived from verified empirical data, it is patently clear that all curricular decisions can not be based on knowledge so defined; we do not know enough. Conversely, if the definition of knowledge is overextended so that, for example, the vast store of assumptions that make up professional lore is perceived as though it were empirically derived knowledge, curricular decisions are void of scholarship. A pressing responsibility of teacher educators is to move as rapidly as possible toward the production of verified knowledge needed in planning programs, to make appropriate use of knowledge that is available, and with firm commitment toward producing and using more adequate knowledge bases for decisions, to recognize without shame those areas where decisions will undoubtedly continue to be based on less than verified knowledge.

Not all the bases used in designing a program can be found in knowledge, however broadly defined; some are feeling and some are valuing. Decisions presumed to be based on knowledge usually are made with ideas that fall somewhere along a continuum stretching from speculation to fact. Speculation is seldom pure; speculation has the benefit of some assumptions, uses generalizations, limited as they may be, and often has some proven facts behind it. Similarly, what is referred to as verified knowledge as a base for decisions frequently encompasses more than proven facts.

To illustrate, the selection of a competency to be included in a program component is based upon a very important assumption, that the possession of the competency by the teacher is positively related to the pupils' achievement of intended objectives. Similarly, decisions made in the process of designing an instructional module rely upon one or more assumptions about cause and effect. Behavior indicators are assumed to be evidence that the competency is present; and the proposed sequencing, articulating, and integrating of training activities, together with the means for mediating between the trainee and the training environment, are assumed to bring about desired outcomes. If teacher behavior is used as the primary criterion in evaluation, an assumption is made that the expected behavior is relevant to the desired pupil behavior. On the other hand, if pupil behavior is the central criterion in evaluating a teacher's competency, it is assumed that pupil behavior is actually tightly related to teacher behavior. Clearly all such assumptions can not now be supported by knowledge at the principle or fact levels. Teacher educators should be giving priority to establishing and using verified knowledge in making an increasing number of program decisions and expressing greater intolerance for sloppy guesses in program designing.

Whatever the definition of knowledge employed, there remains a fundamental consideration of what bodies of knowledge are particularly useful in structuring a teacher education program. Traditionally curriculum designers have called upon accumulated findings in the pure sciences, humanities (for example, class-structure characteristics of a given minority group found by sociologists or ways of knowing as presented by the epistemologists), and the applied sciences (findings from study of operations and conditions in specified settings and with intent to predict or explain actions and their consequences). More recently teaching and schooling have been subjected to systematic study in a style that employs a combination of pure and applied modes, producing primarily knowledge that is descriptive in character and a limited number of prescriptive principles.

The question here is not whether one or all these bodies of knowledge can contribute to designing a teacher education program; they all can. Nor is it whether content within one or all might be part of the curriculum; each has a part in the preparation of teachers. Rather the question is what sources of knowledge will provide guidance in structuring (selecting and organizing content, activities, and environment) the preparatory program. Response to this question sets the framework and provides an advance organizer for program scope and sequence. What is critical in curriculum designing is conscious choice of a point of orientation and consistency in applying that orientation to the selection and organization of content and processes of a program.

Many professional education programs appear to proceed from the supposition that the training sequence ought to provide first for acquisition of theoretical principles, then for study of their application to practice, and finally for practice itself. This sequence is traditional, and its inadequacies are well documented.

Competency-based programs proceed from the supposition that professional preparation should focus on practice; hence, the organizing core is a body of knowledge (loosely defined, to be sure) about teaching, in this case, competencies required for effective teaching. This core directs the selection and use of concepts and skills from a wide range of sources. In other words, with teacher competencies as the organizing focus, knowledge is selected and used because of its relevance to teaching, which considerably improves the chances that students in training will experience meaning and significance in their encounters within the preparatory program.

The appropriate source of knowledge to serve as the organizing focus of teacher education is the professional practice of teaching. Neither does this dictate a competency-based program nor imply a single curricular design. Making teaching the organizing focus does, however, mandate that a conception of teaching be defined at the outset and that relevance to that conception of teaching be the central criterion in the selection and organization of both content and processes of the curriculum.

Balance in Curricula

A tendency for some educators to jump on new ideas and wildly abandon what is in favor of space, time, and personnel for the new is of long standing. Teacher educators have had some notoriety for bandwagon jumping. The wholesale modification of student-teaching programs from campus schools to "representative" public schools, from one or two hours per day to full-time, and from four or six weeks to twelve or eighteen weeks is a case in point. In this instance, it often happened that important components were dropped from programs to make room for the increased amount of student-teaching, that students were scattered widely and got little or no supervision from their college, and that classroom teachers were provided with no preparation for working with students. Consequently, the quality of student-teaching programs was drastically reduced in the name of recommendations intended to raise it. History of the continuing struggle to create balance in allocation of credit and time among general or liberal education, specialization in subject matter, and professional education reveals a sequence of imbalance in one direction, followed by redress, often leading to imbalance in another direction. In the early 1950s and later, following *Sputnik,* academicians bitterly criticized the inadequate preparation of teachers and succeeded in influencing both programs and certification requirements to increase the amount of subject matter in preparatory programs, which frequently resulted in deletion from programs of critically important study of and practice in teaching. Dangers of imbalance toward one or more parts of preservice programs have always been present. Today dangers of imbalance have character and dimensions quite different from those evident in the past.

What is reasonable balance, for example, between independent self-instruction and interdependent socialized instruction? Assuming adequate laboratories, both simulated and real, a young person deciding to become a teacher could wend his way through a maze of activities spirally going from one level to the next level of assessment, training, and evaluation. His behavior could be recorded according to a previously determined program, and he could request output from the computer as he felt the need for it. Such self-instructional programs could be designed for all dimensions of preparation, including what is usually referred to as general education and personal development. Similarly, a teacher in service, without association with other persons, could undertake study of his behavior, and consequences of it, using self-instructional and self-evaluation programs. Given current technological potentials, dispositions of some educators to view teaching as a craft with a set of skills and technics, and the rapid production of self-instructional packages, it is realistic to advance the notion of individual, independent preparation for teaching. That it is possible does not make it right or desirable. Teacher educators must ask, toward what end, under what circumstances, and at what times are independent self-instruction and self-evaluation likely to be most productive. The same question must be asked about the need of trainees to associate with others in the processes of becoming professional teachers. Surely in the total preparation of teachers there are ends sought that demand means characterized by interaction among persons. General communication ability, both written and oral, is one illustration. Other examples are: development of certain intellectual skills such as critical thinking, examination of values and their significance in everyday practice, development of skills, attitudes, and feelings in human relationships, development of concepts and skills of cooperation, and increase in self-understanding and acceptance. These and many other ends generally viewed as important in teacher education programs can not be achieved outside of a social context.

What is reasonable balance in emphases on skills, concepts, and attitudes? To state behavioral objectives with respect to overt, observable skills and to design instructional modules, including assessment, training activities, and evaluation for such objectives is relatively easy. Hence the market is flooded with packages on those teaching behaviors that are most observable and measurable (for example, questioning skill) and almost void of materials on how to use the self as an instrument in the classroom or how to relate to pupils and colleagues with warmth and compassion. More than a few programs are so overweighted toward training in a multiplicity of separate skills that critical attitudes and beliefs, such as prejudice toward both person and ability of minority-group members, go without notice and certainly without any effort to examine them.

Another aspect of balance in curricular offerings relates to provision for training in isolated specifics compared to the opportunity to experience the whole of teaching. Teacher educators know that teaching is in reality something more than the aggregate of specific behaviors, that the whole is greater than the parts. Yet some curricular models make the parts obvious and provide training in details and pieces in such ways as to cover up, treat slightly, or avoid altogether the problem of helping the trainee to integrate and make whole his teaching behavior with respect to the demands of any real situation. It is not surprising that some students complain about being forced to acquire specific skills without ever sensing or testing the role of the specifics in the context of the whole. Although some of the problem here is in the sequencing of opportunities, that is, failure to provide for experience with the whole before concentration of the parts, the more important aspect of the problem is failure to provide reasonable balance in the constant flow of experience back and forth between teaching as an expression of the self in a real setting and activities designed to increase specific skills.

A completely different kind of imbalance is also observable, and its dangers are already clear. It is imbalance in the ways curriculum workers use time, energy, and ability. This includes those who teach in teacher education programs. For many reasons, some teacher educators appear to devote almost all of their time, energy, and thought to producing bits and pieces of programs. Too few persons appear to be working on the whole of a curriculum, considering interrelationships among the parts, and examining the parts for balance and completeness. There is a frightening absence of curriculum designers, in contrast to the great number of materials producers.

A designer treats the whole, giving attention to form, emphasis, balance, articulation, continuity, internal consistency, and unity. The need for attention to the whole is urgent. Curricular models now getting much attention are limited for the most part to the training dimensions of professional preparation. Clearly the total education of a teacher is more than that. Inadequate work is being done on education, and training is being subjected to over-kill. The professional component is analyzed, examined, reformed, and evaluated unendingly, but other large components go untouched. It is time to apply to designing liberal education and specialization components the outstanding features of competency-based programs: concise definition of anticipated outcomes, selection and organization of learning opportunities that are relevant to stated outcomes, and assessment of progress in terms of the same stated outcomes. It is time for all teacher educators, not just those dealing with professional education, to be accountable for the consequences of their curricular decisions. Unless and until all are responsible, there will be danger that parts of programs will be reformed while others, equally important, remain untouched by contemporary developments.

Politics in Designing, Managing, and Evaluating Programs

The politics of designing, managing, and evaluating teacher education programs continues to be a source of major questions and unresolved problems. Questions such as who makes what decisions, where authority rests, and what the roles and responsibilities of participants are have always been present. Now such questions have more specific and complicated referents in practice, and they attract the attention of various publics as well as of educators. For example, the U.S. Office of Education recommended, and in some cases enforced, a principle of parity among school, university, and community personnel in planning, conducting, monitoring, and assessing programs to prepare teachers. In developing the Elementary Education Models, directors were expected to involve representatives from a wide spectrum of locations and specialties. A further expectation was that the models would use a systems approach, including feedback to both program and individuals. These and other expectations for the models made heavy emphasis upon field situations and personnel essential. To the extent that the expectations were met, those models call for different and increased involvement by many persons both in their development and in their use.

Teacher organizations, private funding agencies, and parent groups are becoming more insistent in their demands for a large share of responsible and important involvement in teacher education programs. Agencies in state departments of education are building into new certification standards and procedures requirements that school and college personnel assume joint responsibility for designing, conducting, and evaluating all preservice and continuing teacher education programs. Accreditation standards, adopted in 1970, require that institutions to be accredited show evidence on the performance of their graduates, that such evidence be procured by both school and university personnel, and that it be directly fed into program revision when implied. Involvement of behavioral scientists and specialists in tests and measurement has increased greatly as systems approaches call for constant assessment of trainees and programs.

These are only a few of the many current developments that create a different mix of ideas, persons, and situations involved in curricular decisions. The mix is not well defined or understood, and roles are not clear. On one hand, there is some evidence that university personnel continue to maintain real power and authority at the same time that they try either to make others feel they have power they really do not have or to use token rewards to entice school and community folk to accept the dominance of higher-education institutions. On the other hand, analysis of negotiations between teacher groups and school boards shows that in more than a few instances, classroom teachers' control over certain parts of both pre and inservice teacher education has been built into agreements. If the movement toward increased involvement emerges as a football to be tossed around by groups or individuals seeking self-enhancing power and authority, the hoped-for benefits will surely become barriers to progress in the improvement of programs. When definition of roles and responsibilities is based upon power of numbers, or traditional authority, or thoughtless adherence to the status quo, the consequences are not positive. When expertise is denied in favor of power, the chances of regression in quality of programs is great. The kinds of problems appearing in efforts toward parity in involvement need the scholarship of political scientists, sociologists, and others who have special constructs and methods for study of complex combinations of social systems.

One other aspect of collaboration by representatives of diverse groups needs mention. When persons are brought together with responsibility for designing, monitoring, and evaluating teacher education programs and for recommending persons for certification to teach (as in the new style of certification in the state of New York), the problems, insecurities, and difficulties encountered often consume so much time and energy that little remains for work on the assigned responsibilities. Many hours may be spent in reaching agreements on precise statements of organization (officers, responsibilities, committees, and so forth), additional hours may be spent on trying to build a language for communication, and still more time may be devoted to salving egos or helping an individual to deal with a professional situation. Some cooperating groups gain all the satisfactions members need through these operations and have little time or interest to devote to building a teacher education program. Teacher educators need to be far more sensitive than they are now to the risks accompanying efforts to involve many persons in important decisions and actions in the preparation and certification of teachers.

Assessment and Evaluation of Students and Teachers

Once it is admitted that traditional criteria and procedures for evaluating students and teachers are woefully inadequate, the problem of developing more adequate means must be confronted. That number of courses completed and grades received in a university program do not guarantee competence to teach needs no argument. What, then, are appropriate criteria and procedures?

If a systems approach is used in designing a teacher education program, criteria for assessing and evaluating student progress are determined at the outset of the designing process. These criteria may be in the form of precisely stated competencies with definition of specific behaviors that indicate possession of each competency; or they may be specified knowledge, skills, and attitudes trainees will be expected to demonstrate. It is assumed that a direct path connects the competencies or objectives with training and that they are the outcomes to be examined in assessing both program and students. Although defining criteria to be used in evaluating teaching at any and all levels is a difficult task for all responsible teacher educators, it is less troublesome than determining what evidence shall be admissible in making evaluations.

A focal point in the consideration of admissibility and validity of evidence is whether teacher behavior is adequate as evidence or whether the acceptable evidence must be consequences of that behavior, primarily as present in pupil progress. A few teacher educators still hold tenaciously to one position or the other on that question, but most persons dealing with the problem recognize the need for both types of evidence. Strong reasons can be advanced for being cautious about believing too much in either type of evidence. For example, reliance on teacher behavior forces the assumption that relationships between a given behavior and consequences of it have been established and verified and so can be predicted. Such predicting principles simply have not yet been validated in sufficient number to warrant placing too much confidence in them.

On the other hand, reliance on evidence of intended consequences of teacher behavior, that is, pupil progress, is also based on assumptions that have not yet been validated. Chief among these is the assumption that teacher behavior and pupil progress are directly related. To put it another way, those who insist that the only admissible evidence of teacher competency is pupil progress seem to assume that specified changes in pupil behavior can be shown to be consequences of teacher behavior. Yet no one would seriously argue, with effective educational impact on pupils coming from all sorts of places and activities, that many changes in pupil behavior can be traced directly or exclusively to teacher behavior.

To debate in favor of one position or the other seems to be too ridiculous to consume the time and energies of able teacher educators. Arguing either/or positions is not a fruitful approach to resolving the issue. Teaching is an activity carried on with distinctive purpose, and that purpose has to do with enabling others to progress in directions they desire or directions specified in advance. Clearly, assessment of teaching must take into account all possible evidence that the intent of the teaching is realized. However, to insist that pupil progress is the only admissible evidence may well result in overemphasis on those pupil behaviors easily measured and lack of concern with other important dimensions of both teacher and pupil behavior. Similarly, to insist on teacher behavior as the only evidence of competency may result in failure to search for evidences of consequences and for predictive principles that would contribute so much to the whole process of teacher education. Efforts must go forward on both fronts.

The question of evidence is further complicated by lack of procedures and instruments for collecting and analyzing relevant data. It is tempting to focus evaluation on those behaviors that can be measured with ease and objectivity and to neglect areas where the task is difficult. Risk of such narrow focus and accompanying neglect will be reduced as program designers give more attention to comprehensiveness in statements of objectives or competencies and as conscientious specialists in measurement work toward creating new instruments and procedures for getting evidence on things now not so readily observable and measurable.

Continuity in Education of Teachers

Continuity in the education of teachers is an area to which current curriculum development will have made great contribution if ideas prominent in most proposals come to fruition. Lamentations about the gap between preservice and inservice education have been heard for many years, and even with the best of previous suggestions, a large gap was quite possible because of distribution of responsibility and lack of association among persons and agencies holding certain responsibilities.

To a very large extent, current curricular proposals force reduction of that gap. For one thing, the required involvement of school, university, and community persons in the planning, conducting, and evaluating of teacher education programs brings those people into direct association, dealing with matters in which all have a stake, and under conditions making the sharing of power and responsibility a necessity. But beyond that general mode of operation, there are other and more specific requests that the gap be closed, responsibility be shared, and continuity of educational opportunity for teachers be guaranteed.

As I mentioned earlier, requirements for follow-up of graduates by higher education institutions is one way of providing conditions supporting continuity. If both school and university persons take advantage of the opportunity to come together in working with recent entrants into teaching, not only will all profit from the experience, but also one of the serious obstacles to continuity will have been removed. That obstacle is the failure of those dealing with preservice education to assume a responsibility for graduates and, in like manner, the failure of school personnel to make special provisions for novices and to make those provisions have a direct relationship to higher education institutions.

Very likely the most powerful influence on continuity, on diminishing gaps between phases of teacher education, is the now commonly recommended relationship between continuing education and certification. Such relationships in the past must be described as dismal and unproductive, to say the least. Now it is expected that a teacher will be engaged in advancing his knowledge and skill from the time he decides to prepare for teaching, through various stages of legal licensing, and so long as he wants to involve himself in the practice of teaching.

What gives power to that expectation is the common commitment to competency as the goal of education at all points and as the basis on which to license personnel. Such common commitment is real. Representatives from state departments no longer confine their contacts with institutions preparing teachers to approval visits. Instead, certification officials are on the spot, working with collaborating groups in one center after another, and associating with school, community, and university people in curriculum designing and evaluating activities. What the standards for certification shall be, how and by whom they shall be administered are no longer decisions made in a closed shop at the state education building; they are decisions made by joint deliberations among state, school, university, and community representatives. And in all such enterprises, the focus is on performance and competency. More than ever before, processes of education and licensure have common goals and like ways of working.

The position I have taken in this chapter is that present curricular developments and models have successfully forced curriculum workers to confront once again fundamental questions and problems in relation to designing and conducting teacher education programs. It is argued that promise for the future lies more in the confrontation, with its dialogue and action, and less in materials, whether they be instructional modules, taxonomies, or comprehensive conceptual models. The argument does not deny the outstanding contributions present in the products of this period of activity in curriculum development. Through brief exploration of questions in five areas, the effort has been to identify important contributions and, at the same time, alert teacher educators to unfinished business that urgently needs their attention.

Chapter 13

Profession Anyone?

Herbert A. Thelen

One thing most Americans have and share is their experiences at the receiving end of teaching. During their early years they have accommodated to a wide array of teaching styles, personalities, and demands. They have talked over their classroom experiences with friends and parents. They have seen classroom fantasies on TV, and they have read "all about" education and classrooms in the newspapers and magazines. As a result of this common experience and discussion of it, practically everybody "knows" what teachers do and what teaching is.

Teachers call the class to order. They tell the students what to do. They assign work. They demand, hear, and correct recitations. They pass judgment on students, encouraging some and discouraging others. Listening to students is a sign of friendliness; being strict with students is a token of scholarship. Familial dignity carries over into classrooms, and teachers are to comport themselves within the boundaries of morality publicly professed by the school board and parents. Methodologically, the essential (although not

priceless) ingredients of teaching are the sacred text, the daily catechism, and the year-end confirmation to certify the true or sincere
believers.

A person may study teaching empirically and education
philosophically to his heart's content, but he can never quite eradicate the great expectations of this cultural archetype nor can his
practices very far depart from them. Like the image of Mother, this
understanding of teaching is built into the culture simply by virtue
of common and prolonged experience. It acts like a force to restrain
change and to secure order. It is at once the guardian and avenging
angel of every classroom.

On the basis of similarity of attitudes one can hypothesize
that the cultural archetype may be descended from the *pedagogue:*
"Among the Greeks and Romans, the pedagogue was originally a
slave who attended the younger children of his master, and conducted them to school, to the theater, etc., combining in many cases
instruction with guardianship" (*Century Dictionary of the English
Language,* 1891, p. 4351). In that model, the teacher stands in the
place of parents; he is an adjunct member of the household, hired
by parents, and inferior in status to them. His power over children
is "official," that of a civil servant, a prerogative of office rather
than a consequence of education; his authority is legitimated by
certification rather than by wisdom; and his objectives derive from
social-class aspirations rather than from individual needs of children.

These cultural expectations of the teacher and teaching are
as real in teaching as are IQs, developmental phases, sex, subject
matter, and achievement; and they are probably the most influential determinants of what happens. It is embarrassingly obvious
that teacher education should be concerned with developing the
candidate's awareness of the cultural archetype and of his reactions
to it. I do not think it is too extreme to assert that the essential
differences among teacher-training programs can best be demonstrated along a continuum between unconscious endorsement of the
archetype (mindlessness) and conscious analysis and use of its expectations as facts to be taken into account and worked with.

What the cultural archetype and its pattern of expectations
mean varies among individuals and groups. People accept them as
part of the natural order; but, like gravity and sex, they do not

necessarily like them. For some, the archetype means opportunity and a secure society; for others it means alienation and denial. Moreover, the great expectations do not constitute a specific job description, and they may give rise to kaleidoscopic permutations of teacher behaviors. The enduring and compelling force of the cultural archetype resides not in specific stipulations and prohibitions; it is instead in the spirit or ethos inherent in the pattern. Regardless of their reason or merit in other frames of reference, practices that violate this spirit produce guilt and tend to activate countermeasures.

Borrowman (1971, pp. 71–79) writes that by 1827 the concept of teaching as a profession was close to the surface and that it probably expressed the consensus of educators when it was made official in the charter of the National Education Association in 1870. The paraphernalia of a profession—normal schools and university programs, state and local certification, research and professional associations—was developed piecemeal. The special-knowledge characteristic of professions was located first in standard works on moral and mental philosophy and later in the pedagogical systems of Pestalozzi and Herbart. In the 1890s, during the fantastic flowering of intellect in America, the new social sciences emerging in universities were connected to pedagogy; and the new scientific study of education offered the prospect of the continuous and systematic growth of the special knowledge that would give substance to the profession. But even these new social institutions and vistas of knowledge would not, by themselves, make teaching a profession. A third element, the sense of vocation—the commitment to an ideal, spirit, or ethos—was needed. And it was found in the great movement toward social reforms that swept all aspects of American life. By 1895 the school was no longer to be merely a device for training citizens; it was to become an instrument of social reform (Cremin, 1962, pp. 168–176). This ideology galvanized education, pulled together the various elements, and generated the new archetype, teaching as a profession. Cremin sees the founding of Teacher's College at Columbia in 1899 as the outcome of the merger of professionalism and progressivism into a "full-fledged reformist philosophy of teacher preparation. . . . In progressivism teachers soon found that they had an ideology that dignified in the noblest terms their own quest for status, while in professionalism progressives had the key to their demand for scientifically trained pedagogues who could bring into being a new society 'more worthy, lovely, and harmonious' " (1962, p. 175). These were the seminal days of James, Parker, Thorndike, and Dewey. The professional archetype, orchestrating practical institutions, systematic development of scientific knowledge, and ideological commitment gained momentum and, in 1919, spawned the Progressive Education Association. Cremin traces the gradual erosion of the movement—and the profession—from its beginning in the 1930s to its last significant hurrah in the eight-year study, which ended in 1940.

Four forces can be identified that brought down the Progressive-Professional movement: the disintegration of the science of education into the pursuit of the proliferating separate social sciences carried on in educational settings and mostly unconcerned with pedagogy; the ebbing of the Progressive movement in national life and the failure to find any other ideological thrust to give viability to the profession; the capitulation of schools and all other parts of the educational apparatus to social, economic, and political exigencies; and the reassertion of the cultural archetype, no longer held at bay by vigorous intellectual activity and inspired experimentation.

It seems to me that certain things can be learned from this melancholy account: Education is a complex enterprise. Its quality depends to a very high degree on the voluntary exercise of courage, insight, and commitment by thousands of teachers and other educational functionaries. Their efforts can not be coordinated by force (supervision) nor can their behavior be programed by administrators (procedures) or even by elite computers. The basis of coordination has to be a shared commitment to an educational vision: the concept of a profession. Incongruence sensed between operational and conceptual systems will generate the tensions that can improve both and may lead to the establishment, through internalization-seeking dialogue, of the professional archetype.

In this chapter, I shall take it that teaching is to be a profession; that preservice training is to induct persons into the profession; and that inservice learning, practical experimentation, scientific research, and substantive philosophical inquiry are all to enhance the character and effectiveness of the profession.

Bricklayer or Cathedral-Builder?

Do you remember the fine old story about the two bricklayers? They were asked "What are you doing?" One replied, "I am laying bricks." The other said, "I am building a cathedral." The first man is a tradesman; the second has the soul of an artist or professional. The difference is in the meaning of the activity. It is not in how expertly or skillfully the bricklayers daub mortar onto each brick; it is not in the number of hours of supervised practice they had; it is not in how much information they have about the job; it is not in their loyalty to the boss; it is not in their familiarity with other constructions. It is in how they savor and feel about what they are doing, in their sensing of relationships between their work and that of others, in their appreciation of potentialities, in their sense of form, in their need for and enjoyment of significance, in their identification of self with civilized aspirations, in their whole outlook on life.

A similar distinction can be made between teachers who hold class or teach school and teachers who educate children and between training programs that turn out manpower and those that turn out professionals. It may be that both training programs have courses in educational psychology and foundations, both have supervised practice teaching, both have a unit or two on the teaching profession, both have methods courses, and both worry about the student's knowledge of the subjects he is to teach. The programs may offer the same ingredients, but in one case the ingredients represent separate requirements to meet or hurdles to leap whereas in the other case, the ingredients are inputs assimilated into a style of life and intentionality (May, 1969, pp. 223–245), a system of thought, feeling, and action.

The tradesman-teacher operates by scanning his memory of various courses for specific examples or instructions to follow or emulate, in contrast to the professional-teacher, who reflects his internalized sense of education against the specific situation and spontaneously creates appropriate structures of response. Putting it another way, the first teacher looks for the particular weapon or tool to use, but the other teacher mobilizes his entire being in a holistic response to the total situation. The first teacher is unidimensional, responding to an idea, feeling, performance, or attitude as if it existed by itself; the second teacher responds, usually without conscious analysis at the time, to the pattern of these components, to his apprehension of meanings in the various ways of life in the situation.

If you feel that the above paragraphs are vague, mystical, sentimental, or wishful, then you are a true child of our times. Our hard-won–technical-social ethos has driven the quest for meaning from the public to the private realm. Phrases like the *adaptive wisdom of the body* or the *relations between man and universe* are dismissed as bad biology or as theology.

The major value in society is getting things done, and the prototype of modern enterprise is the assembly line and what is known as research and development. Houses, space vehicles, TV sets, computer programs, medical treatment, political campaigns, curricula, and teacher-training programs are all produced on a powerful insight: that a complex product or service can be fabricated by assembling simple, standardized components, modules, subroutines, roles, or other units. The assembly may be as complicated as a city or as simple as the linear accumulation of course credits toward a diploma. Each module is created by specially trained workers; and in their eyes, the module, not the assembly, is the end. No worker has to have more than a small fraction of the skills and understandings required to produce the whole assembly. He may not even know what other parts will ultimately have to mesh with his.

Should supervising teachers know educational psychology? Should the professors of foundation courses know how to teach? Should methods instructors understand the educational issues in the nation? Should all of them participate in writing (and revising) state certification requirements? Should all these parts be continually modified and reinterpreted as the various instructors seek to relate their activity to that of the others? Should we be bricklayers or cathedral-builders? Tradesmen or professionals? Technicians or

adventurers? Where and what is the equivalent of the master to
whom professional trainees used to be apprenticed? How can people
be trained into an exciting style of professional life when nobody
around them lives it?

Community by the Pool

The persons and organizations whose attitudes and actions
affect the overall state of education constitute the educational system. If each part (for example, school or classroom) goes its solitary
way, unaffected by and without consequence for any other part,
then there is no system, and the teachers are entrepreneurs. If cooperation or negotiation among parts is required for the operation
of each, then there is a network of interdependency and teachers
are citizen-tradesmen. Finally, if the authority that governs cooperation and negotiation is the commitment of each part to some overall purpose, value, or concept, to the development of which each
part contributes, then the system is full-fledged and the teacher is
a professional.

The whole that is implemented through the parts and that
regulates their interdependent functioning is the concept and sense
of the profession of education. Two difficulties stand in the way of
developing this educational system. First, educators do not have any
clear concept of a whole profession; and second, each part is captive to political, social, economic, and other exigencies. To overcome
these obstacles, we shall somehow have to buck up the parts, free
them from servitude to noneducational masters, and help them
negotiate a vital place for themselves within the shared conception
of an educational system, educational in the full sense of the term.
And we shall have to develop this conception as a nationwide
understanding that can stir the conscience, elicit voluntary effort,
respond to social and political facts, and find participatory roles for
everyone whose conduct directly affects education. The conception
of an educational system is a mental construction and its sense is
like that of nation in the exquisite definition that "A nation is a
bunch of people who think they are a nation—and," I may add,
"act like it." A profession is composed of people who think they are
professionals and who seek through the practical inquiry of their

lives, both alone and together, to clarify and live up to what they mean by being a professional.

The only way to generate the profession is through inter-actions of the various parts. They must give each other information, share experience, plan together, and take part in all that we usually mean by formal and informal communications. They must also engage in reflective and humane communion that builds the sense of community. In 1927, Dewey pointed out: "Wherever there is conjoint activity whose consequences are appreciated as good by all singular persons who take part in it, and where the realization of the good is such as to effect an energetic desire and effort to sustain it in being just because it is a good shared by all, there is so far a community" (Dewey, 1927, p. 149).

In education, the required dialogue will have to be about perennial issues and values even as it creates new organizational forms and procedures. Marin puts it this way: "We might [instead] confront directly such issues as the relation between individual and state; the definitions of cultural and private value; our underlying historical direction; the nature of political reality and religious meaning; the relation of knowledge and experience. But because we are not accustomed to talking in clear detail about those issues, they are reduced . . . to fogged and meaningless arguments about schooling" (1972, p. 44).

The issues Marin identifies are national and perennial. Pro-fessionals ought to participate in a national dialogue. Schooling is a set of more or less traditional procedures and organizations, the particular provisions for education supplied in the local community. Talking in clear detail about the issues, that is, engaging in intel-lectually disciplined discussion, brings together the two levels of dialogue in a wedding of the conceptual and practical. Let us con-sider the two levels separately.

In the familiar face-to-face associations of families, organiza-tions, and neighborhoods, I think it is fair to assume that Dewey's image of community resonates with our longings and with some of our most cherished personal experiences. In our present postindus-trial period, the development of community is essential. This recog-nition is explicit in such educational projects as Operation Follow Through, Neighborhood Educational Advisory Councils, most poverty programs, and some open schools and communes. It seems to me that the usual failure of these projects leaves their participants with four conclusions. Extraordinarily hard work at all hours of day and night is required for even a small result, but even so, the ideal of community seems more right than ever; and the assembly line and research and development technologies, as normally understood and applied, do not work. Our faith in them has misled us and accounts, in large measure, for our difficulties.

For dialogue at the national level, Dewey pinned considerable hope on the development of communications technology. National TV, radio, movies, conferences, associations, journals, federal bureaucratic networks, and all the rest certainly do provide the tools, but they have not noticeably developed the profession. The national communication technologies make plenty of input available to educators in local communities, but this input is of no avail except as persons, through local dialogue, search out its private and public implications for their joint action.

It is true that people watch TV, read books, and try to influence legislation. Scientists and practitioners find out things, publish them, and sometimes tell about them on talk shows. The president sends up a trial balloon. Newspapers, TV, and articles in journals register reactions. Personages take positions, offer rationales, demonstrate logic. Legislation is or is not passed. And federal agencies scatter inducements to local groups to mend their ways.

The public dialogue is unorganized and haphazard. To clarify it, I offer (with well-merited diffidence) the allegory of the dialogic pool. This contains and is composed of the expressed concerns, ideas, metaphors, slogans, recollections of past events, opinions, scientific findings, and popular know-how that constitute the content of public discussion. It is into this pool that scientists (for example)' toss their findings. The findings make a small eddy and then, perhaps, sink without a trace (onto a library shelf from which they may or may not ever be exhumed), or they get scooped out of the pool, worked over, and thrown back in a new, more manageable form, a report of an application, a novel they stimulated. Perhaps they float under the nose of some politician who is fishing for good vote-getting issues, and he refers to them in a speech (torrent) that provokes a nationwide reaction (flood). The scientist who tossed them into the pool may later haul out something that accidentally catches his eye only to discover that it is a total misrepresentation or an immoral application of what he thinks his findings were.

This pool, with its dialogic crosscurrents, bleaching action, and dissolving and aggregating powers, injects the outcomes of individual experiences into society. There may be any number of little input streams from the various specialized communities (scientific, economic, welfare, black) down which they may float their wisdom in elegant little packages, but unless the tide is running in the pool, the packages just accumulate, like delta sand, doing no good and, worse, blocking navigation upstream, in the pursuit of public interests, to the source of knowledge.

In all this fishing out, working over, throwing back, and recycling of ideas, there is a continual sorting process. Some notions are in the pool for a day, others for years. These latter grow like coral reefs, associating to themselves other relevant thoughts. In the large pool, they form small floating islands of established concerns, and, from time to time, some islands are beached and others are in the middle of the maelstrom. These ever-changing but always identifiable islands are landmarks in the dialogic pool.

These permanent islands are the premises of the dialogue, the roots of the deeper questions that float in and out of active concern. There is no final answer to these questions, which is why they are perennial, but their existence and continual reinterpretation over the centuries forms, orients, and charts the history of human communities.

We educators must become adept, after local screening and formulation, at getting our better ideas into this national pooled discourse. Further, we must develop the habit of fishing in the pool, skillfully extracting intriguing ideas, and working them over with our partners. But the most difficult and essential requirement is that we discern among the islands of the pool an agenda for continuing, long-range educational dialogue, and, even more, that we see this educational dialogue as integral to the total economic, political, and spiritual dialogue of society. As we develop these capabilities, we shall learn that changes in the operation of schools and training programs are inevitable by-products of professional dialogue and that action is the consummation of ideas rather than a separate end in itself.

From Morass to Music

The nature of present educational discussion developed from the circumstances of the educational enterprise within society. The circumstances are: that education processes and thought are dominated by a preindustrial traditional orientation (the cultural archetype); that the educational system is part and parcel of an overall society whose dominant orientation is industrial (the assembly line and research and development ethos); and that the function of present discussion in education is mainly to resolve discrepancies between the two orientations and bring the educational system more organically within the societal system. But even during this process, the new romanticism of the postindustrial society (with its mixture of reformism and reconstructionism) is upon us. Instead of resolving discrepancies between the two established orientations, discussion will have to take on a larger, more complex, qualitatively different function—that of creatively seeking integration among all three orientations.* The creative conjoint seeking will involve a conscious effort to develop our capability for a new mode of discourse that I call professional dialogue.

To examine the nature of present discussion and how it will have to change, let us start with some fragments taken from faculty meetings. In each fragment I shall juxtapose ideas that were uttered at different times within the same meeting and simply allowed to stand on the record.

Since true learning is a voluntary process, it must be gratifying to the student. You do not really learn anything without hard work.

A teacher who tells the class what to do, how to do it, and when to stop doing it is hiding his sense of inadequacy under a cloak of authoritarianism. He is meeting the students' needs for security-giving structure.

---

* This is an appropriate place to acknowledge gratefully many profitable hours of discussion with the staffs of the Education Policy Research Centers at Syracuse and Stanford.

A teacher who habitually asks the kids what they think is floundering and grasping at straws. He is genuinely concerned for development of the kids' interests and sophistication.

A teacher should work hard to make his presentations interesting and even exciting. When kids get excited and start whispering to each other, the teacher should call them to order.

If a child finds class work dull and uninteresting and does not learn, he should be put in a class to drill endlessly on fundamentals. Drilling on fundamentals is the dullest of all classroom activities.

If a child loves learning and doing school work and achieves very well, he should be rewarded with the privilege of getting out of class.

The faculty should get ready to go on strike if the school board adopts the proposed system of merit pay. Competition for grades is a necessary spur to learning for children.

A B grade means that the child is at the 70th percentile. A B grade means that the child is pretty well living up to his own ability. (Correlation between the two measures is zero.)

A good teacher is one whose children all master the subject. If a teacher gives As to more than 30 percent of the class, there is something wrong with him or his course.

The purpose of education is individual self-realization and effective participation in society. The best measure of educational progress is standardized verbal-achievement tests.

A teacher should treat everybody as an individual, which means responding differently to different students. The most important characteristic of a good teacher is fairness, which means treating everybody just the same.

It is important that boys and girls be in the same classroom so they can learn to get along together. Classrooms should be dignified places and all whispering, silliness, or signs of undue intimacy should be suppressed.

We should have a committee to draw up a code of ethics for our teachers. Everyone knows that the only real crime is whatever results in a parent's complaining to the principal.

Our principal is gung-ho for participatory democracy in the classroom. Just make sure it cannot be heard in the hall.

Classes should follow their own inquiries. All classes in tenth-grade English must cover the same things.

Present discussion is based on the assumptions that contradictions are an occupational disease; that there is no effective way to deal with contradictions; that if there were, teachers would be incapable of implementing it; that all opinions of teachers have equal warrant; that the content of discussion in schools is unimportant because what really matters is fellowship, loyalty, or interpersonal relations; and that practices are so fixed and sacred that a new idea could not be adopted anyway.

Professional dialogue will be based on a different assumption: that teachers can develop the capability of professional discipline. Professional discipline is composed of skills, attitudes, sets, knowledge, and techniques, but what makes it whole is the incorporation of these components within a special mode of personal striving that goes on under the conditions of dialogue. An individual cannot develop this capability by himself, although solitary meditation is necessary to it. The capability does not develop through fellowship, although this relationship may facilitate it. An individual can not get very far merely by studying Dewey, even though without it he will surely be an educational ignoramus. Similarly, participating in ideological protest, raising one's family life to the level of art, cooperating in service to the community, and writing a chapter like this do provide useful experiential input, but they may or may not be exercises in professional discipline.

The difference between discussion and dialogue can be conveyed most cogently by an analogy. Let us compare four string instrumentalists individually practicing their scales and passages versus playing as a quartet. In both cases, the operation occurs in the same room at the same time; the players are affected by each other's behavior; each privately gets something out of it; and much of the content of performance is the same. The obvious difference is that the quartet makes music and that the members are not free to practice in accordance with their own wishes.

In a beginning quartet, effort is coordinated through the written score, which programs a sequence of external demands that each player must meet, and individuals are typically anxious about creditably getting over the tough spots. (This is like leader-dominated recitation.) But as professional discipline develops, the score becomes only a set of familiar guideposts, objective existential cues, and the authority for coordinating effort becomes a shared feeling of the quality to strive for along with a shared intention to attain this quality.

Discipline is not merely proficiency in skills, aesthetic appreciation, and knowledge of requirements. It is also meditative awareness of these elements and anticipation of their potentially significant conjoint consequences, and it is the voluntary commitment of each participant to use this awareness intelligently to shape his performance and insight toward the evolving end.

Anatomy of Dialogue

The stuff of intelligence is awareness, and in the conversion of undisciplined discussion to professional dialogue, four features need to be singled out for special attention. That these features differ markedly from one person to the next is a potential source of strength for the profession.

Experiential Universe. Experiences of its members are the profession's direct contact with existential reality, the world of people, acts, emotions, and materials. One's experience is not defined by the job he holds, although job descriptions suggest something about one's opportunity for different sorts of experience. The distinction between twenty years of experience and one year of experience repeated twenty times is worth making. Persons differ both in how and what they experience, which is uniquely determined by the personal–social life context of their jobs. Two persons in identical situations have different experiences.

A number of implications flow from this simple, obvious, and often-ignored fact. First, since the uniqueness of experience in seemingly similar jobs is the ultimate source of creativity within the profession, we must learn to respect each other's experiences. If we do not, we shall (as at present) cut off from the profession the input that it most saliently needs.

Second, all further processes of awareness, theorizing, and application are limited and biased by one's experience or, more precisely, by how his experience is internalized. That is, each person, through experiencing, develops what appear to the observer to be basic assumptions about the nature, meaning, utility, processes, and expectations of education. Regardless of what he says, each person acts as if he has a theory or rationale of education. These typically hidden rationales determine the quality of further experience. They generate selective resistance, distortion, or insensitivity to new stimuli as well as openness and reaching out. In many persons, these unaware rationales seem like builtin individual variants of the cultural archetype or the assembly line ethos. These variants may embody some new insight or creative approach, although considerable digging may be required to find it.

Quest for Awareness: Educational Relevance. With awareness, the person is transmuted from involuntary reactor to autonomous actor. Without awareness, intelligence and self-direction are not possible, and education reduces to training.

It is at the level of awareness, somewhere between the levels of experience and theory, that the problems of the profession come into the starkest focus. Each specialty—research, teaching, administration—not only attends to some of the raw materials of experience, it also deliberately shuts out other aspects, often overriding the clamor of its own intuitions. Awareness is a kind of knowledge, and knowledge destroys innocence. What are the things we dare not, in our various jobs, be aware off? What are the humane intuitions we have to suppress because knowledge is too confounding or even painful? A partial list would include: the researcher whose concepts restrict mastery learning to specific performances; the inner-city teacher who feels that he can keep order only by sacrificing interest in individual pupils; the teacher-trainer who settles for grinding out technicians because his students are too immature for education; the theorists and leaders who connive with publishers to convince teachers that going at one's own rate is all there is to individualization; the bureaucrats and school boards who allow Moynihan's and Coleman's work to persuade them that inner-city schools are hopeless; the teachers who willingly go along with upper-status parents who insist on ability grouping; and the one thousand and one other instances in which the criterion of plausibility displaces the criterion of fidelity to experience.

People's awarenesses differ, then, by virtue of different experiential content, subconscious and expedient patterns of defense, job specifications of what is relevant, and skills attuned to realizing some kinds of awareness but not others (as when a teacher's vocabulary for describing pupils is so limited that he can only sort them out as bright and dull). Articulated awarenesses of the various participants in a dialogue constitute its manifest content and differences among awarenesses tend to drive the group toward greater public reason and greater private meaning. Development of awareness during dialogue is the pipeline, however leaky or constricted, between the culture or orientation of the profession and the real world that education as a vocation must accept and respect.

Organization of Awareness: Theory. Man is a pattern-seeking animal. Inconsistency and conflict among his awarenesses is painful, which, incidentally, helps to account for the abortion of an awareness that one senses could not, if allowed to fructify, fit into the already more consciously developed pattern. The name for selecting, suppressing, and distorting awareness to fit a preconceived pattern or thought is neurosis. The neurosis so prevalent in education that it is practically an occupational disease is suppression and distortion of educational intuition by the sacred preconceived pattern of practices that we call schooling. Apart from strong publicly exerted social and political pressures, there is an additional special reason for the susceptibility of our profession to this sort of neuroticism: Our experiences with teaching-learning processes is so multidimensional that it defies comprehension. We intuit this multi-dimensionality: We sense that we are in fact (regardless of the rhetoric of curriculum-makers) dealing with the whole child and with classroom microsocieties; that as we talk to a child we are also responding in some way to his parents and community; that when we give a grade we are at one and the same time acknowledging past performance, encouraging or dissuading from further pursuits, assessing growth, and rewarding or punishing service to our aspirations. Given this bewildering complexity in which past, present, and future, experience, awareness, and theory are inextricably mingled with thought, feeling and action, it is no wonder that we seek simplistic theories and then legitimate them with passionate ideologies in the hope of gaining protection from the disorderly and terrifying onslaught of experiential common sense.

Yet each simple theory or procrustean concept does contain some piece of the truth. Our neurosis is not in having limited theories, but in trying uncritically to make too much of our experience fit them and in ignoring the experiences that do not. The ideal educator would know the competing theories and their ideologies—psychotechnical, process, discourse, and doctrinal (types identified in 1972 by my colleagues in the Department of Curriculum and Instruction at the University of Chicago)—and then he would disregard them. He would assimilate each as the embodiment of a form, design, or mode of thought and action, and these forms would become a repertoire of templates, a propositional inventory for constructing strategies of conduct.

It is in this connection that our colossal misinterpretation of the contribution of behavioral science to education becomes appallingly evident. We have simply misread the intelligence of research. Findings are fragments of awareness, but their meaning is in the experience that produced them, not in their predictive or authoritative scientific truth. To be useful to education, a piece of research must be regarded primarily as a thoroughly explicated course of conduct in a carefully described and therefore severely limited situation. (The fact that most accounts of research completely fail as narratives makes them practically useless for educators.*) Seen in this way, research is useful to the extent that it clarifies coherent prototypes or that it models segments of our broader educational experience. Research is deleterious if we allow the prestige of its scientific findings to override our intuitive reservations. It is simply neurotic to assume that learning outcomes should replicate experimental results; and before reaching that conclusion we should ask ourselves what relevance the processes of the experiment and the hidden assumptions of the researcher have for the vocation, not merely for the technique, of education. Thus, for example, research can show us how to condition responses to certain kinds of stimuli, but we ourselves must decide to what extent and in what circumstances the conditioning process in all of its ramifica-

* Thanks to Professor Joseph J. Schwab.

tions (including those "controlled out" by the experimental design) may be educational or antieducational.

Unifying Principle: Vocation. The essence of dialogue is the quest for relationships among experience, awareness, and theory. These diverse, often seemingly intransigent elements can be accepted and used only to the extent that they can be ordered by means of a unifying principle. I believe that the unifying principle that can make diverse inputs a source of strength rather than a perpetuation of chaos is the love that is manifested through the sense of vocation.

Today we no longer look to Providence as the unifying inspiration of our lives or our professions. Where, then, is this inspiration to be found? The search for it has spawned a fantastic variety of movements organized around consumerism, new politics, political ideologies, drug cults, ecumenism, Eastern mystiques, and so on. Like Shaw's black girl in search of God, we have sought our unifying principle in psychological theories, utopias of romantics and ideologues, technical inventions, clothed and unclothed encounters, and political slogans. But these searches have failed. They are useful to organize and promote awareness but useless to organize the larger dialogue in which awareness is only one component, although it is a major one. The search, to be successful, must guide us into a style of life in which the quests for form and context illuminate both. The outcomes of this search will be both public and private. The public outcome will be educational policy to which all the various parts and resources of the societal-educational system may contribute and through which the parts can voluntarily coordinate their semiautonomous effort. The private outcome will be meaning and growth within individuals. At any moment, the outcomes so far achieved will serve as inputs whose interaction will drive further dialogue, and, as this occurs, the nature and sense of the unifying and guiding principle, vocation, will become increasingly clear and trustworthy.

Commitment to the joint search for vocation is the authority under whose aegis the conduct and nurturance of professional dialogue—and its material by-product, the educative system—will gradually evolve.

What is the nature of this sense of vocation that is so desperately needed?

Substance of Vocation

Just as the substance of awareness is experience and the substance of theory is awareness, the substance of the unifying principle of vocation is concern. The qualities of humaneness—compassion and enlightenment—are central to any vocation. Concern without compassion is empty, and concern without enlightenment is futile. Humane studies in philosophy, theology, literature, and cultural anthropology can be seen as attempts to identify and explicate the perennial concerns of men and societies. I do not believe that the concerns of a profession can or should ever be authoritatively defined. They have to be defined in terms salient and vital to each culture, each period, each situation. It seems to me that a vocation is defined by its duties in respect to its comprehension of these concerns.

Underlying the shifting definitions of concerns are propositions (metaconcerns) that capture the logic of the enterprise; and they point to the questions that education, because it is education, must always seek situationally effective answers to. Thus the concerns of a vocation have a dual nature: They consist of the questions that have to be asked in order to carry out the functions of the profession and, at the same time, the demands inherent in the larger humane, societal, and transcendent aspirations that the profession is to serve. It is because of this dual relevance, this looking outward and inward at the same time, that the sense of vocation—its patterning of concerns—is the unifying principle of the profession.

These considerations give pause to any individual who thinks he alone can formulate the concerns or underlying propositions for the profession. Still, the reality of the profession is a lot of people thinking, speculating and being concerned together. Since I am one of those people, as a sort of closing benediction to this long chapter, I would like to offer three propositions that seem to me to express our most fundamental concerns in a way useful for guiding our meditation and inquiry into every activity throughout the entire educational system. These concerns are for authenticity, legitimacy, and productivity. I define them as follows:

An activity has authenticity for a participant if he understands it in such terms that he can participate in it intelligently; if he can assimilate the experience it engenders with other past experiences; and if it is meaningful to him. In authentic activity, one feels alive, challenged, and turned on, and he can control the extent and manner of his investment in such feelings. He listens to others, who are accepted as meaningful in the situation, and he senses activities as dramatic, as episodes with beginning, middle, and end.

An activity is legitimated by reason, as distinguished from capricious-seeming teacher demand, acting-out impulse, mere availability, or impenetrable habit. An activity may be legitimated by group purposes, disciplines of knowledge, career demands, test objectives, requirements, societal issues, laws, or by any other larger, organized context that enables the activity to go beyond its own particulars to become a prototype or model for a broad class of enterprises throughout life. Some present bases of legitimacy in classrooms have little relevance to education; others are central.

An activity is productive to the extent that it is effective for some purpose. The purpose may be as clear as completing a defined task or as esoteric as arriving at a sense of the meeting. It is awareness of purpose that makes means-ends thinking possible, allows consciousness and self-direction, tests self-concepts against reality, and makes practice add up to capability.

We shall develop the profession of education through dialogue that overlaps all parts and levels of the educational enterprise. The dialogue will respect and utilize experience, awareness, and theories of all participants. These substantive elements will be integrated by shared concerns for the authenticity, legitimacy, and productivity of each activity. The outcomes of dialogue will be public policy for action and private reconstruction of meanings. The capability of each person, which will develop and be developed by his participation in dialogue, is professional discipline, and the accumulation of this capability will shape anew the humble vocation and proud profession of education.

Chapter 14

Liberal Arts Perspective

Leon D. Epstein

No one should claim to speak for all or even for most liberal arts professors on the subject of teacher education. Views must vary as greatly as do experiences in different disciplines, institutions, generations, and responsibilities. Without a systematic survey of professorial attitudes, the most that one of us can attempt is to describe the perspective of those liberal arts professors whose situations are much like one's own and whose views are familiar from collegial associations.

In my case, this means writing primarily from observations of faculty members at a major state university campus whose liberal arts departments are committed to important graduate training and research programs along with large-scale undergraduate teaching. I know most about my own colleagues in political science, somewhat less about other social scientists, and considerably less about the

214

humanities and natural science professors whose views I encountered while I was a liberal arts administrator. Even this limited familiarity, I should emphasize, excludes the significant minority of liberal arts professors who directly participate in teacher education. I know only of their existence, as joint appointees of liberal arts departments and the department of curriculum and instruction of the school of education. I know only at second hand about the contribution of academic subject-matter specialists to the revision of secondary school programs, of which the new mathematics is the most famous example. The perspective of these participants may be decidedly different from that of the professors whose views I seek to represent. But the latter, whose relations to teacher education are only incidental to their other work, seem the more usual, at least in liberal arts departments in my kind of university.

By describing certain relevant characteristics of the situation of many liberal arts professors, I hope to explain their limited involvement. I want to do so in a spirit of neutrality, however unfashionable that has become in educational controversies. It is as facts of academic life that I suggest seven distinguishing marks of the liberal arts perspective, numbered for convenience although their substance overlaps.

First and most important in determining the other characteristics is the commanding commitment to academic subject matter. The liberal arts professor shares this commitment with many professional school colleagues, differing only in the degree to which the stress is on exclusively academic learning as opposed to what is derived from experience. Subject matter provides the focus of knowledge, whether of facts, analysis, principles, concepts, theories, or research methods. How to communicate the knowledge is decidedly secondary. It may be helpful in earning a living, particularly in some fields, but knowledge of one's subject is what is crucial for self-esteem as well as for peer-group rankings.

At least two general types of academic subject-matter commitment are found among liberal arts professors. One is associated with the apparently diminishing tradition of humanistic scholarship and the other with a more highly specialized, scientific, and professional training. But these types have much in common. The humanist defines his subject matter more broadly and perhaps less rigorously. He loves it no less. And he thinks it no less important to know about it. I emphasize this because I believe it mistaken to regard the subject-matter identification of liberal arts professors as a product only of recent tendencies toward narrower specialization, more scientific learning, and greater professionalization of graduate work. These tendencies are real enough, and they have contributed to the nature of the subject-matter commitment in ways that I shall try to elucidate later. But the older humanistic tradition has made its contribution, too. The present generation of faculty members is not the only one who has been attracted to graduate studies and so to university positions because of an interest in a particular subject or, more precisely, because of an interest in learning more about it. Such a commitment has loomed larger in the liberal arts faculty of a university than has any primarily teaching commitment even though professors have been known to enjoy teaching their subject in addition to learning about it.

I can best illustrate my point about the humanistic contribution and at the same time underscore the theme of professorial subject-matter commitment by drawing upon Highet's *The Art of Teaching*. As a classics professor at Columbia, famous for his writing and his teaching, Highet is surely a splendid example of the humanist tradition. Moreover, his book on teaching has been popular among liberal arts professors, and aspiring liberal arts professors, for over twenty years. There is a good reason for this popularity. Not only is the book written with style, learning, and reasonableness, but it also says what liberal arts professors have always believed. Notably, Highet specifies that the first and most necessary of the qualities of a good teacher is that he know the subject that he teaches, and that this requisite knowledge requires the kind of understanding that comes only from advanced and continued learning at the higher levels of subject matter and at the frontiers where new discoveries are made. Highet's second essential of good teaching is closely related: The teacher must like the subject that he teaches. He adds third and fourth essentials of a different kind, namely, that the teacher should like his pupils and that he should know the young as such (1950, pp. 12–35). But it is plain where the priority lies.

Significantly, the subject-matter emphasis holds despite the apparent inclusion of secondary teaching along with college teaching in the context of Highet's discussion. Here Highet may differ from other liberal arts professors, but only in specifically taking noncollegiate teaching into account. There is good reason to believe that his university peers would similarly accept the primacy of subject-matter learning for teaching generally if they too contemplated noncollegiate education. The primacy follows from the experience of liberal arts faculty members. And, as Highet exemplifies, the older, broader, and more humanistic tradition is part of this determining experience.

Within a university and particularly within its liberal arts college, it is not clear to me that the apostles of the humanistic tradition are any less highly organized around their subject matter than are their newer and more professional-minded colleagues. The academic department is every professor's fortress, and the liberal arts department is firmly linked to a body of knowledge about a definable subject. Subjects have become more specialized, and so subdepartments or entirely new departments have been added to accommodate the specializations. The pattern, however, is well established. It has not been substantially affected in the past, any more than it is now, by occasional experiments in general and interdisciplinary education. Most liberal arts professors have remained outside such experiments altogether even if they have tolerated them in their colleges. Some have participated to the extent of contributing their specialized subject matter to symposium courses listed under interdisciplinary rubrics, while others have developed an essentially new subject matter that itself finds a new departmental home. Only a few have sought to establish themselves as generalists. To do so goes against the academic grain. It is very different from collaboration among specialists, legitimated by the subject-matter learning of each, and it is very different from the development of a new discipline from elements of older fields combined with new research findings.

There seems little doubt about the durability of the disciplinary structure. It helps explain the limited success of the general education programs started after World War II and the trend away from such programs in the 1960s (Bell, 1966; Jencks and Riesman, 1968, pp. 498–499, 504). And it helps explain why liberal arts professors conceive of education generally, precollegiate as well as collegiate, as rightly organized around certain recognized subjects of learning. The suspicion is strong that generally labeled courses or curricula, claiming to synthesize or to be interdisciplinary, really conceal loose and uninformed notions. Social science, for example, is not a subject that anyone can claim to have mastered or even to have had the chance to master in his university training.

One other aspect of the subject-matter commitment needs to be noted. That is its academic rather than practitioner emphasis. Liberal arts professors insist on scholarly credentials for entry into their university teaching fields, and they are almost as certain to believe that similarly derived credentials are essential for good teaching generally. In their own departments, the symbol is the doctor of philosophy degree, embodying the certification of advanced knowledge of a given subject matter and of research training in gathering new knowledge of that subject matter. Occasionally, especially in an older generation, the requisite demonstration of scholarship has been accomplished outside the formal doctoral route. But such demonstration is supposed to have been the rough equivalent of the product of graduate training. It has almost never meant acceptance of experience as a substitute for academic learning. At most, a liberal arts department might regard practitioner experience as enhancing the capacity of a professor otherwise equipped as a scholar. So it has been in political science, where legislative, administrative, or even campaigning experience is treated as a useful but neither a necessary nor a frequent supplement to conventional academic learning.

Where the situation has differed is in those fields that, although often attached to liberal arts colleges, are really outside the traditional mainstream. Journalism, social work, and the performing arts come to mind. Practitioners as such need to be appointed here in order to teach prospective practitioners, and they do not always combine the requisite experience with scholarly backgrounds. Insofar as appointments of nonscholars are made in a given situation, the faculty departs from the conventions of the liberal arts. But insofar as scholarship is required, either to the exclusion of work experience or in addition to it, the particular faculty resembles a liberal arts department, as now occurs especially in journalism but also in certain other originally practioner-oriented fields. The point remains that academic credentials are crucial to liberal arts status. The way for a field to gain status is to require credentials for all or for almost all of its professors.

No departure from the academic character of subject-matter learning is involved in the increased mobility between universities and government and industry. Physicists and economists, for example, move back and forth for both short and long periods, but they do so as specialists whose academic subject-matter training, including the Ph.D. degree, equips them with the scholarly credentials required by governmental and industrial-research establishments no less than by universities. They are not like businessmen in relation to an economics department, politicians to a political science department, or even creative writers to an English literature department, all of whom tend to be no more than visiting lecturers. Rather, the previously cited physicists and economists, even while in nonuniversity employment, are the fellow professionals of faculty members sharing their specialization. They contribute to the same journals and belong to the same academic associations. They are potential professorial colleagues, in a way that is not established solely by experience as practitioners in a particular field. And, be it well noted, they are potential colleagues even though their careers may have had little or no involvement with teaching. Nothing more sharply indicates the significance of the subject matter commitment of university professors.

The second closely related characteristic of the liberal arts perspective can be described much more briefly. It is the belief in the teacher's freedom and autonomy, once scholarly peers are satisfied concerning subject-matter competence. There is little disposition to check systematically classroom performances of junior colleagues or even to supervise closely the work of graduate teaching assistants. Efforts by administrators or external authorities to impose such checking or supervision are unpopular among most professors, junior, and senior. So are campaigns for any degree of uniformity in teaching methods, grading, or course content. The prevailing ethos is highly individualistic. Quite conventional professors are usually prepared to tolerate the eccentric and the bizarre among their colleagues as the price for their own freedom. If a colleague's performance must be judged, then only the scholarly peer group, usually the department and certainly not a hierarchical management, is equipped to make the judgment. But such judgment, in my university experience, is almost always favorable or no worse than neutral with respect to teaching performance. I am uncertain whether this reflects an unwillingness or an unability to find adverse evidence. In either case, I suspect that it is connected to the professor's preference for noninterference with his colleague's teaching and with his own.

The consequent absence of much emphasis on critical evaluation of classroom performance can be justified if it is assumed that subject-matter competence itself is the overwhelmingly important criterion for good teaching. With that assumption, all that is needed is rigorous evaluation of scholarly work, especially as evidenced by publications, and many professors of my acquaintance have been both willing and able to offer that evaluation. Here negative findings are frequent, although perhaps not usual. The contrast to the customarily favorable or neutral evaluation of classroom performance is striking. The characteristically nonnegative evaluation of classroom performance does not seem to have greatly changed during the recent upsurge of interest in the systematic gathering of student opinions of their teachers. This is not so much because of an absence of professorial attention to the student opinions as because of the generally favorable opinions, in varying degrees, registered by the students. The student evaluations, although helpful in many ways, do not provide much evidence for adverse professorial judgment.

The third characteristic may seem a partial rewording of the second, but it is worth calling attention to the liberal arts professor's belief that teaching is an art rather than a science, if only to explain further the tolerance extended to classroom performance. Most liberal arts professors have never been interested in systematic methods of teaching. They doubt whether the methods are reducible to a science (Highet, 1950, p. vii). And so they doubt whether the general study of methods can exist in respectable academic form (Conant, 1963, p. 138). If it does, it is not their professional subject. Their profession is chemistry, economics, history, or some other academic subject. Liberal arts professors identify themselves this way

in relation to each other and in relation to other specialists in the
same subject who happen to be working outside a university. It is
true that they also consider themselves teachers, at any rate university teachers or professors, but mainly in relation to portions of
the lay public (including their less advanced students). The word
educator is avoided whenever possible despite (or perhaps because
of) the use of this term in *Who's Who* for all school and college
personnel, administrators and professors alike.

Among liberal arts professors, Jencks and Riesman are certainly correct in saying that "teaching is not a profession in the way
that research is" (1968, p. 531). This need not mean that most
professors neglect their own teaching. It is often their main occupation. But they are unlikely themselves to have had any systematic
teacher training, and they are unlikely to provide any for their
students or to encourage them to seek it elsewhere. The closest that
liberal arts professors tend to come to teacher training is to believe
that something about teaching can be learned from example, particularly by a graduate student from his major professor, and that a
few years of experience will be helpful in improving classroom
performance. These beliefs may be linked to occasional treatment of
graduate teaching assistantships as useful apprenticeships for prospective professors, and they may also lead to sympathy for the
practice-teaching programs provided by schools of education. But
they do not support anything like a specialization in methods of
teaching or in curriculum planning. Here, diametrically different
from his attitude toward his own subject matter, the liberal arts
professor subscribes to the cult of the amateur.

There are obvious negative sides to this cult. Not only do
many liberal arts professors ignore systematic teacher training, but
some have also been openly hostile to that which exists in schools of
education, particularly to the study of methods (Barzun, 1954, pp.
9, 180). Others have attacked teacher certification requirements
that involve specific training courses (Conant, 1963, p. 7). But
generally an absence of interest seems more typical than overt
hostility. After all, liberal arts professors are not threatened or
seriously troubled by whatever it is schools of education are trying
to do. And in recent years, as schools of education have increasingly
identified themselves with the scholarly standards and even the

scholarly subjects of the liberal arts, there is a growing realization that their old emphasis on methods may be diminishing.

The amateur approach to teaching also has a positive side. It is the belief in the importance of liking, really of loving, one's subject, in other words, amateurism in the literal sense of the term. This is the quality, it will be recalled, that Highet places second only to knowledge of subject matter as the essential for good teaching and that seems to follow from the emphasis on knowledge itself. To know a subject thoroughly and deeply is to love it, because of the subject's original attractions and because of the subsequent learning. It is understandable that liberal arts professors look for enthusiasm about subject matter in any prospective colleague. Practically, when considering a new young appointee, this means enthusiasm about a specialized research project, often a doctoral dissertation, on the ground that one has to be enthusiastic about one's own work in order to demonstrate a continuing interest in the subject matter more generally. If it seems unwarranted to assume that the enthusiasm exhibited in this form will automatically make for successful classroom communication even at the introductory undergraduate level, it is at least reasonable to believe that without this kind of enthusiasm successful classroom teaching is most improbable. It is a necessary although not so clearly a sufficient condition for first-rate teaching.

Beyond thinking that experience, largely on one's own, will usually help develop the art of teaching, liberal arts professors seem to have no doctrine about the requisites that should be added to knowledge and enthusiasm. Professors certainly vary considerably in the degree and the kind of attention they give to their own teaching performances. Humanities professors, of whom Highet is a good example, are most plainly conscious of the value of artistry itself. After all, given their subject matter, it is natural that professors of literature, art appreciation, and perhaps history should be concerned with the aesthetics of their presentations. They are not the only professors seeking to dramatize their subjects, but they are the likeliest to know how to do so just as they are the likeliest to think it important to try. Natural and social scientists, apart from those with native dramatic talents to exploit, tend to limit their aspirations to developing nonaesthetic skill in exposition. Perhaps it is really skill that most professors mean when they talk about the art of teaching. This fits the belief that the way to learn how to teach, if it can be learned at all, is from one's own practice and trial and error rather than from a science of methods. Professors may believe that almost everything else can be learned from systematically gathered knowledge, but not how to teach. (Nor, it ought to be added, do professors believe that academic administration is learned in this way; here, too, the cult of the amateur prevails, as is evidenced by the preference for academic colleagues to assume university administrative positions.)

Fourth in my accounting of the liberal arts perspective is the customary acceptance of lecturing in classroom teaching. Most liberal arts professors, at least in large universities, do the great bulk if not all of their undergraduate classroom teaching by some version of the lecture method. The word *classroom* is an important modifier. Professors teach in many ways outside the classroom. In fact, they are not in formal classroom situations during many working hours. But when they are in undergraduate classrooms, in contrast to graduate seminar rooms, they most often come primarily as lecturers. Understandably, then, they are bound to regard their classroom roles as different in kind from those of primary and secondary school teachers who are expected to do something other than lecture. And they can regard their subject-matter knowledge as the overwhelmingly important basis for competency as lecturers, whatever else might be needed for other methods of teaching.

I need to qualify this emphasis in certain respects. Professors do not ordinarily defend the lecture as the best way to impart factual information. Their own prized subject-matter knowledge is more about understanding than about facts. Moreover, they are aware of the printing press, the mimeograph machine, and even xerography as means of communicating information; professors surely use these means, as their output of written publications amply indicates. But they will defend the lecture as a way to increase understanding of particularly difficult material or as a way to raise the level of interest through effective, even dramatic, oral presentation assisted by laboratory demonstration or other visual aids. Except in very large lecture classes, a value is attached to the opportunity for immediate questioning afforded the student and for interchange generally between a live professor and his students. The exception noted for very large classes is significant because it is by no means rare or even unusual, and because it is more frequent now than in earlier times. If so, the consequence is to make for greater, or more thoroughgoing, dependence on the lecture method. There are professors who deplore any such trend because they prefer the lecture class of only about thirty to seventy on the ground that it permits considerable exchange between teacher and students. Other professors, less typical of those accustomed to large universities, have always deplored lectures as the major undergraduate teaching method and express preferences for a Socratic technique or for some other highly individualized style requiring very small classes or even one-to-one tutorial situations. More professors, as well as more students, may come to prefer these methods, but the lecture remains now as in the past the principal means by which liberal arts professors communicate in their undergraduate classrooms.

The fifth professional characteristic is to assume that college teaching is of adults rather than children. Like many of the other characteristics noted here, it is one that liberal arts faculties share with other college-level faculties, one that they believe sets their work apart from that of secondary school teachers. So sharp a distinction makes little sense if it is thought to rest solely on the difference between high school seniors and college freshmen. The small increase in age could hardly be expected to transform learning behavior from a childhood pattern to an adult pattern. Besides, any reasonable person grants that some high school students are either already adult learners or capable of such status and that some college students are not. But the collegiate assumption about teaching adults derives from no simple belief in the difference between the ages of seventeen and eighteen. Rather it comes from the belief that college learning is and ought to be different from high school learning and that only those equipped by native intellectual capacity, prior school training, and serious inclination are rightly admitted to college. Moreover, those admitted are supposed to remain only by continued demonstration of ability and willingness to learn.

These qualifications, not just age, are the bases for distinguishing college students. Perhaps, therefore, it is misleading to use the term *adult*. Admittedly, college students are in no usual sense any more adult than others of their same age who do not go to college, and until just lately most undergraduate college students, ages eighteen to twenty-one, were not adults in legal usage. Furthermore, adult education has specifically pertained to a generation beyond college age. But I use adult here anyway, because it most nearly expresses the attitudes of professors in dealing with their students in contrast to their conceptions of precollege students. I speak only about the professorial attitudes toward students as learners. Whether most professors regard their students as adults in other respects is disputable. Nor do I go so far as to say that there is a peer-group relationship between professors and students, especially undergraduate students.

More significant than academic admission standards in distinguishing many college students is the voluntary nature of enrollment. Some, it is true, are subject to selection or rejection by particular institutions of their choice, but in the United States they have almost always been able to gain admission to a college somewhere. The main restraints against enrolling altogether have been economic rather than intellectual. Otherwise, college students can be said to select themselves. Despite various degrees of parental encouragement, there has been a strong voluntary element in college enrollment, certainly a much stronger one than in high school enrollment.

I should not want to leave the impression that there is an unawareness of changes in the nature of this voluntary tradition. I teach in a large state university whose enrollments have greatly increased under the impact of new assumptions about the need or desirability of higher education. I know of the pressures in some communities and in some families that make it seem almost obligatory to seek and gain college admission. And I know full well the consequent pressures to retain, and even to graduate, students who have come only more or less willingly to college and who have pursued their studies with hardly any interest. In fact, the type is not entirely new in a state university; it has only become more numerous. But even now, in my experience, motivated students remain dominant. They would want to come even without community and family pressures. Certainly most of the unmotivated do not come. Much of the old basis for the assumption about adult learning is still valid, even in mass higher education. No doubt, the assumption holds more fully in highly selective institutions, particularly certain private colleges, and least fully in community colleges or in some other public institutions serving a diverse local population. It may have become more widely operative on major state university campuses, especially during the 1960s, as it became possible for those campuses to increase their selectivity, *de facto* if not *de jure,* because other state institutions developed to absorb new applicants. One may call this an elitist element in the tradition of American colleges and universities (Bigelow, 1971, p. xliv). Insofar as it is an elitism based on educational merit, liberal arts professors are almost certain to subscribe to it now just as they have in the past. It survives in many places although the United States seems at the brink of universal rather than merely mass higher education (Trow, 1970, pp. 1–42).

Admittedly, even within a particular college, the degree of adult learning differs by course level. An introductory course, if not literally required, tends to have many students whose enrollment in that particular course is not entirely by free choice. But in advanced undergraduate courses, which are what most professors teach, it is fair to assume that almost all students have chosen the courses because of some interest in their subject matter, whether or not they are pursuing the relevant majors. Most of even these students are not prospective specialists in the particular field. Rather they are nonspecialized students who share the professorial interest in the subject matter without wanting to devote their lives to it. The significant point is the common interest that can be assumed from the start. It provides the basis not only for much of the pleasure that professors find in their teaching, but also for thinking that at least most of that teaching is very different from the classroom efforts needed in meeting the diverse and less highly formed interests of secondary school students.

Another way to put the matter is to say that there is less distance between college professors and their students than between high school teachers and their students. At least, college professors feel that there is less distance. The language here may suggest too much. It seems accurate only when tied closely to the view that college students are more often capable of sharing a highly developed subject-matter interest with their teachers than high school students are with their teachers. In other respects, the teacher-student distance in college may be greater than in high school. Relatively greater age difference is one possibility, and so is the professor's attachment to a professional field other than teaching itself.

Sixth in my listing is the liberal arts professor's separation from the teaching of tool subjects at the introductory level. If he is not separated from it, he certainly believes that he should be. And he has tried hard, probably with increasing success in the 1950s and 1960s, to accomplish the separation. The most straightforward and the preferred way is to require proficiency in tool subjects, particularly English composition, reading skills, elementary mathematics, and beginning foreign language, as a condition for admission to college. Professors at highly selective institutions have usually had the advantage of such admission requirements, enforced by entrance examinations and not just by high school records. State university faculties, unable ordinarily to be so demanding, have tended to require only that certain relevant courses be on the high school record of apparent accomplishment. These formal requirements, however, fall short of the academic preparatory courses insisted upon by the most rigorous private colleges, and state university professors know that many of their admissible high school graduates are not well equipped in the tool subjects despite their earlier course records. The obvious answer has been to provide the essential training in college (to make sure, as the professorial joke goes, that everyone has a good high school education even if it takes four years of college). But except in hard times, professors at state universities (in contrast to many state colleges) do not directly teach any large portion of the needed tool subjects. The customary solution is to have graduate teaching assistants staff the courses in English composition, elementary mathematics, and beginning foreign language, even though the graduate teaching assistants are no more likely than their professors to regard such classroom work as the content of what they want to teach. It is not even clear that the assistants always teach the tool subject as expected, especially in English. Like their professors, they too are committed to a subject-matter learning (literature rather than composition, to adhere to the example of English), and so they may also adopt the view that the tool subjects are not the university's rightful business. In that case, especially if the graduate assistants openly revolt against their chores as happened in the English department on my campus, it may become expedient to eliminate the tool-subject teaching almost completely. The alternative of finding a corps of permanently sub-professorial instructors would seldom be attractive even if it were possible.

Faced with a situation of this sort, liberal arts professors naturally suggest that the high schools devote themselves more thoroughly to training their graduates in the tool subjects. Professors have probably always believed that high schools, no less than elementary, junior, and middle schools, should concentrate heavily on this type of learning along with certain basic and traditional academic background material. The fact that professors themselves do not want to teach the relevant subjects hardly means that they do not want someone else to do so. They are concerned that their prospective students be prepared for college learning. This seems only a sensible division of labor. But it ought to be observed that it is a division between high school and college teaching, or really between the kind of teaching relevant to a high school, even though it has to be done in college, and the more advanced teaching that most liberal arts professors consider their appropriate role.

The seventh and last characteristic of the liberal arts perspective is the professorial tendency toward greater specialization. I said earlier that I thought that subject-matter commitments were overwhelmingly important even before and apart from any recent specialization, but that newer tendencies in the direction of specialization must also be taken into account. Certainly this is true insofar as more liberal arts professors might be removed from teaching all but the most advanced undergraduates (while they concentrate on graduate students and their own research) or might be removed from teaching undergraduates on any regular or frequent basis. The result, in such cases, would be to put professorial work at an even greater distance from high school teaching and from the direct products of high school teaching. Incidentally, too, the liberal arts professors thus removed from nonspecialized undergraduates are removed as well from those undergraduates intending to become school teachers.

No one doubts that increasing specialization has occurred and that it has had some of the impact indicated. More professors now, as contrasted to twenty-five years ago, function at advanced levels largely or wholly removed from unspecialized undergraduate teaching. Others, it may also be granted, spend smaller proportions of their time with undergraduates than they and their colleagues did when research opportunities were more limited, teaching loads heavier, and graduate students fewer. It is doubtful, however, that these changes are so widespread either within universities or among them as to cause a sharply different liberal arts perspective from that which has traditionally existed.

Perhaps in the early and mid-1960s, professors seemed to be moving more decidedly away from undergraduate teaching. Clark Kerr was, I believe, describing this movement at its zenith in time and probably also at a vanguard institution, Berkeley in particular and the University of California pretty generally, when he wrote (originally in 1963–1964) his partly critical account of the neglect of undergraduate teaching (1966, pp. 64–65). Not only were graduate enrollments and research funding then greatly increasing, but also the demand for professors was temporarily rising so much faster than the supply of new Ph.D.'s that, especially at major universities and other prestige institutions, professors were able to secure reductions in their hours of undergraduate classroom teaching. This successful bargaining, with the threat to go elsewhere in the highly favorable market situation, admittedly says a great deal about the inclinations of professors. There is no reason to believe that the inclinations are temporary; they are consistent with characteristic subject-matter commitments and the accompanying tendency to specialized learning. But the widespread indulgence of such inclinations now seems to have been temporary. For the next decade or two, neither the graduate training and research situation nor the general market for faculty service is conducive to such successful bargaining by most professors, even in major universities. And, it should be stressed, this means that liberal arts professors, with relatively few exceptions, will remain committed to large portions of undergraduate teaching. The reductions actually achieved, even if not reversed in the 1970s, affect most professors only marginally. They teach fewer separate undergraduate courses, often fewer courses altogether, but they still teach undergraduates, perhaps in larger numbers than before, and such teaching is still a major portion of their responsibilities, even if it is not as dominating as it was.

It can not be otherwise at strictly undergraduate colleges, including the most prestigious, and it can not be radically different for most liberal arts professors at state universities, however highly developed their graduate and research programs. They may, it is true, teach a smaller proportion of the undergraduate class hours, especially at the freshman and sophomore levels, as graduate assistants do more of it (though less characteristically in the 1970s than in the 1960s), but the professorial teaching roles remain at least at the junior and senior levels. Anyway, regardless of what has happened to the proportion of all undergraduate teaching done by professors, there is little doubt that most liberal arts professors spend substantial amounts of time and energy teaching undergraduates. As suggested before, teaching can be a principal occupation, even if one does not perceive it as one's profession.

To be fair, the most frequent argument about recent tendencies of liberal arts colleges has not been based on the view that professors disengaged themselves from undergraduate teaching altogether, but on the view that they have become much more professionally specialized in their teaching even at the undergraduate level. This is the view of Jencks and Riesman. What they call the university college (1968, p. 24), which mainly prepares students for graduate or professional schools, is said to have superseded the old liberal arts tradition both in major universities and in select private colleges, thus becoming an influential model for faculties in the much larger number of less prestigious institutions. Jencks and Riesman believe that in this way increasingly specialized academics determine the nature of undergraduate education. They sound a note of regret, but mainly accept the university college as an inevitable result of the long-run development of academic work in the United States.

Not all observers of the same phenomenon see it so neutrally or with such detachment. Arrowsmith, writing as a classics professor and more recently as an educational consultant, is a good example of the adverse reaction to growing specialization, professionalism, and scientific training in universities and their impact on teaching. In the name of an older humanistic tradition, he attacks the "elitism of the learned professions" for their destruction of liberal education in the universities (1971, p. 13). Specifically he deplores the consequences for prospective teachers as for undergraduate students generally since he believes that the dominating professionals seek to teach only preprofessionals in their own learned disciplines. Arrowsmith may well regard academic specialization as inevitable, but he would remove its practitioners from control of undergraduate education and presumably from the actual teaching of most undergraduates. Who would then staff the liberal arts colleges, at least in major universities, is not clear. There do not seem to be many prospective professors who share the older and broader humanistic background, and they are not likely to be produced by the graduate programs that Arrowsmith deplores. His own liberal arts commitment to subject matter leads neither to a nonacademic reliance on experience rather than learning nor to training primarily in methods of teaching, curriculum planning, and school management.

Stressing the common liberal arts perspective, however, is not a means to gloss over Arrowsmith's critique of the impact of increasingly specialized learning. I contend only that the impact, although substantial, has not been as drastic as he suggests, partly because it represents a long-run tendency implicit in professorial commitments. Probably I am reflecting my own experience as a modestly specialized professor who is accustomed to spending time and effort in undergraduate teaching, in ways that have not dramatically changed as a result of the greater professionalization of the last quarter century. But I believe that my experience is usual in my age group and in my field. Also I find most of my newer and more highly trained professional colleagues to be just as concerned about responding, and at least as able to respond, to the nonprofessional interests of students as I am. The limitations that exist seem more persistent than novel. Perhaps the situation is different in the humanities, where specialization may detract from an earlier emphasis on the aesthetic appreciation of art and literature.

Regardless of the relative influence of recent specialization, I realize that the seven characteristics that I have described will confirm the view that most liberal arts professors are detached from the concerns of teacher education. Given that view, a critic who would improve teacher education regards liberal arts professors as a serious part of the problem (Bigelow, 1971, p. xli). The point ought to be granted as long as the liberal arts professors continue to teach most of the subjects that prospective school teachers study during undergraduate years. Although liberal arts professors are not immune from suggestions about the needs of prospective teachers, especially when those prospective teachers are numerous in particular courses or institutions, they are likely to teach in ways basically conditioned by the perspective that I have tried to explain. The characteristics of that perspective, attractive or not, have to be taken into account. They are not readily altered since they derive from societal demands, including those for specialization, and not just from self-serving concerns of the professors themselves.

The question that remains is how unfortunate it is, or whether it is unfortunate at all, for most liberal arts professors to be detached from the concerns of teacher education. It is by no means evident that their detachment precludes their making a useful contribution to the preparation of teachers. Conveying knowledge, understanding, and appreciation of their subject matter, in ways that liberal arts professors are both capable of and interested in doing, seems at least as relevant for prospective teachers as it is for college students generally. Might not most liberal arts professors contribute to teacher education simply by being themselves? Lest this sound too much like being content that liberal arts professors help prospective teachers without being conscious of the particular task—without really trying—I quickly add that the performance would benefit from a systematic effort to learn what prospective teachers find most useful about their liberal arts courses. Such an effort, involving a modest interchange between education school professors (as well as their students) and particular liberal arts professors, seems entirely feasible. It must already be occurring in informal, if not formal, ways. It does not basically alter the characterized detachment, but it mitigates the consequences.

Another reason for doubting the unfortunate consequences of the detachment is that the term fits no more than most liberal arts professors. As I said in the beginning of this chapter, a significant minority is more directly participating in teacher education.

This minority may well be sufficient or nearly sufficient for the purpose. After all, no one proposes or wants that all or even any large share of liberal arts professors become actively involved in specific school of education courses or in revising secondary school curricula. The important point is to have the collaboration of some subject matter specialists from liberal arts departments. If the need, or effective demand, is not now being met, the limited necessary recruitment should cause little difficulty. I am impressed that even in my own field of political science, without the traditional relations to high school curricula of history, English, mathematics, and other established fields, highly competent professionals have helped to develop an experimental secondary level course based upon advanced and innovative conceptions of the subject matter. It hardly matters that most political science professors have had nothing directly to do with this development or that most of them might not want to be concerned with it. The many do not have to be called. Enough professors, here as in other fields, are willing and able.

Chapter 15

Responsibilities of the Dean for Reform

Donald J. McCarty

Teacher education is neither appreciated nor honored in our society. Its cultural function is perceived by many even in the university community to be skill development of the most rudimentary kind. The most cruel jokes are invented to depict its plight (those who can perform some useful work do so; those who can not work teach; those who can not teach, teach teachers). Small wonder that schools of education suffer from incredibly low prestige. A recent Wisconsin symposium on productivity in the public sector put it succinctly when its final report pointed out that inadequate teacher training is a weak spot throughout education (Gissler, 1972, pp. 840–850).

Stephen J. Knezevich, Edward A. Krug, Henry S. Lufler, and John R. Palmer of the University of Wisconsin at Madison critiqued the first draft of this chapter; their comments were both helpful and incisive.

One seldom finds any really positive support for professional education.

Reform in teacher education is, therefore, an absolute necessity. It is widely perceived to be inefficient and resistant to new technology. For example, university professors still spend inordinate amounts of time traveling to schools supervising student teachers instead of using video tapes. Computers and other forms of mechanization are frequently resisted. While teacher educators stress the need to treat the learner as an individual, they continue to lecture to large groups. Education students invariably rate their education courses as inferior to those obtained in the liberal arts and sciences.

All higher education is now suspect, but teacher education is seen to be particularly impervious to change. It is accused of anti-intellectualism and low standards. Too much attention is supposedly given to inputs like methods courses and not enough to what difference these factors make in outputs such as demonstrated teaching ability in the classroom. None of these criticisms is new, but in the face of soaring government costs and the call for improvements in productivity, teacher education, vulnerable as it is in light of its second-rate status, is destined to have a difficult time unless it reforms itself dramatically.

Given this brief, bleak analysis, what options are open to those with a strong desire to build an exemplary preservice and in-service teacher preparation program?

Not surprisingly the most common administrative ploy within the university has been incrementalism: Current policies and practices are modified slightly in response to a specific pressure. Ordinarily, a faculty committee, usually aided by a few students, is formed and charged with reviewing the present program and with presenting changes to the entire faculty for approval. Since committees are notoriously slow and methodical in their deliberations, the product that emerges is hardly revolutionary. Ratification dutifully takes place, and business goes on much as before. Usually, faculty members are not even aware of the modest revisions enacted.

A tactic preferred by more energetic reformers is the creation of a new unit within an ongoing institution. Vito Perrone took this alternative when he developed his innovative program at the University of North Dakota (Silberman, 1970). Through bypassing the school of education he broke up all the encrusted patterns and traditions. The beauty of this approach is the opportunity to start from ground zero without immediately facing a seemingly insurmountable list of constraints.

The trauma of replacing dissidents is exchanged for the excitement of employing true believers. Sooner or later, however, if these new ventures are to be accepted as legitimate, they must make their peace with the established rules and regulations of the university community; otherwise they remain as appendages and suffer the depredations reserved for deviants.

Another alternative is illustrated by the renewal center concept, a current favorite of the Office of Education. Given that the traditional college or university governance system is difficult to change, according to this notion, might it not be productive to withdraw completely from this arcane environment and begin anew where the action is, in the school community itself. This radical substitute for schools of education is based on the assumptions that teaching is a craft and that the best way to learn a skill is to practice it.

On the surface renewal centers are appealing because they seem so logical and pragmatic. New experiments in learning can be launched in field situations, and inservice activities can be directed to specific improvements in teaching. No longer does the teacher have to sit at the feet of the theoretician; he can learn from his peers who really know what to do on Monday. To separate teacher education from the universities, of course, reduces it to a craft.

The distinction of craftsmen is that they have a predetermined end. The carpenter knows what he is making; the navigator has to get the ship into port. The difficulty with teaching is that the ends are mysterious. In an important sense, even the best teacher does not know what he is doing. If he did know, the remedy for poor teaching would be technical or skill instruction.

The approach typified by those who call for the political leader is worthy of close examination because it is very appealing on the surface. The politician is an expert in pragmatic decision-making, and he is determined to see that his policies are adopted. Political administrators are accustomed to dealing with the real world. They know how to conquer resistance in a number of ways:

cooptation, reward and punishment, guile, fear, salesmanship, imperiousness, or outright political manipulation. Of necessity, means rather than ends often take precedence.

Finally in this list of reformers and methods for reform we have the systems man, whose catechism is equally prescriptive. He believes objectives must be defined, activities must be implemented to fit these objectives, and assessment measures must be derived to test achievement. Feedback is the dynamic component; the system is revised as new information is received and catalogued, and the process is repeated over and over again. It is a neat and mechanistic approach with a loyal band of supporters.

Not one of these models is fully attractive to me. At the same time I am aware that teacher education has been extremely inhospitable to reform from within. Yet few want the federal government involved in planning detailed programs, and few with even a nodding acquaintance with state legislative bodies want programs designed to fulfill only their parochial curricular requirements.

The crucial dimensions of improved teacher education—innovation, experiment, reform—do not emanate from overworked schools of education living on bare-bones budgets any more than they can from federal, state, or local bodies acting independently.

Neither is the university faculty, with its time-honored mechanisms of modest structural changes and minor additions to or deletions from the curriculum, a likely source of substantial reform. Professors are unusually adept at practicing the occult art of strategic concession instead of blatant resistance. They are after all highly individualistic human beings and are not terribly interested in extensive reform since it involves working with others on policies and ideas, efforts that do not contribute significantly to their own careers. This is the main reason teacher education has been so static.

Since every professor is the keeper of his own goal, the current most viable force for constructive change within the university is the administration. It is the administrator alone who is held responsible for overall program achievement. Schools of education need deans who are ready to use the legitimate authority that their position implies. (The faculty has substantial protection through its power to recall the dean if need be.) I am not suggesting

at all that deans suddenly become arbitrary or disingenuous, only
that they have ideas and be willing to express and act on them.
Leadership is explicit on this point. Once an administrator takes a
clear position and others have to respond to his initiatives, his
leadership role is enhanced.

Unfortunately most deans now spend the bulk of their time
assisting faculty members: To make great teaching possible is their
leadership challenge. The emphasis on service to others takes inordinate amounts of time: Interpersonal conflicts must be resolved,
budgets have to be submitted, countless invitations to speak must
be met, and innumerable meetings have to be attended. These
management routines sap the strength and energy of administrators
and divert them from true leadership tasks. Propounding the mission of a school or department of education and keeping the vision
in front of its members is frequently sacrificed to routine concerns.

What are some of the precise impediments a dean faces in
his attempts at reform? Erickson (1972, pp. 1–4) suggests that the
present open system in higher education is characterized by such
diffusion of power that no one can do much to alter things. To
some degree this indictment is an accurate one. The reforming dean
is often powerless.

Within his own organization examples of diffusion of power
abound: Faculty members bypass their department chairmen and
go directly to the deans with or without the chairmen's knowledge;
some faculty members even bypass their deans; competition among
departments for resources reduces effective communication; urgent
requests by higher echelons for information and predictions take
precedence over school priorities; and rapid turnover of top administrators at the presidential and chancellor level creates uncertainties. The upshot is that the dean has to adjust to a nonhier-
archical structure in a continuous state of flux.

The dean has important external reference groups to consider as well. Most teacher education institutions are not on the best
terms with their main client groups, public school teachers and local
school systems. Many teachers have short-lived allegiance to the
schools of education that spawn them. After all, it is hardly possible
to inculcate the kind of professional norms and loyalties demanded
by medical schools, for example, in a brief exposure to a few edu-

cation courses of which practice-teaching is the most exciting. Teachers give primary loyalty to the union or the education association because these organizations protect their welfare for longer periods during a career. In addition, quality is often not a factor in a potential teacher's choice of university. Since almost every college in the country turns out teachers mostly as an afterthought, the market is surfeited. Those institutions that try to develop and maintain expensive exemplary programs are submerged under the unceasing flood of low-cost competitors.

Public school teachers often take advanced degrees in education, but the underlying impulse is not love and respect for the discipline, education, but escalation on the salary schedule. Schools of education accommodate their clients by easing residence expectations, eliminating foreign language requirements, simplifying course demands, and substituting action research for basic research.

Teachers pursue the degrees, but curse the local system regulations that force them to attend summer and evening school classes. Moreover, they are convinced that it is impossible to lay down principles of teaching and that the best teacher is likely to be the one who is improvising and experimenting in his class. They are perplexed by the "scientific" articles that appear regularly in educational journals and that are invariably laced with what to them are indecipherable statistical notations. These prevailing attitudes appear in one form or another in practically all surveys of teachers' opinions.

The successful unionization of teachers, a possibility considered remote twenty years ago, provides an entirely new environment. Unions are readying legislative proposals that would place the control of teacher education firmly in the hands of classroom teachers. If teacher unions or associations attempt to undertake the whole job of teacher education, the knowledge base is certain to suffer, and we will be wallowing in the mystique of best practice, a return to the limitations of apprenticeship, and an end to the hope of professionalism. Whatever the outcome, the long-standing shared responsibility among state departments, public school systems, and college and universities is likely to be shattered.

Local school systems, like teachers, do not hold teacher education in high esteem. Their attitude seems to be that it makes no difference how or where one is trained to satisfy certification demands since teaching is principally a skill learned best in the public school trenches.

One of the strongest challenges to teacher education from outside the university walls comes from state departments of education. In fact, they, not schools of education, are now initiating the main reforms in teacher education. The performance-based–teacher education movement is a case in point; state initiative in Florida, New York, Texas, and Washington nurtured it. Increased state power may ultimately, however, be quite destructive of the freedom to innovate. Consider how a compulsory and standardized teacher preparation design enforced by state codes would threaten diversity in programing and institutional autonomy. Signs are unmistakable that pressures from the state are intensifying along these lines.

Federal intervention in teacher education has also increased. The Office of Education is heavily staffed with noneducationists and career bureaucrats, most of whom have never confronted a pupil in a real classroom. These individuals now exhibit more confidence in the views of liberal arts professors, commercial research organizations, and minority group spokesmen with a touch for the sensational than they do in the views of professional educators. The federal educational bureaucracy sees itself as a catalyst for change and prescribes through its requests for proposals what innovations it prefers at any one time. Unfortunately, federal administrators change so frequently that few of these programs exist long enough to be thoroughly researched or tested. The National Study Commission on Undergraduate Education and the Education of Teachers, directed by Paul Olson at the University of Nebraska and supported by the federal government, is a case in point. Olson is utterly opposed to educationists and advocates greater emphasis on community and parent needs, elimination of credentials, client control, value consciousness, and the like. These proposals, to say the least, are difficult to evaluate.

Not the least of the dean's concerns in any university is the reputation of the school of education in relation to the arts and science faculty and the elite professional schools, particularly engineering, law, and medicine. In most cases, he is at a distinct disadvantage. Poorer salaries, heavier teaching assignments, and crushing service obligations differentiate the professer of education from his more favored colleagues in the other colleges. Educationists suffer a second-class citizenship in academia; seldom are they tapped for distinguished chairs, and rarely are they appointed or elected to prestigious faculty committees. It is generally assumed that not much basic, theoretical research is going on in education and what research is going on is oriented toward immediate concerns and current fads.

These visible marks of inferiority are reinforced by budgetary discriminations; schools of education are often poorly funded. Ironically, education courses have been salable and profit-making. However, the surplus proceeds have been diverted by college presidents to more valued and more expensive subjects; the allocation of money is an important indicator of institutional value systems.

It is easy to explicate the administrative impediments to change; it is difficult to provide guidance to the individual who wishes to make a difference. Much of the intellectual criticism of teacher education has been a continual litany of despair. Although the specific facts and words are right, the music seems strangely out of tune with political reality. To be specific, a special opinion poll conducted for the Charles F. Kettering Foundation indicates that the public thinks of education largely in a conservative way (Gallup, 1972, pp. 33–42). The inevitable conclusion is that the public is not looking for radical or costly educational innovations; it seeks not to deschool society, but to hold schools accountable for teaching basic and practical skills.

The real issue is the delicate matter of arriving at some notion of what we want schools to do, of what teachers should accomplish, and of what kinds of teachers should emerge from teacher education. Innovation as an abstraction is unsatisfying. We need innovation calculated on the basis of a realistic philosophy of education, both for the individual and for society. Much of what has been under discussion in the literature, including, I think, performance-based teacher education, has been detached from this principle.

Let me turn now to specific suggestions. I believe that deans have failed to fight hard for the policies they consider important. They have generally been supportive of the professoriat (although that support has rarely been returned), perhaps out of necessity at a time when college jobs were plentiful and the desire to retain staff was paramount. Under current budgetary stringencies, however, deans no longer have a valid excuse for failing to provide purpose and direction.

My intent is not to exclude professors of education from deliberations. The faculty must participate in important policy decisions; for the dean to act unilaterally is to guarantee failure. As the most concerned, the faculty should in fact be the most active. But quality participation from those who have the most to gain or lose is not automatic. Educationists seek scholarly status within the university, and significant numbers of them worship first at the altar of knowledge production (though this goal is sometimes more of a pretension than an accomplishment). Given this situation, the dean must take the initiative.

I sense a readiness for a more direct style of governance, particularly in situations where primary financial support comes from the university budget. The most undisciplined members in schools of education have been the grantsmen who benefitted from soft money. The new scenario restores some of the power abdicated by deans and department chairmen to these modern buccaneers. Enterprising deans must use the discretionary funds available in any school of education to nudge their faculties along.

Deans of schools of education, in short, should suggest new program directions, circulate their proposals to their colleagues inside and outside the university, argue persuasively for their consideration, accept criticism in good faith, but insist on movement toward reform.

The most desirable help a dean can receive as he pursues the course of installing new programs is substantial input from students and the liberal arts faculty. The former must pass through the curricular experiences, and the latter provides the subject-matter knowledge that all fledgling teachers must have. Achieving a working partnership with these two groups has baffled most reformers; no matter how representatives are chosen, the question of credibility immediately arises. But we must uphold the principle of participatory democracy even when we are accused of fraudulence. For students, an elective system should be devised and the successful candidates woven into the decision-making process with the exact procedures differing from campus to campus.

Dealing with the liberal arts constituency is considerably more complicated. Students are transients and their commitment temporary; liberal arts professors are specialists whose status and rank are marginally related to their contributions to schools of education. Fortunately, every institution has a few arts and science professors who are willing to help. Only the best minds should be enlisted for this service, and their energy and intelligence should not be dissipated on meaningless chores. These people should be asked to respond critically to solid proposals, to suggest new directions, and to use their judicious temperament on crucial problems. Endless and directionless committee meetings are certain to drive them permanently away.

The dean must also assume responsibility for establishing cordial relations with teachers in service. What matters at this juncture is the integration of the significant experiences and unique perspectives of the teacher in service with the expertise of the college professor, who, by definition, is responsible for studying the educational process in all its complexities. Barring societal revolution, most individuals who will be teaching for the next twenty years are now in place. The need in the future, therefore, will be for inservice education of practitioners, not preservice education. If various forms of training, career education, performance-based teacher education, or human relations training, to cite a few examples, are to be successful, teachers in service must accept them and feel comfortable about them. A massive reeducation process is in order. Part of it should be conducted on site and part in the university so that rigid separation between practice and theory can be counteracted.

If institutional inertia is to be successfully assailed, the dean must be a dedicated and courageous person. Academic reform is a war of attrition, and defeat is predictable if resolve is lost. Although the dean must share his power and willingly release some resources for cooperative use, his primary task is to establish worthy targets. To do otherwise is to abdicate responsibility.

References

American Association of Colleges for Teacher Education. *Bulletin,* 1972, *25*(9), 1.

ANDREWS, T. *New Directions in Certification.* Washington, D.C.: Association of Teacher Educators, 1971.

ARROWSMITH, W. "Teaching and the Liberal Arts: Notes Toward an Old Frontier." In D. Bigelow (Ed.), *The Liberal Arts and Teacher Education.* Lincoln: University of Nebraska Press, 1971.

BARR, A. S. *Characteristic Differences in the Teaching Performance of Good and Poor Teachers of the Social Studies.* Bloomington, Ill.: Public School Publishing, 1929.

BARZUN, J. *Teacher in America.* Garden City, N.Y.: Doubleday, 1954.

BELL, D. *The Reforming of General Education: The Columbia College Experience in the National Setting.* New York: Columbia University Press, 1966.

BIGELOW, D. "Introduction: Revolution or Reform in Teacher Education." In D. Bigelow (Ed.), *The Liberal Arts and Education.* Lincoln: University of Nebraska Press, 1971.

245

BOBBITT, F. "Some General Principles of Management Applied to the Problems of City-School Systems." In *Twelfth Yearbook of the National Society for the Study of Education*, Part I. Chicago: University of Chicago Press, 1913.

BOBBITT, F. "Discovering and Formulating the Objectives of Teacher-Training Institutions." *Journal of Educational Research*, October 1924, *10*, 187–196.

BORROWMAN, M. L. "Teacher Education: History." In *The Encyclopedia of Education*. New York: Macmillan, 1971.

BROUDY, H. *A Critique of Performance-Based Teacher Education*. Washington, D.C.: American Association of Colleges for Teacher Education, 1972.

CARDOZO, M. W. "Accreditation of Law Schools in the United States." *Journal of Legal Education*, 1966, *18*, 420–424.

Century Dictionary of the English Language. New York: Century, 1891.

CHARTERS, W. W. "The Objectives of Teacher-Training." *Educational Administration and Supervision*, September 1920, *6*, 301–308.

CHARTERS, W. W., AND WAPLES, D. *The Commonwealth Teacher-Training Study*. Chicago: University of Chicago Press, 1929.

CONANT, J. B. *The American High School Today*. New York: McGraw-Hill, 1959.

CONANT, J. B. *The Education of American Teachers*. New York: McGraw-Hill, 1963.

CONNER, W. H., AND SMITH, L. M. *Analysis of Patterns of Student Teaching*. St. Louis: Washington University, 1967.

CREMIN, L. A. *The Transformation of the School*. New York: Knopf, 1962.

CRONBACH, L. J. "The Logic of Experiments on Discovery." In L. S. Shulman and E. R. Keisler (Eds.), *Learning by Discovery*. Chicago: Rand McNally, 1966.

CUNNINGHAM, L. L. *Educational Reform in Ohio: Redefinition and Regeneration*. Columbus: College of Education, The Ohio State University, 1971. (Mimeographed.)

DANIEL, F., AND CRENSHAW, J. W. *What Has Been and Should Be the Role of the State Education Agencies in the Development and Implementation of Teacher Education Programs?* Washington, D.C.: U. S. Office of Education, 1971.

DEWEY, J. *The Public and Its Problems*. New York: Holt, Rinehart, and Winston, 1927.

DUBIN, R., AND TAVEGGIA, T. C. *The Teaching-Learning Paradox*.

Eugene, Ore.: Center for the Advanced Study of Educational Administration, 1968.

EDELFELT, R. A. "Whither NCATE?" *The Journal of Teacher Education,* Spring 1970, *21,* 3–4.

Education: A Framework for Expansion. Cmnd. 5174. London: HMSO, 1972.

ELAM, S. *Performance-Based Teacher Education: What Is the State of the Art?* Washington, D.C.: American Association of Colleges for Teacher Education Committee on Performance-Based Teacher Education, 1971.

ELAM, S. *A Résumé of Performance-Based Teacher Education.* Washington, D.C.: American Association of Colleges for Teacher Education, 1972.

ELLUL, J. *The Technological Society.* New York: Vintage, 1964.

ERICKSON, D. A. "Moral Dilemmas of Administrative Powerlessness." *Administrator's Notebook,* April 1972, *20,* 1–4.

FORMAN, S. "One Librarian's View of NCATE 'Standards'." *Teacher's College Record,* May 1971, *72,* 519–523.

FRIEDENBERG, E. Z. *Coming of Age in America.* New York: Random House, 1965.

FRINKS, M. L. *Emerging State Agency—Institutions of Higher Learning Relationships and Procedures in Planning and Effecting Improvements in the Preparation and Certification of Educators.* Denver: Education Commission of the States, 1970.

GAGE, N. L. *Teacher Effectiveness and Teacher Education: The Search for a Scientific Basis.* Palo Alto, Calif.: Pacific Books, 1972.

GALLUP, G. H. "Fourth Annual Gallup Poll of Public Attitudes Toward Education." *Phi Delta Kappan,* September 1972, *54,* 33–44.

GISSLER, S. "Productivity in the Public Sector: A Summary of a Wingspread Symposium." *Public Administration Review,* November/December 1972, *32,* 840–850.

HASLAM, M. B. *An Analysis of the Development of Perspectives Toward Teaching Among Student Teachers.* Unpublished doctoral dissertation. State University of New York, Buffalo, 1971.

HAWKINS, D. "Learning the Unteachable." In L. S. Shulman and E. R. Keisler (Eds.), *Learning by Discovery.* Chicago: Rand McNally, 1966.

HERNDON, J. *The Way It Spozed To Be.* New York: Simon and Schuster, 1968.

HERNDON, J. *How to Survive in Your Native Land.* New York: Simon and Schuster, 1971.

HIGHET, G. *The Art of Teaching.* New York: Knopf, 1950.

HOMANS, G. C. *The Human Group.* New York: Harcourt Brace Jovanovich, 1950.

IANNACONE, L., AND BUTTON, H. W. *Functions of Student Teaching: Attitude Formation and Initiation in Elementary School Teaching.* St. Louis: Washington University, 1964.

JACKSON, P. W. *Life in Classrooms.* New York: Holt, Rinehart, and Winston, 1968.

JAMES, LORD OF RUSHOLME (Chm.). *Teacher Education and Training: A Report by a Committee of Enquiry Appointed by the Secretary of State for Education and Science.* London: HMSO., 1972.

JENCKS, C. "The Coleman Report and the Conventional Wisdom." In F. Mosteller and D. Moynihan (Eds.), *On Equality of Educational Opportunity.* New York: Random House, 1972.

JENCKS, C., AND RIESMAN, D. *The Academic Revolution.* Garden City, N.Y.: Doubleday, 1968.

KERR, C. *The Uses of the University.* New York: Harper and Row, 1966.

KUHN, T. *The Structure of Scientific Revolutions.* Chicago: University of Chicago Press, 1964.

LANGER, S. *Philosophy in a New Key.* New York: New American Library, 1948.

LEAR, J. "Defining the New Physician." *Saturday Review,* January 1967, pp. 122–125.

LINDSEY, M. (Ed.) *New Horizons for the Teaching Profession.* Washington, D.C.: National Education Association, 1961.

MARIN, P. "Has Imagination Outstripped Reality?" *Saturday Review,* July 1972, pp. 40–44.

MAUL, R. C. "NCATE Accreditation." *The Journal of Teacher Education,* Spring 1970, *21,* 47–52.

MAY, R. *Love and Will.* New York: Norton, 1969.

MAYOR, J. R., AND SWARTZ, W. G. *Accreditation in Teacher Education: Its Influence on Higher Education.* Washington, D.C.: National Commission on Accrediting, 1965.

MERRILL, E. C. "New NCATE Standards." In *AACTE Yearbook.* Washington, D.C.: American Association of Colleges for Teacher Education, 1970.

MITZEL, H. E. "Teacher Effectiveness." In C. W. Harris (Ed.), *Encyclopedia of Educational Research* (3rd ed.). New York: Macmillan, 1960.

National Association of State Directors of Teacher Education and Certification. *Proposed Standards for State Approval of Teacher Education.* Salt Lake City: Utah State Department of Education, 1971.

National Center for Educational Statistics. *Earned Degrees Conferred: 1968–1969, Part B—Institutional Data.* Washington, D.C.: Government Printing Office, 1971.

National Commission on Teacher Education and Professional Standards. *Negotiating for Professionalization.* Washington, D.C.: National Education Association, 1970.

National Council for Accreditation of Teacher Education. *Standards for Accreditation of Teacher Education: The Accreditation of Basic and Advanced Preparation Programs for Professional School Personnel.* Washington, D.C., 1970.

National Council for Accreditation of Teacher Education. *Annual List, 1970–71.* Washington, D.C., 1971.

NORTHRUP, F. S. C. *The Logic of the Sciences and Humanities.* New York: Meridian, 1959.

Office of the State Superintendent of Public Instruction, State of Washington. *1971 Guidelines and Standards for the Preparation of Professional Education Personnel.* Olympia, Wash., 1971.

POPHAM, W. J. "Teaching Skill Under Scrutiny." *Phi Delta Kappan,* June 1971, *52,* 599–602.

PRICE, D. *Little Science, Big Science.* New York: Columbia University Press, 1963.

RICE, J. M. *Scientific Management in Education.* New York: Arno, 1969.

ROSENOW, E. C. "The Present Status of the AMA Accreditation of Continuing Medical Education." *Journal of Medical Education,* October 1965, *40,* 998–1002.

SILBERMAN, C. E. *Crisis in the Classroom.* New York: Random House, 1970.

SMITH, B. O. "Teaching: Conditions of Its Evaluation." In *The Evaluation of Teaching.* Washington, D.C.: Pi Lambda Theta, 1967.

SMITH, B. O. *Teachers for the Real World.* Washington, D.C.: American Association of Colleges for Teacher Education, 1970.

STEPHENS, J. M. "The Residual Theory Again: An Analytical Study." *Educational Theory,* July 1955, *5,* 158–166.

STEPHENS, J. M. "Nondeliberative Factors in Teaching." *Journal of Educational Psychology,* January 1956a, *47,* 11–24.

STEPHENS, J. M. "Nondeliberative Factors Underlying the Phenomenon of Schooling." *Educational Theory*, January 1956b, *6*, 26–34.

STEPHENS, J. M. *The Process of Schooling*. New York: Holt, Rinehart, and Winston, 1967.

STINNETT, T. M. "Thoughts about NCATE." *The Journal of Teacher Education*, Winter 1969, *20*, 505–508.

STINNETT, T. M. "Accreditation of Teacher Education Institutions and Agencies." *Phi Delta Kappan*, September 1970, *52*, 25–31.

SUTHERLAND, D. *Gertrude Stein*. New Haven: Yale University Press, 1951.

TROW, M. "Reflections on the Transition from Mass to Universal Higher Education." *Daedalus*, Winter 1970, *99*, 1–42.

University of the State of New York, The State Education Department. *Taking Your Talents Across State Lines*. Albany, N.Y., undated.

WALLEN, N. E., AND TRAVERS, R. M. W. "Analysis and Investigation of Teaching Methods." In N. L. Gage (Ed.), *Handbook of Research on Teaching*. Chicago: Rand McNally, 1963.

WASSERMAN, M. *The School Fix, NYC, U.S.A.* New York: Outerbridge and Dienstfrey, 1970.

WIGGINS, W. S. "Accreditation: The Profession's Response to Public Responsibility." *Journal of Medical Education*, July 1966, *41*, 33–44.

Index

A

Accrediting: alternatives to, 125–129; controversy about, 112–114; and curricular development, 188; historical background of, 115–119; improvement of, 129–138; licensing contrasted with, 136–137; program approval contrasted with, 85–86; by regional associations, 127; scale of, 114

Administrators: responsibility of for reform, 7, 234–244; training of, 55, 62–64

American Association of Colleges for Teacher Education (AACTE): Committee on Performance-Based Teacher Education of, 15; formation of, 116; responsibility of for standards, 119, 121

ARROWSMITH, W., 230–231

B

BARR, A. S., 14, 15, 24

Board of Education, agenda of, 67–69

BOBBITT, F., 142

C

California, licensing legislation in, 106–110

Certification related to continuing education, 192. *See also* Licensing

CHARTERS, W. W., 13–14, 15, 24

Colorado, proposed PBTE for, 90–91

Competency-based teacher education. *See* Performance-based teacher education

CONANT, J. B., 45, 50, 113, 118, 119, 131, 133, 220, 221

Coordinating boards for higher education: growth of, 76–77; role changes of, 86–87

Council for National Academic Awards, 165, 170, 171, 173

CREMIN, L. A., 51, 196–197

CRENSHAW, J. W., 88

CRONBACH, L. J., 20–21

251